Totus Tuus
Catechesis on the Blessed Virgin Mary

Totus Tuus
Catechesis on the Blessed Virgin Mary

Saint John Paul II

Edited by
Geoffrey W.M.P. Lopes da Silva

Domina Nostra Publishing
Providence, Rhode Island

Published in 2023 by
Domina Nostra Publishing
555 N. Main Street, #1329
Providence, RI. 02904 USA
Email: info@DominaNostraPublishing.com
Website: www.DominaNostraPublishing.com

The mosaic featured on the cover of this book can be found in the Sanctuary of Saint John Paul II (*Sanktuarium Świętego Jana Pawła II*) at the "Be Not Afraid" John Paul II Centre (*Centrum Jana Pawła II „Nie lękajcie się!"*) in Krakow, Poland.

First printing, 2023

ISBN 978-0-9741900-8-2

This book is humbly dedicated to

Domina Nostra, Beata Maria, Mater Ecclesiae.[1]

"*Ecce enim ex hoc*
beatam me dicent omnes generationes"
(*Lucam* 1, 48).[2]

[1] Our Lady, Blessed Mary, Mother of the Church.
[2] "For behold, henceforth all generations will call me blessed" (*Luke* 1:48).

Table of Contents

Preface 11
Introduction 13
Abbreviations for the Books of the Bible 14
Other Abbreviations 17

The Catecheses

1 Mary is the Pattern of the Church's Holiness 20
2 Mary is the Virgin Mother of God 23
3 Mary was United to Jesus on the Cross 26
4 The Church Grew in Understanding of Mary's Role 30

5 To Honour Mary is to go to Jesus 33
6 Mary is the Model of Persevering Silence 36
7 Mary Shows us God's Respect for Women 39
8 Mary Sheds Light on Role of Women 42

9 The Second Vatican Council's Teaching on Mary 45
10 The Purpose and Method of Exposure of Marian Doctrine 48
11 Mary in the Trinitarian Perspective 51
12 Mary in the Protogospel 54

The Annunciation of the Lord
to the Blessed Virgin Mary

13 Announcement of the Messianic Maternity 57
14 Motherhood Comes from God 60
15 Women Involved in the Salvation of the People 64
16 The Moral Nobility of Woman 67
17 The Daughter of Sion 70
18 The New Daughter of Sion 74
19 "Full of Grace" 77
20 The Perfect Holiness of Mary 80
21 The Immaculate Conception 83
22 The *Immaculata:* Redeemed through preservation 86
23 The *Immaculata:* The Dogmatic Definition of the Privilege 89
24 Holy Throughout Life 92
25 She who Believed 95

The Perpetual Virginity of the Blessed Virgin Mary

26 The Virginity of Mary, the Truth of Faith 98
27 The Purpose of Virginity 102
28 The Value of the Virginal Conception of Jesus 105
29 Mary, Model of Virginity 108
30 Mary and Joseph Lived the Gift of Virginity 111
31 The Church Presents Mary as Ever-Virgin 113

The Visitation of the Blessed Virgin Mary to Saint Elizabeth

32 Mary Offers a Sublime Model of Service 116
33 Mary, the New Eve, Freely Obeyed God 118
34 The Visitation is a Prelude to the Mission of Christ 121
35 Mary Sings the Praises of God's Mercy 124
36 The Nativity Shows Mary's Closeness to Jesus 126
37 The Church Proclaims Mary as the Mother of God 129

The Childhood and Hidden Years of Jesus

38 Teacher of the Son of God 132
39 The Presentation of Jesus in the Temple 134
40 The Prophecy of Simeon Associated Mary to the Painful Destiny of the Son 137
41 The Presentation of Jesus in the Temple Reveals the Cooperation of the "Woman" in the Redemption 139
42 Jesus, Lost and then Found in the Temple 142
43 Mary in the Hidden Life of Jesus 145

The Public Ministry of Jesus

44 Mary at the Wedding of Cana 148
45 At Cana, Mary Leads Jesus to Perform His First Miracle 151
46 Mary's Participation in the Public Life of the Son 154
47 At the Cross, Mary is a Participant in the Drama of Redemption 157
48 Mary's Unique Cooperation with Redemption 160
49 Woman, Behold Your Son! 163
50 Behold, Your Mother 165
51 Mary and the Resurrection of Christ 168
52 Mary and the Gift of the Spirit 171

The Assumption of the Blessed Virgin Mary

53 The Dormition of the Mother of God 174
54 The Assumption of Mary, the Truth of Faith 177

55 The Assumption of Mary in the Tradition of the Church 180
56 The Queen of the Universe 183

Holy Mary, Mother of the Church

57 Mary, the Pre-Eminent Member of the Church 186
58 Mary, Type and Model of the Church 189
59 Mary, Model of the Motherhood of the Church 192
60 Mary, Model of the Virginity of the Church 195
61 Mary, Model of the Holiness of the Church 198
62 Mary, Model of the Church in Divine Worship 201
63 Mother of the Church 204
64 The Intercession of the Heavenly Mother of Divine Grace 208
65 Mary, Mediatrix 211
66 The Cult of the Blessed Virgin 214

Devotion to the Blessed Virgin Mary

67 The Nature of Marian Devotion 218
68 Marian Devotion and the Worship of Images 221
69 Prayer to Mary 225
70 The Mother of Unity and Hope 228

Appendix of Marian Prayers

1 The Angelic Salutation (*Salutatio angelica*) 232
2 The *Sub tuum* 232
3 The *Salve Regina* 233
4 The Holy Rosary (*Sanctum Rosarium*) 233
5 The *Magníficat* 235
6 The *Angelus* and the *Regina Cœli* 236
7 The *Memorare* 237
8 A Child's Prayer to Mary 238
9 Mary, Help of Those in Need (*Sancta Maria, succurre miseris*) 238
10 The Litany of Loreto (*Litaniæ Lauretanæ*) 238
11 Pious Invocations (*Piæ Invocationis*) 241
12 The Akathist Hymn to the *Theotókos* 242

Indices

Index of Scriptural Citations 248
Index of Magisterial Documents 251
Index of Names 253

Preface

Totus Tuus: Catechesis on the Blessed Virgin Mary collects the 70 addresses given by Pope Saint John Paul II at his weekly general audiences between September 1995 and November 1997.

The Latin phrase *Totus Tuus* was chosen as the title of this collection of catecheses on the Blessed Virgin Mary because it served as the motto of Saint John Paul II's episcopacy and papacy. In his 2002 Apostolic Letter *Rosarium Virginis Mariæ* (cf. n. 15), Saint John Paul II explained how he borrowed the motto from Saint Louis Marie Grignion de Montfort's 1712 book *True Devotion to Mary*.

Totus tuus ego sum, et omnia mea tua sunt.
Accipio te in mea omnia.
Præbe mihi cor tuum, Maria.

I belong entirely to you, and all that I have is yours.
I take you for my all.
O Mary, give me your heart.

In editing this volume, it was important to ensure that the catecheses of Saint John Paul the Great on the Blessed Virgin Mary were accessible to a wide audience It is my hope that *Totus Tuus: Catechesis on the Blessed Virgin Mary* will serve as a comprehensive introduction to Mariology, the theological study of the Holy Mother of God, who "lives only in Christ and for Christ!"[1]

I pray that this book will bring comfort, inspiration, and a deeper understanding of the role of the Blessed Virgin Mary in our lives to all who read it.

Sancta María, Mater Ecclésiæ, ora pro nobis!

Geoffrey W.M.P. Lopes da Silva
Publisher and Executive Editor

9 April 2023
Dominica Resurrectionis

[1] "*Non enim vivit Maria nisi in Christo ac pro Christo!*" (Sanctus Ioannes Paulus II, Epistula Apostolica *Rosarium Virginis Mariæ* (16 October 2002), n. 15; *Acta Apostolicæ Sedis*, 94 (2002), p. 15.

Introduction

Pope Saint John Paul II's catecheses on the Blessed Virgin Mary were given during his weekly Wednesday audiences from September 1995 to November 1997. During this period, Saint John Paul II dedicated his teachings to the life, mission, and role of the Blessed Virgin Mary. These catecheses provide a rich and comprehensive understanding of the Church's doctrine on the Blessed Virgin Mary.

Saint John Paul II's teachings on the Blessed Virgin Mary were influenced by his own devotion to Our Lady and his deep understanding of Sacred Scripture and Sacred Tradition. Throughout his papacy, Saint John Paul II emphasized the importance of the New Evangelization and the role of the Blessed Virgin Mary in this task.

This book provides a valuable resource for those seeking a deeper understanding of the Church's teachings on the Mother of God. These addresses of Saint John Paul II offer insight and inspiration for all who seek a deeper relationship with Our Lady.

Each catechesis originally contained numbered sections by Saint John Paul II. The editor has further numbered subsequent paragraphs for easy reference and citation.

Beginning with the catechesis given on 12 March 1997 (n. 46, p. 154), each subsequent address was preceded with a text from Sacred Scripture. These texts have been retained for this volume.

All footnotes are the editor's, which often provides the Latin of cited texts wherever applicable and available, as Latin remains the official language of the Catholic Church.

The terms ordinary form of the Roman Rite and extraordinary form of the Roman Rite are used and refer to the post-Vatican II or modern liturgy and the pre-Vatican II or traditional liturgy (cf. Pope Benedict XVI, Apostolic Letter given "*motu proprio*" *Summorum Pontificum* (7 July 2007), art. 1).

An Appendix of Marian Prayers has also been included. These prayers are referenced in the texts of several catecheses, and their inclusion elinimates the need to reference another source.

Abbreviations for the Books of the Bible

I. Biblical Order

OLD TESTAMENT
VETUS TESTAMENTUM

Gn	Genesis
Ex	Exodus
Lv	Leviticus
Nm	Numbers
Dt	Deuteronomy
Jos	Joshua
Jgs	Judges
Ru	Ruth
1 Sm	1 Samuel (1 Kings)
2 Sm	2 Samuel (2 Kings)
1 Kgs	1 Kings (3 Kings)
2 Kgs	2 Kings (4 Kings)
1 Chr	1 Chronicles (1 Paralipomenon)
2 Chr	2 Chronicles (2 Paralipomenon)
Ezr	Ezra (1 Esdras)
Ne	Nehemiah (2 Esdras)
Tb	Tobit (Tobias)
Jdt	Judith
Est	Esther
1 Mc	1 Maccabees
2 Mc	2 Maccabees
Jb	Job
Ps	Psalm(s)
Prv	Proverbs
Eccl	Ecclesiastes (Qoheleth)
Sg	Song of Songs (of Solomon)
Wis	Wisdom (of Solomon)
Sir	Sirach (Ecclesiasticus)
Is	Isaiah
Jer	Jeremiah
Lam	Lamentations (of Jeremiah)
Bar	Baruch
Ez	Ezekiel
Dn	Daniel
Hos	Hosea (Osee)
Jl	Joel
Am	Amos
Ob	Obadiah
Jon	Jonah (Jonas)
Mi	Micah (Micheas)
Na	Nahum
Hab	Habakkuk (Habacuc)
Zep	Zephaniah (Sophonias)
Zec	Zechariah (Zacharias)
Hag	Haggai (Aggeus)
Mal	Malachi (Malachias)

NEW TESTAMENT
NOVUM TESTAMENTUM

Mt	Matthew
Mk	Mark
Lk	Luke
Jn	John
Acts	Acts of the Apostles
Rom	Romans
1 Cor	1 Corinthians
2 Cor	2 Corinthians
Gal	Galatians
Eph	Ephesians
Phil	Philippians
Col	Colossians
1 Thess	1 Thessalonians
2 Thess	2 Thessalonians
1 Tm	1 Timothy
2 Tm	2 Timothy
Tit	Titus
Phlm	Philemon
Heb	Hebrews
Jas	James
1 Pt	1 Peter
2 Pt	2 Peter
1 Jn	1 John
2 Jn	2 John
3 Jn	3 John
Jud	Jude
Rev	Revelation
or Apoc	Apocalypse

II. Alphabetical

Acts	Acts of the Apostles
Am	Amos
Apoc	Apocalypse (Revelation)
Bar	Baruch
1 Chr	1 Chronicles (1 Paralipomenon)
2 Chr	2 Chronicles (2 Paralipomenon)
Col	Colossians
1 Cor	1 Corinthians
2 Cor	2 Corinthians
Dn	Daniel
Dt	Deuteronomy
Eccl	Ecclesiastes (Qoheleth)
Eph	Ephesians
Est	Esther
Ex	Exodus
Ez	Ezekiel
Ezr	Ezra (1 Esdras)
Gal	Galatians
Gn	Genesis
Hab	Habakkuk (Habacuc)
Hag	Haggai (Aggeus)
Heb	Hebrews
Hos	Hosea (Osee)
Is	Isaiah
Jas	James
Jb	Job
Jdt	Judith
Jer	Jeremiah
Jgs	Judges
Jl	Joel
Jn	John
1 Jn	1 John
2 Jn	2 John
3 Jn	3 John
Jon	Jonah (Jonas)
Jos	Joshua
Jud	Jude
Jgs	Judges
1 Kgs	1 Kings (3 Kings)
2 Kgs	2 Kings (4 Kings)
Lam	Lamentations (of Jeremiah)
Lk	Luke
Lv	Leviticus
Mal	Malachi (Malachias)
1 Mc	1 Maccabees
2 Mc	2 Maccabees
Mi	Micah (Micheas)
Mk	Mark
Mt	Matthew
Na	Nahum
Ne	Nehemiah (2 Esdras)
Nm	Numbers
Ob	Obadiah (Abdias)
1 Pt	1 Peter
2 Pt	2 Peter
Phil	Philippians
Phlm	Philemon
Prv	Proverbs
Ps	Psalm(s)
Rom	Romans
Ru	Ruth
Rv	Revelation (Apocalypse)
Sg	Song of Songs (of Solomon)
Sir	Sirach (Ecclesiasticus)
1 Sm	1 Samuel (1 Kings)
2 Sm	2 Samuel (2 Kings)
Tb	Tobit (Tobias)
1 Thess	1 Thessalonians
2 Thess	2 Thessalonians
1 Tm	1 Timothy
2 Tm	2 Timothy
Tit	Titus
Wis	Wisdom (of Solomon)
Zec	Zechariah (Zacharias)
Zep	Zephaniah (Sophonias)

III. Latin

Index siglorum

Adb	Prophetia Abdiæ
Act	Actus Apostolorum
Ag	Prophetia Aggæi
Am	Prophetia Amos
Ap	Apocalypsis Ioannis
Bar	Liber Baruch
Cant	Canticum canticorum
1 et 2 Chr	Libri I et II Chronicorum (= 1 et II Paralipomenon)
Col	Epistola beati Pauli apostoli ad Colossenses
1 et 2 Cor	Epistolæ I et II beati Pauli Apostoli ad Corinthios
Dan	Prophetia Danielis
Deut	Liber Deuteronomii
Eph	Epistola beati Pauli Apostoli ad Ephesios
Esd	Liber Esdræ (= I Esdræ)
Est	Liber Esther
Ex	Liber Exodus
Ez	Prophetia Ezechielis
Gal	Epistola beati Pauli Apostoli ad Galatas
Gen	Liber Genesis
Hab	Prophetia Habacuc
Hebr	Epistola ad Hebræos
Iac	Epistola Iacobi
Ier	Liber Ieremiæ
Io	Evangelium secundum Ioannem
1, 2, et 3 Io	Epistolæ I, II et III Ioannis
Iob	Liber Iob
Ioel	Prophetia Ioel
Ion	Prophetia Ionæ
Ios	Liber Iosue
Is	Liber Isaiæ
Iud	Epistola Iudæ
Iudic	Liber Iudicum
Iudt	Liber Iudith
Lam	Lamentationes (= Threni)
Lc	Evangelium secundum Lucam
Lev	Liber Leviticus
1 et 2 Mac	Libri I et II Maccabæorum
Mal	Prophetia Malachiæ
Mc	Evangelium secundum Marcum
Mic	Prophetia Michææ
Mt	Evangelium secundum Matthæum
Nah	Prophetia Nahum
Neh	Liber Nehemiæ (= II Esdræ)
Num	Liber Numeri
Os	Prophetia Osee
1 et 2 Petr	Epistolæ I et II Petri
Phil	Epistola beati Pauli Apostoli ad Philippenses
Phm	Epistola beati Pauli Apostoli ad Philemonem
Prov	Liber Proverbiorum

Ps	Liber Psalmorum
Qoh	Liber Qohelet (= Ecclesiastes)
1 et 2 Reg	Libri I et II Regum (= III et IV Regum)
Rom	Epistola beati Pauli Apostoli ad Romanos
Rut	Liber Ruth
1 et 2 Sam	Libri I et II Samuelis (= I et II Regum)
Sap	Liber Sapientiæ
Sir	Liber Siracidæ (Ben Sira = Ecclesiasticus)
Soph	Sophoniæ Prophetia
1 et 2 Th	Epistolæ I et II beati Pauli Apostoli ad Thessalonicenses
1 et 2 Tim	Epistolæ I et II beati Pauli Apostoli ad Timotheum
Tit	Epistola beati Pauli Apostoli ad Titum
Tob	Liber Thobis
Zac	Prophetia Zachariæ

Other Abbreviations

AAS	*Acta Apostolicae Sedis* (Latin), Acts of the Apostolic See
Adh. ap.	*Adhortatio Apostolica* (Latin), Apostolic Exhortation
B.C.	Before Christ
ca.	*circa* (Latin), around
Const. ap.	*Constitutio Apostolica* (Latin), Apostolic Constitution
cf.	*confer* (Latin), compare
DS	*Enchiridion symbolorum definitionum et declarationum de rebus fidei et morum* [Compendium of Creeds, Definitions, and Declarations on Matters of Faith and Morals] Heinrich Joseph Dominicus Denzinger (1819–1883)
Ep. ap.	*Epistula Apostolica* (Latin), Apostolic Epistle (Letter)
etc.	*et cetera* (Latin), and other things
ibid.	*ibidem* (Latin), in the same place
i.e.	*id est* (Latin), that is to say
Litt. enc.	*Litterae Encyclicae* (Latin), Encyclical Letter
n.	number
no.	number
nos.	numbers
op. cit.	*opus citatum* or *opere citato* (Latin), the work cited or the cited work
p.	page
pp.	pages
PP.	*Papa* (Latin), Pope or Pope and Pontiff
P.G.	*Patrologia Graeca* (or *Patrologiae Cursus Completus, Series Graeca*)
P.L.	*Patrologia Latina* (or *Patrologiae Cursus Completus, Series Latina*)
S.C.	*Sources Chrétiennes* (French), Christian Sources
v.	verse
vol.	volume
vv.	verses
†	died

The Catecheses

1
MARY IS THE PATTERN OF THE CHURCH'S HOLINESS

1.1 After pausing in the previous catecheses[1] to reflect more deeply on the identity and mission of the Church, I now feel the need to turn our gaze to the Blessed Virgin, she who is the perfect realisation of the Church's holiness and its model.

1.2 This is exactly what the Fathers of the Second Vatican Council did: after explaining the doctrine on the reality of the People of God in salvation history, they wanted to complete it with an illustration of Mary's role in the work of salvation. In fact, the purpose of the eighth chapter of the conciliar Constitution *Lumen gentium*,[2] is to emphasise the ecclesiological significance of Marian doctrine, but likewise to shed light on the contribution that the figure of the Blessed Virgin offers to our understanding of the Church's mystery.

2.1 Before explaining the Council's Marian itinerary, I would like to take a reflective look at Mary just as, at the Church's beginning, she is described in the Acts of the Apostles. At the beginning of this New Testament text, which describes the life of the first Christian community, and after recording the names of the Apostles one by one (1:13), Luke states: "All these with one accord devoted themselves to prayer, together with the women and Mary the mother of Jesus, and with his brethren" (1:14).[3]

2.2 The person of Mary stands out clearly in this picture; she is the only one, with the Apostles, mentioned by name. She represents one face of the Church, different from and complementary to the ministerial or hierarchical aspect.

3.1 In fact, Luke's statement mentions the presence in the Cenacle of some women, thus showing the importance of the feminine contribution to the Church's life from the very beginning. This presence is closely linked to the perseverance of the community in prayer and harmony. These traits perfectly express two basic aspects of women's specific contribution to ecclesial life. Better suited to outward activity, men need women's help to be brought back into personal relationships in order to progress towards the union of hearts.

---

[1] The previous papal catechesis was on the Creed, divided into four parts and given over the span of 10 years; God the Father (1985–1986), God the Son (1986–1989), God the Holy Spirit (1989–1991), and the Church (1991–1995).

[2] The Dogmatic Constitution on the Church *Lumen Gentium*, Latin for "Light of the Nations", is one of the principal documents of the Second Vatican Ecumenical Council (1962–1965), promulgated by Pope St Paul VI on 21 November 1964.

[3] "*Hi omnes erant perseverantes unanimiter in oratione cum mulieribus et Maria matre Iesu et fratribus eius*" (*Act* 1, 14).

3.2 "Blessed among women" (cf. *Lk* 1:42),[1] Mary eminently fulfils this feminine mission. Who better than Mary can encourage all believers to persevere in prayer? Who better than she can promote harmony and love?

3.3 Recognising the pastoral mission entrusted by Jesus to the Eleven, the women in the Cenacle, with Mary in their midst, joined in their prayer and at the same time witnessed to the presence in the Church of people who, although they have not received that mission, are likewise fully-fledged members of the community gathered in faith in Christ.

4.1 Mary's presence in the community, which was waiting in prayer for the outpouring of the Spirit (cf. *Acts* 1:14), calls to mind her part in the Incarnation of the Son of God by the work of the Holy Spirit (cf. *Lk* 1:35). The Virgin's role in that initial stage and the role she plays now, in the manifestation of the Church at Pentecost, are closely linked.

4.2 Mary's presence at the first moments of the Church's life is remarkably highlighted by comparison with her previous, very discreet participation during Jesus' public ministry. When the Son began his mission, Mary remained in Nazareth, even though this separation did not exclude significant contacts such as the one at Cana. Above all, it did not prevent her from taking part in the sacrifice of Calvary.

4.3 In the first community, however, Mary's role assumes notable importance. After the Ascension and in expectation of Pentecost, Jesus' Mother is personally present at the first stages of the work begun by her Son.

5.1 The Acts of the Apostles stress that Mary was in the Cenacle "with his [Jesus'] brethren" (*Acts* 1:14), that is, with his relatives, as has always been the Church's interpretation.[2] It was not so much a family gathering as the fact that under Mary's guidance, Jesus' natural family came to be part of Christ's spiritual family: "Whoever does the will of God", Jesus had said, "is my brother, and sister, and mother" (*Mk* 3:35).[3]

---

[1] "*Benedicta tu inter mulieres*" (*Lc* 1, 42).

[2] "*Ad hoc quandoque obiicitur Scripturam fratrum et sororum Iesu facere mentionem* (cf. *Mc* 3, 31-35; 6, 3; *1 Cor* 9, 5; *Gal* 1, 19). *Ecclesia hæc loca semper intellexit tamquam non alios filios Virginis Mariæ denotantia: Iacobus utique et Ioseph, « fratres » Iesu* (*Mt* 13, 55), *filii sunt cuiusdam Mariæ Christi discipulæ* (cf. *Mt* 27, 56), *quæ significanter tamquam « altera Maria »* (*Mt* 28, 1) *denotatur. Agitur de proximis propinquis secundum quamdam notam Veteris Testamenti expressionem* (cf. *Gn* 13, 8; 14, 16; 29, 15; etc.)" (*Catechismum Catholicæ Ecclesiæ*, editio typica (1997), n. 500).

"Against this doctrine the objection is sometimes raised that the Bible mentions brothers and sisters of Jesus (cf. *Mk* 3:31-35; 6:3; *1 Cor* 9:5; *Gal* 1:19). The Church has always understood these passages as not referring to other children of the Virgin Mary. In fact James and Joseph, 'brothers of Jesus,' are the sons of another Mary, a disciple of Christ, whom St Matthew significantly calls 'the other Mary' (*Mt* 13:55; 28:1; cf. *Mt* 27:56). They are close relations of Jesus, according to an Old Testament expression (cf. *Gen* 13:8; 14:16; 29:15; etc.)" (*Catechism of the Catholic Church*, Second Edtion (1997), n. 500).

[3] "*Qui enim fecerit voluntatem Dei, hic frater meus et soror mea et mater est*" (*Mc* 3, 35).

5.2 On the same occasion, Luke explicitly described Mary as "the mother of Jesus" (*Acts* 1:14), almost as if he wished to suggest that something of the presence of the Son ascended into heaven has remained in the presence of the mother. She reminded his disciples of Jesus' face and, with her presence in the community, is the symbol of the Church's fidelity to Christ the Lord.

5.3 The title of "Mother", in this context, proclaims the attitude of thoughtful closeness with which the Virgin followed the Church's life. Mary was to open her heart to the Church to show the marvels done in her by the almighty and merciful God.

5.4 From the very beginning, Mary carried out her role as "Mother of the Church": her action encouraged understanding between the Apostles, whom Luke describes as being of "one accord", far from the disputes that had occasionally arisen among them.

5.5 Lastly, Mary expressed her motherhood towards the community of believers not only by praying to obtain for the Church the gifts of the Holy Spirit necessary for her formation and her future, but also by teaching the Lord's disciples about constant communion with God.

5.6 She thus became the Christian people's teacher of prayer, of encounter with God, a central and indispensable element, so that the work of the Pastors and the faithful would always have its beginning and its inner motivation in the Lord.

6 From these brief remarks it can clearly be seen how the relationship between Mary and the Church is a fascinating comparison between two mothers.[1] It clearly reveals Mary's maternal mission and the Church's commitment ever to seek her true identity in contemplation of the face of the *Theotókos*.[2]

6 September 1995

---

[1] The traditional term "Holy Mother Church" refers to the Church as the mother and teacher (*mater et magistra*) of believers.

[2] *Theotókos* (Θεοτόκος) is Greek for "God-bearer", more often translated as *Mater Dei* or *Dei Génetrix* (literally "birther of God") in Latin and as "Mother of God" in English.

2
MARY IS THE VIRGIN MOTHER OF GOD

1.1 In the Constitution *Lumen gentium*, the Council states that "joined to Christ the head and in communion with all his saints, the faithful must in the first place reverence the memory 'of the glorious ever Virgin Mary, Mother of our God and Lord Jesus Christ'" (n. 52).[1] The conciliar Constitution uses these terms from the Roman Canon of the Mass, thereby stressing how faith in the divine motherhood of Mary has been present in Christian thought since the first centuries.

1.2 In the newborn Church Mary is remembered with the title "Mother of Jesus". It is Luke himself who gives her this title in the Acts of the Apostles, a title that corresponds moreover to what is said in the Gospels: "Is not this… the son of Mary?", the residents of Nazareth wonder according to the Evangelist Mark's account (6:3);[2] "Is not his mother called Mary?", is the question recorded by Matthew (13:55).[3]

2.1 In the disciples' eyes, as they gathered after the Ascension, the title "Mother of Jesus" acquires its full meaning. For them, Mary is a person unique in her kind: she received the singular grace of giving birth to the Saviour of humanity; she lived for a long while at his side; and on Calvary she was called by the Crucified One to exercise a "new motherhood" in relation to the beloved disciple and, through him, to the whole Church.

2.2 For these who believe in Jesus and follow him, "Mother of Jesus" is a title of honour and veneration, and will forever remain such in the faith and life of the Church. In a particular way, by this title Christians mean to say that one cannot refer to Jesus' origins without acknowledging the role of the woman who gave him birth in the Spirit according to his human nature. Her maternal role also involves the birth and growth of the Church. In recalling the place of Mary in Jesus' life, the faithful discover each day her efficacious presence in their own spiritual journey.

3.1 From the beginning, the Church has acknowledged the virginal motherhood of Mary. As the infancy Gospels enable us to grasp, the first Christian continuities themselves gathered together Mary's recollections about the mysterious circumstances of the Saviour's conception and birth. In particular,

[1] "*Et in qua fideles Christo Capiti adhærentes atque cum omnibus sanctis Eius communicantes, memoriam etiam venerentur oportet 'in primis gloriosæ semper Virginis Mariæ, Genitricis Dei et Domini nostri Iesu Christi'*" (Concilium Vaticanum II, Const. dogm. de Ecclesia, *Lumen gentium*, 52: *AAS* 57 [1965], p. 58).

[2] "*Nonne iste… filius Mariæ*" (*Mc* 6, 3).

[3] "*Nonne mater eius dicitur Maria…?*" (*Mt* 13, 55).

the Annunciation account responds to the disciples' desire to have the deepest knowledge of the events connected with the beginnings of the risen Christ's earthly life. In the last analysis, Mary is at the origin of the revelation about the mystery of the virginal conception by the work of the Holy Spirit.

3.2 This truth, showing Jesus' divine origin, was immediately grasped by the first Christians for its important significance and included among the key affirmations of their faith. Son of Joseph according to the law, Jesus in fact, by an extraordinary intervention of the Holy Spirit, was in his humanity only the son of Mary, since he was born without the intervention of man.

3.3 Mary's virginity thus acquires a unique value and casts new light on the birth of Jesus and on the mystery of his sonship, since the virginal generation is the sign that Jesus has God himself as his Father.

3.4 Acknowledged and proclaimed by the faith of the Fathers, the virginal motherhood can never be separated from the identity of Jesus, true God and true man, as "incarnate of the Virgin Mary",[1] as we profess in the Nicene-Constantinopolitan Creed.[2] Mary is the only Virgin who is also a Mother. The extraordinary co-presence of these two gifts in the person of the maiden of Nazareth has led Christians to call Mary simply "the Virgin", even when they celebrate her motherhood.

3.5 The virginity of Mary thus initiates in the Christian community the spread of the virginal life embraced by all who are called to it by the Lord. This special vocation, which reaches its apex in Christ's example, represents immeasurable spiritual wealth for the Church in every age, which finds in Mary her inspiration and model.

4.1 The assertion: "Jesus was born of the Virgin Mary" already implies in this event a transcendent mystery, which can find its most complete expression only in the truth of Jesus' divine sonship. The truth of Mary's divine motherhood is closely tied to this central statement of the Christian faith: she is indeed the Mother of the Incarnate Word, in whom is "God from God... true God from true God".[3] The title "Mother of God", already attested by Matthew in the equivalent expression "Mother of Emmanuel", God-with-us (cf. *Mt* 1:23), was explicitly attributed to Mary only after a reflection that embraced about two centuries. It is third-century Christians in Egypt who begin to invoke Mary as *Theotókos*, Mother of God.

---

[1] "*Et incarnátus est de Spíritu Sancto ex María Vírgine...*" (*Symbolum Nicænum-Constantinopolitanum*: *Missale Romanum, editio typica tertia emendata* (2008), Ordo Missæ, n. 18; *DS* 150).

[2] The Nicene-Constantinopolitan Creed (*Symbolum Nicænum-Constantinopolitanum*) was drawn up at the First Council of Nicaea (325 AD) and then modified and expanded at the First Council of Constantinople (381 AD). Better known at the Nicene Creed (*Symbolum Nicænum*), it is sung or said at Mass on all Sundays and Solemnities.

[3] "*Deum de Deo... Deum verum de Deo vero*" (*Symbolum Nicænum-Constantinopolitanum*).

4.2 With this title, which is broadly echoed in the devotion of the Christian people, Mary is seen in the true dimension of her motherhood: she is the Mother of God's Son, whom she virginally begot according to his human nature and raised him with her motherly love, thus contributing to the human growth of the dime person who came to transform the destiny of mankind.

5.1 In a highly significant way, the most ancient prayer to Mary ("*Sub tuum præsídium*..." "We fly to thy patronage...")[1] contains the invocation: "*Theotókos*, Mother of God". This title did not originally come from the reflection of theologians, but from an intuition of faith of the Christian people. Those who acknowledge Jesus as God address Mary as the Mother of God and hope to obtain her powerful aid in the trials of life.

5.2 The Council of Ephesus[2] in 431 defined the dogma of the divine motherhood, officially attributing to Mary the title *Theotókos* in reference to the one person of Christ, true God and true man.

5.3 The three expressions which the Church has used down the centuries to describe her faith in the motherhood of Mary: "Mother of Jesus", "Virgin Mother" and "Mother of God", thus show that Mary's motherhood is intimately linked with the mystery of the Incarnation. They are affirmations of doctrine, connected as well with popular piety, which help define the very identity of Christ.

13 September 1995

[1] *Sub tuum præsídium* (We fly to thy patronage), see Appendix of Marian Prayers, page 232.
[2] The First Council of Ephesus, the 3rd Ecumenical Council of the Church, was convoked in 431 by the Byzantine Emperor Theodosius II (401–450) and Pope Saint Celestine I († 432), primarily to address and formally condemn the Nestorian and Pelagian heresies.

3
MARY WAS UNITED TO JESUS ON THE CROSS

1.1 Saying that "the Virgin Mary... is acknowledged and honoured as being truly the Mother of God and of the Redeemer" (*Lumen gentium*, n. 53),[1] the Council draws attention to the link between Mary's motherhood and Redemption.

1.2 After becoming aware of the maternal role of Mary, who was venerated in the teaching and worship of the first centuries as the virginal Mother of Jesus Christ and therefore as the Mother of God, in the Middle Ages the Church's piety and theological reflection brought to light her co-operation in the Saviour's work.

1.3 This delay is explained by the fact that the efforts of the Church Fathers and of the early Ecumenical Councils, focused as they were on Christ's identity, necessarily left other aspects of dogma aside. Only gradually could the revealed truth be unfolded in all its richness. Down the centuries, Mariology would always take its direction from Christology. The divine motherhood of Mary was itself proclaimed at the Council of Ephesus primarily to affirm the oneness of Christ's person. Similarly, there was a deeper understanding of Mary's presence in salvation history.

2.1 At the end of the second century, Saint Irenaeus,[2] a disciple of Polycarp,[3] already pointed out Mary's contribution to the work of salvation. He understood the value of Mary's consent at the time of the Annunciation, recognising in the Virgin of Nazareth's obedience to and faith in the angel's message the perfect antithesis of Eve's disobedience and disbelief, with a beneficial effect on humanity's destiny. In fact, just as Eve caused death, so Mary, with her "yes", became "a cause of salvation" for herself and for all mankind (cf. *Adv. Haer.*, III, 22, 4; *SC* 211, 441).[4] But this affirmation was not developed in a consistent and systematic way by the other Fathers of the Church.[5]

---

[1] "*Virgo enim Maria... ut vera Mater Dei ac Redemptoris agnoscitur et honoratur*" (CONCILIUM VATICANUM II, Const. dogm. de Ecclesia, *Lumen gentium*, 53: *AAS* 57 (1965), p. 58).

[2] Saint Irenaeus († c. 202 AD) was Bishop of Lugdunum in Gaul (now Lyons in France), a disciple of Saint Polycarp, and is a Father of the Church. His feast day is 28 June in the Ordinary Form of the Roman Rite, 3 July in the Extraordinary Form, and 23 August in the Eastern Orthodox churches.

[3] Saint Polycarp (c. 69 – c. 155) was Bishop of Smyrna and a martyr. He is believed to have been a disciple of Saint John the Evangelist. His feast day is 23 February in the Ordinary Form of the Roman Rite and 26 January in the Extraordinary Form.

[4] "*Sic et Maria habens prædestinatum virum, et tamen virgo, obediens, et sibi, et universe generi humano causa facta est salutis*" (SANCTUS IRENÆUS LUGDUNENSIS, *Adversus hæreses*, lib. III, cap. XXII, 4: *PG* 7, 959).

[5] The Fathers of the Church or Church Fathers are "all those writers of the first twelve centuries whose works on Christian doctrine are considered of weight and worthy of respect" (DONALD ATTWATER, *A Catholic Dictionary* (1958), p. 190).

2.2 Instead, this doctrine was systematically worked out for the first time at the end of the tenth century in the *Life of Mary* by a Byzantine monk, John the Geometer. Here Mary is united to Christ in the whole work of Redemption, sharing, according to God's plan, in the Cross and suffering for our salvation. She remained united to the Son "in every deed, attitude and wish" (cf. *Life of Mary*, Bol. 196, f. 122 v.).

2.3 Mary's association with Jesus' saving work came about through her Mother's love, a love inspired by grace, which conferred a higher power on it: love freed of passion proves to be the most compassionate (cf. *ibid.*, Bol. 196, f. 123 v.).

3.1 In the West Saint Bernard,[1] who died in 1153, turns to Mary and comments on the presentation of Jesus in the temple: "Offer your Son, sacrosanct Virgin, and present the fruit of your womb to the Lord. For our reconciliation with all, offer the heavenly victim pleasing to God" (*Serm. 3 in Purif.*, 2: *PL* 183, 370).[2]

3.2 A disciple and friend of Saint Bernard, Arnold of Chartres,[3] shed light particularly on Mary's offering in the sacrifice of Calvary. He distinguished in the Cross "two altars: one in Mary's heart, the other in Christ's body. Christ sacrificed his flesh, Mary her soul". Mary sacrificed herself spiritually in deep communion with Christ, and implored the world's salvation: "What the mother asks, the Son approves and the Father grants" (cf. *De septem verbis Domini in cruce*, 3: *PL* 189, 1694).[4]

3.3 From this age on other authors explain the doctrine of Mary's special cooperation in the redemptive sacrifice.

4.1 At the same time, in Christian worship and piety contemplative reflection on Mary's "compassion" developed, poignantly depicted in images of the *Pietà*.[5] Mary's sharing in the drama of the Cross makes this event more

---

[1] Saint Bernard of Clairvaux (1090–1153), "the Mellifluous Doctor," was a member of the Order of Cistercians, abbot, confessor, and is a Doctor of the Church. His feast day is 20 August.

[2] "*Offer filium tuum, Virgo sacrata, et benedictum fructum ventris tui Domino repræsenta. Offer ad nostram omnium reconciliationem hostiam sanctam, Deo placentem*" (SANCTUS BERNARDUS CLARÆ-VALLENSIS, *In Purificatione B. Mariæ*, Sermo III, 2: *PL* 183, 370).

[3] Arnold of Chartres, Abbot of Bonneval († after 1156) was a disciple and friend of Saint Bernard of Clairvaux.

[4] "*Nimirum in tabernaculo illo duo videres altaria, aliud in pectore Mariae, aliud in corpore Christi. Christus carnem, Maria immolabat animam… Cum quod mater peteret, Filius approbaret, Pater donaret*" (ERNALDUS BONAEVALLIS, *De septem verbis Domini in cruce*, tractatus III: *PL* 189, 1694-1695).

[5] *Pietà* (Italian for "pities"), is an image, generally carved in stone or cast in metal, of the dead body (*corpus*) of Christ lying in the arms of His mother. The most well-known representation of this is Michelangelo's *La Pietà* in Saint Peter's Basilica in Rome.

deeply human and helps the faithful to enter into the mystery: the Mother's compassion more clearly reveals the Passion of the Son.

4.2 By sharing in Christ's redemptive work, Mary's spiritual and universal motherhood is also recognised. In the East, John the Geometer told Mary: "You are our mother". Giving Mary thanks "for the sorrow and suffering she bore for us", he sheds light on her maternal affection and motherly regard for all those who receive salvation (cf. *Farewell Discourse on the Dormition of Our Most Glorious Lady, Mother of God,* in A. Wenger, *L'Assomption de la Très Sainte Vierge dans la tradition byzantine*, p. 407).

4.3 In the West too, the doctrine of the spiritual motherhood developed with Saint Anselm,[1] who asserted: "You are the mother… of reconciliation and the reconciled, the mother of salvation and the saved" (cf. *Oratio* 52, 8: *PL* 158, 957 A).[2]

4.4 Mary does not cease to be venerated as the Mother of God, but the fact that she is our Mother gives her divine motherhood a new aspect that opens within us the way to a more intimate communion with her.

5.1 Mary's motherhood in our regard does not only consist of an affective bond: because of her merits and her intercession she contributes effectively to our spiritual birth and to the development of the life of grace within us. This is why Mary is called "Mother of grace" and "Mother of life".

5.2 The title "Mother of life", already employed by Saint Gregory of Nyssa,[3] was explained as follows by Blessed Guerric of Igny,[4] who died in 1157:

"She is the Mother of the Life from whom all men take life: in giving birth to this life herself, she has somehow given rebirth to all those who have lived it. Only one was begotten, but we have all been reborn" (*In Assumpt.* I, 2: *PL* 185, 188).[5]

---

[1] Saint Anselm d'Aosta of Canterbury (c. 1033 – 1109) was Archbishop of Canterbury, a Benedictine monk, the founder of scholasticism, and is a Doctor of the Church. His feast day is 21 April.

[2] "*Ergo, o domina, mater es iustificationis et iustificatorum, genitrix es reconciliationis et reconciliatorum, parens es salutis et salvatorum*" (Sanctus Anselmus Cantuariensis, *Orationes*, oratio LII: *PL* 158, 957 A).

[3] Saint Gregory of Nyssa (c. 335 – c. 394) was Bishop of Nyssa and a Cappadocian Father. His feast day is 9 March in the Roman Catholic Church, 10 January in the Eastern churches, 14 June in the Lutheran church, and 19 July in the Anglican Communion.

[4] Blessed Guerric of Igny (c. 1070 – 1157) was a Cistercian and the 2nd Abbot of Igny in France. His feast day is 19 August.

[5] "*Mater siquidem est Vitæ qua vivunt universi; quam dum ex se genuit, nimirum omnes qui ex ea victuri sunt, quodammodo regeneravit. Unus generabatur, sed nos omnes generabamur*" (Beatus Guerricus Igniacensis, *In Assumptione B. Mariæ*, sermo I, 2: *PL* 185, 188).

5.2 A thirteenth century text, the *Mariale*, used a vivid image in attributing this rebirth to the "painful travail" of Cavalry, by which "she became the spiritual mother of the whole human race". Indeed, "in her chaste womb she conceived by compassion the children of the Church" (*Q*. 29, par. 3).[1]

6.1 The Second Vatican Council, after stating that Mary "in a wholly singular way co-operated in the work of the Saviour", concludes: "for this reason she is a mother to us in the order of grace" (*Lumen gentium*, n. 61),[2] thus confirming the Church's perception that Mary is at the side of her Son as the spiritual Mother of all humanity.

6.2 Mary is our Mother: this consoling truth, offered to us ever more clearly and profoundly by the love and faith of the Church, has sustained and sustains the spiritual life of us all, and encourages us, even in suffering, to have faith and hope.

25 October 1995

[1] *Mariale quotidianum sive brevissima Mariana obsequia*, 29, 3.
[2] "*Quam ob causam mater nobis in ordine gratiæ exstitit*" (Concilium Vaticanum II, Const. dogm. de Ecclesia, *Lumen gentium*, 61: *AAS* 57 (1965), p. 63).

4
THE CHURCH GREW IN UNDERSTANDING OF MARY'S ROLE

1.1 In our preceding catecheses we saw how the doctrine of Mary's motherhood passed from its first formula, "Mother of Jesus", to the more complete and explicit, "Mother of God", even to the affirmation of her maternal involvement in the redemption of humanity.

1.2 For other aspects of Marian doctrine as well, many centuries were necessary to arrive at the explicit definition of the revealed truths concerning Mary. Typical examples of this faith journey towards the ever deeper discovery of Mary's role in the history of salvation are the dogma of the Immaculate Conception and the Assumption, proclaimed, as we know by two of my venerable predecessors, respectively, the Servant of God Pius IX[1] in 1854, and the Servant of God Pius XII[2] during the Jubilee Year of 1950.

1.3 Mariology is a particular field of theological research: in it the Christian people's love for Mary intuited, frequently in anticipation, certain aspects of the mystery of the Blessed Virgin, calling the attention of theologians and pastors to them.

2.1 We must recognise that, at first sight, the Gospels offer scant information on the person and life of Mary. We would certainly like to have had fuller information about her, which would have enabled us to know the Mother of God better.

2.2 This expectation remains unsatisfied, even in the other New Testament writings where an explicit doctrinal development regarding Mary is lacking. Even Saint Paul's letters, which offer us a rich reflection on Christ and his work, limit themselves to stating, in a very significant passage, that God sent his Son "born of woman" (*Gal* 4:4).[3]

---

[1] Blessed Pope Pius IX (1792–1878), born Giovanni Maria Mastai-Ferretti, was elected the 255th Bishop of Rome on 16 June 1846. He reigned for nearly 32 years, making his papacy the longest in the history of the Church. He defined *ex cathedra* the dogma of the Immaculate Conception of the Blessed Virgin Mary in 1854 and convened the First Vatican Council in 1869, which would decree the dogma of Papal Infallibility. In the 1950s and again in 2000, the body of Blessed Pius IX was found to be incorrupt. He was beatified by Saint John Paul II in 2000. His feast day is 7 February.

[2] Venerable Pope Pius XII (1876–1958), born Eugenio Maria Giuseppe Giovanni Pacelli, was elected the 260th Bishop of Rome on 2 March 1939. He defined *ex cathedra* the dogma of the Assumption of the Blessed Virgin Mary.

[3] "*Factum ex muliere*" (*Gal* 4, 4).

2.3 Very little is said about Mary's family.[1] If we exclude the infancy narratives, in the Synoptic Gospels we find only two statements which shed some light on Mary: one concerning the attempt by his "brethren" or relatives to take Jesus back to Nazareth (cf. *Mk* 3:2 1; *Mt* 12:48); the other, in response to a woman's exclamation about the blessedness of Jesus' Mother (*Lk* 11:27).

2.4 Nevertheless, Luke, in the infancy Gospel, in the episodes of the Annunciation, the Visitation, the birth of Jesus, the presentation of the Child in the temple and his finding among the teachers at the age of 12, not only provides us with some important facts, but presents a sort of "proto-Mariology" of fundamental interest. His information is indirectly completed by Matthew in the account of the annunciation to Joseph (*Mt* 1:18-25), but only with regard to the virginal conception of Jesus.

2.5 Moreover, John's Gospel deepens our knowledge of the value for salvation history of the role played by the Mother of Jesus, when it records her presence at the beginning and end of his public fife. Particularly significant is Mary's presence at the Cross, when she received from her dying Son the charge to be mother to the beloved disciple and, in him, to all Christians (cf. *Jn* 2:1-12; *Jn* 19:25-27). Lastly, the Acts of the Apostles expressly numbers the Mother of Jesus among the women of the first community awaiting Pentecost (cf. *Acts* 1:14).

2.6 However, in the absence of further New Testament evidence and reliable historical sources, we know nothing of Mary's life after the Pentecost event nor of the date and circumstances of her death. We can only suppose that she continued to live with the Apostle John and that she was very closely involved in the development of the first Christian community.

3.1 The sparse information on Mary's earthly life is compensated by its quality and theological richness, which contemporary exegesis has carefully brought to light.

3.2 Moreover, we must remember that the Evangelists' viewpoint is totally Christological and is concerned with the Mother only in relation to the joyful proclamation of the Son. As Saint Ambrose[2] observed, the Evangelist, in expounding the mystery of the Incarnation, "believed it was better not to seek further testimonies about Mary's virginity, in order not to seem the defender

[1] Tradition names the parents of the Blessed Virgin Mary as Joachim and Ann, who have been venerated as saints since the early days of Christianity. Their feast day is 26 July in the Ordinary Form of the Roman Rite. In the Extraordinary Form, Saint Anne's feast day is on 26 July and that of Saint Joachim is on 16 August.

[2] Saint Ambrose of Milan († 397) was Bishop of Milan and is a Doctor of the Church. His feast day is 7 December.

of the Virgin rather than the preacher of the mystery" (*Exp. in Lucam*, 2, 6: *PL* 15, 1555).[1]

3.3 We can recognise in this fact a special intention of the Holy Spirit, who desired to awaken in the Church an effort of research which, preserving the centrality of the mystery of Christ, might not be caught up in details about Mary's life, but aim above all at discovering her role in the work of salvation, her personal holiness and her maternal mission in Christian life.

4.1 The Holy Spirit guides the Church's effort, committing her to take on Mary's own attitudes. In the account of Jesus' birth, Luke noted how his mother kept all these things, "pondering them in her heart" (*Lk* 2:19),[2] striving, that is, to "put together" (*symballousa*), in a deeper vision, all the events of which she was the privileged witness.

4.2 Similarly, the people of God are also urged by the same Spirit to understand deeply all that has been said about Mary, in order to progress in the knowledge of her mission, intimately linked to the mystery of Christ.

4.3 As Mariology develops, the particular role of the Christian people emerges. They co-operate, by the affirmation and witness of their faith, in the progress of Marian doctrine, which normally is not only the work of theologians, even if their task is indispensable to deepening and clearly explaining the datum of faith and the Christian experience itself.

4.4 The faith of the simple is admired and praised by Jesus, who recognised in it a marvellous expression of the Father's benevolence (cf. *Mt* 11:25; *Lk* 10:21). Down the centuries it continues to proclaim the marvels of the history of salvation, hidden from the wise. This faith, in harmony with the Virgin's simplicity, has led to progress in the recognition of her personal holiness and the transcendent value of her motherhood.

4.5 The mystery of Mary commits every Christian, in communion with the Church, "to pondering in his heart" what the Gospel revelation affirms about the Mother of Christ. In the logic of the *Magníficat*,[3] after the example of Mary, each one will personally experience God's love and will discover a sign of God's tenderness for man in the marvels wrought by the Blessed Trinity in the woman "full of grace".

8 November 1995

[1] "*Et ideo qui Incarnationis incorruptum susceperat probare mysterium, non putavit uberius prosequendum virginitatis Mariae testimonium; ne defensor magis Virginis, quam assertor mysterii crederetur*" (Sanctus Ambrosius Mediolanensis, *Expositio Evangelii secundum Lucam*, lib. II, 6: *PL* 15, 1555).

[2] "*Conferens in corde suo*" (*Lc* 2, 19).

[3] For the text of the *Magníficat* or Canticle of the Blessed Virgin Mary (*Canticum Beatæ Mariæ Virginis*), see the Appendix of Marian Prayers, p. 235.

5
TO HONOUR MARY IS TO GO TO JESUS

1.1 After following in our previous catecheses how the Christian community's reflection on the figure and role of the Blessed Virgin in salvation history took shape from the earliest times, let us pause today to meditate on *the Marian experience of the Church.*

1.2 The development of Mariological thought and devotion to the Blessed Virgin down the centuries has contributed to revealing ever better the Church's Marian aspect. Of course, the Blessed Virgin is totally related to Christ, the foundation of faith and ecclesial experience, and she leads to him. That is why, in obedience to Jesus, who reserved a very special role for his Mother in the economy of salvation, Christians have venerated, loved and prayed to Mary in a most particular and fervent way. They have attributed to her an important place in faith and piety, recognising her as the privileged way to Christ, the supreme Mediator.

1.3 The Church's Marian dimension is thus an undeniable element in the experience of the Christian people. It is expressed in many ways in the life of believers, testifying to the place Mary holds in their hearts. It is not a superficial sentiment but a deep and conscious emotional bond, rooted in the faith which spurs Christians of the past and present to turn habitually to Mary, to enter into a more intimate communion with Christ.

2.1 After the most ancient prayer, formulated in Egypt by the Christian communities of the third century, to implore "the Mother of God" for protection in danger, numerous invocations were addressed to her, whom the baptised consider most powerful in her intercession with the Lord.

2.2 Today, the most common prayer is the *Hail Mary,*[1] whose first part consists of words from the Gospel (cf. *Lk* 1:28, 42). Christians learn to recite it at home from their earliest years and receive it as a precious gift to be preserved throughout life. This same prayer, repeated tens of times in the Rosary, helps many of the faithful to enter into prayerful contemplation of the Gospel mysteries and sometimes to remain for long intervals in intimate contact with the Mother of Jesus. Since the Middle Ages, the *Hail Mary* has been the most common prayer of all believers who ask the Holy Mother of the Lord to guide and protect them on their daily journey through life (cf. Apostolic Exhortation *Marialis cultus*, nn. 42-55).

---

[1] For the text of the *Ave Maria* (Hail Mary), see the Appendix of Marian Prayers, p. 232.

2.3 Christian people have also expressed their love for Mary by multiplying expressions of their devotion: hymns, prayers and poetic compositions, simple or sometimes of great quality, imbued with that same love for her who was given to men as Mother by the Crucified One. Some of these, such as the Akathist Hymn and the *Salve Regina*,[1] have deeply marked the faith life of believers.

2.4 The counterpart of Marian piety is the immensely rich artistic production in the East and West, which has enabled entire generations to appreciate Mary's spiritual beauty. Painters, sculptors, musicians and poets have left us masterpieces which, in shedding light on the various aspects of the Blessed Virgin's greatness, help to give us a better understanding of the meaning and value of her lofty contribution to the work of Redemption.

2.5 In Mary, Christian art recognises the fulfilment of a new humanity which corresponds to God's plan and is therefore a sublime sign of hope for the whole human race.

3.1 This message could not fail to be grasped by Christians called to a vocation of special consecration. In fact, Mary is particularly venerated in religious orders and congregations, in institutes or associations of consecrated life. Many institutes, primarily but not only female, include Mary's name in their title. Nevertheless, over and above its external expressions, the spirituality of religious families, as well as of many ecclesial movements, some of which are specifically Marian, highlight their special bond with Mary as the guarantee of a charism fully and authentically lived.

3.2 This Marian reference in the lives of people particularly favoured by the Holy Spirit has also developed the mystical dimension, which shows how the Christian can experience Mary's intervention in the innermost depths of his being.

3.3 This reference to Mary binds not only committed Christians but also simple believers and even the "distant", for whom it is frequently their only link with the life of the Church. Pilgrimages to Marian shrines, which attract large crowds of the faithful throughout the year, are a sign of the Christian people's common sentiment for the Mother of the Lord. Some of these bulwarks of Marian piety are famous, such as Lourdes, Fatima, Loreto, Pompei, Guadalupe and Czêstochowa! Others are known only at the national or local level. In all of them, the memory of events associated with recourse to Mary conveys the message of her motherly tenderness, opening our hearts to God's grace.

---

[1] For the texts of the Akathist Hymn to the *Theotókos* and the *Salve Regina* (Hail Holy Queen), see the Appendix of Marian Prayers, p. 242 and 233.

3.4 These places of Marian prayer are a wonderful testimony to God's mercy, which reaches man through Mary's intercession. The miracles of physical healing, spiritual redemption and conversion are the obvious sign that, with Christ and in the Spirit, Mary is continuing her work as helper and mother.

4.1 Marian shrines often become centres of evangelisation. Indeed, even in the Church today, as in the community awaiting Pentecost, prayer with Mary spurs many Christians to the apostolate and to the service of their brothers and sisters. Here I would especially like to recall the great influence of Marian piety on the practice of charity and the works of mercy. Encouraged by Mary's presence, believers have often felt the need to dedicate themselves to the poor, the unfortunate and the sick, in order to be for the lowliest of the earth a sign of the motherly protection of the Blessed Virgin, the living icon of the Father's mercy.

4.2 It can be clearly seen from all this how the Marian dimension pervades the Church's whole life. The proclamation of the Word, the liturgy, the various charitable and cultural expressions find in Mary an occasion for enrichment and renewal.

4.3 The People of God, under the guidance of their Pastors, are called to discern in this fact the action of the Holy Spirit who has spurred the Christian faith onward in its discovery of Mary's face. It is he who works marvels in the centres of Marian piety. It is he who, by encouraging knowledge of and love for Mary, leads the faithful to learn from the Virgin of the *Magníficat* how to read the signs of God in history and to acquire a wisdom that makes every man and every woman the architects of a new humanity.

15 November 1995

6
MARY IS THE MODEL OF PERSEVERING SILENCE

1.1 After reflecting on the Marian dimension of ecclesial life, we are now going to cast light on the immense spiritual wealth Mary communicates to the Church by her example and her intercession.

1.2 We would first like to pause and briefly reflect on some significant aspects of Mary's personality, which offer all believers valuable guidance in accepting and fulfilling their own vocation.

1.3 Mary has gone before us on the way of *faith*: believing the angel's message, she was the first to welcome the mystery of the Incarnation and did so perfectly (cf. *Redemptoris Mater*, n. 13). Her journey as a believer began even earlier than her divine motherhood and developed more deeply throughout her earthly experience. Hers was a daring faith. At the Annunciation she believed in what was humanly impossible, and at Cana she urged Jesus to work his first miracle, pressing him to manifest his messianic powers (cf. *Jn* 2:1-5).

1.4 Mary teaches Christians to live their faith as a demanding and engaging journey, which, in every age and situation of life, requires courage and constant perseverance.

2.1 Mary's *docility* to the divine will was linked to her faith. Believing in God's word, she could accept it fully in her life and, showing herself receptive to God's sovereign plan, she accepted all that was asked of her from on high.

2.2 The Virgin's presence in the Church thus encourages Christians to listen to the word of the Lord every day, to understand his loving plan in various daily events, and to co-operate faithfully in bringing it about.

3.1 This is how Mary teaches the community of believers to look to the future with total abandonment to God. In the Virgin's personal experience, *hope* is enriched with ever new reasons. Since the Annunciation, Mary concentrates the expectations of ancient Israel on the Son of God, incarnate in her virginal womb. Her hope was strengthened during the successive stages of Jesus' hidden life in Nazareth and his public ministry. Her great faith in the word of Christ, who had announced his Resurrection on the third day, prevented her from wavering, even when faced with the drama of the Cross. She retained her hope in the fulfilment of the messianic work and steadfastly, after the darkness of Good Friday, awaited the morning of the Resurrection.

3.2 On their difficult path through history, between the "already" of salvation received and the "not yet" of its fulfilment, the community of believers know they can count on the help of the "Mother of Hope". After experiencing Christ's victory over the powers of death, she communicates to them an ever new capacity to await God's future and to abandon themselves to the Lord's promises.

4.1 Mary's example enables the Church better to appreciate the value of *silence*. Mary's silence is not only moderation in speech, but it is especially a wise capacity for remembering and embracing in a single gaze of faith the mystery of the Word made man and the events of his earthly life.

4.2 It is this silence as acceptance of the Word, this ability to meditate on the mystery of Christ, that Mary passes on to believers. In a noisy world filled with messages of all kinds, her witness enables us to appreciate a spiritually rich silence and fosters a contemplative spirit.

4.3 Mary witnesses to the value of a *humble and hidden* life. Everyone usually demands, and sometimes almost claims, to be able to realise fully his own person and qualities. Everyone is sensitive to esteem and honour. The Gospels frequently mention that the Apostles were ambitious for the most important places in the kingdom and they argued among themselves as to which of them was the greatest. In this matter Jesus had to teach them the need for humility and service (cf. *Mt* 18:1-5; 20:20-28; *Mk* 9:33-37; 10:35-45; *Lk* 9:46-48; 22:24-27). Mary, on the contrary, never sought honour or the advantages of a privileged position; she always tried to fulfil God's will, leading a life according to the Father's plan of salvation.

4.4 To all those who often feel the burden of a seemingly insignificant life, Mary reveals how valuable life can be if it is lived for love of Christ and one's brothers and sisters.

5.1 Mary, moreover, witnesses to the value of a life that is *pure* and full of *tenderness* for all men. The beauty of her soul, totally offered to the Lord, is an object of admiration for the Christian people. In Mary, the Christian community has always seen the ideal woman, full of love and tenderness because she lived in purity of mind and body.

5.2 Faced with the cynicism of a certain contemporary culture, which too often seems not to recognise the value of chastity and degrades sexuality by separating it from personal dignity and God's plan, the Virgin Mary holds up the witness of a purity that illumines the conscience and leads to a greater love for creatures and for the Lord.

6.1 Furthermore, Mary appears to Christians of all times as the one who feels deep *compassion* for the sufferings of humanity. This compassion does not consist only in an emotional sympathy, but is expressed in effective and concrete help when confronted with humanity's material and moral misery.

6.2 In following Mary, the Church is called to take on the same attitude towards all the earth's poor and suffering. The maternal attention of the Lord's Mother to the tears, sorrows and hardships of the men and women of all ages must spur Christians, particularly at the dawn of the new millennium, to increase the concrete and visible signs of a love that will enable today's humble and suffering people to share in the promises and hopes of the new world which is born from Easter.

7.1 Human affection for and devotion to the Mother of Jesus surpasses the Church's visible boundaries and fosters sentiments of *reconciliation.* As a mother, Mary desires the union of all her children. Her presence in the Church is an invitation to preserve the unanimity of heart which reigned in the first community (cf. *Acts* 1:14) and, consequently, to seek ways of unity and peace among all men and women of goodwill.

7.2 In interceding with her Son, Mary asks the grace of unity for all humanity, in view of building a civilisation of love, overcoming tendencies to division, temptations to revenge and hatred, and the perverse fascination of violence.

8.1 The motherly *smile* of the Virgin, reproduced in so much Marian iconography, expresses a fullness of grace and peace that seeks to be shared. This expression of her serenity of spirit effectively contributes to giving the Church a joyful face.

8.2 Welcoming, in the Annunciation, the angel's invitation to "rejoice" (*khaire* [*chàire*] = rejoice: *Lk* 1:28),[1] Mary was the first to share in the messianic joy foretold by the Prophets for the "daughter of Sion" (cf. *Is* 12:6; *Zep* 3:14-15; *Zec* 9:9), and she passes it on to humanity in every age.

8.3 Invoking her as *causa nostræ lætítiæ*,[2] the Christian people find in her the capacity to communicate the joy that is born of hope, even in the midst of life's trials, and to guide those who commend themselves to her to the joy that knows no end.

22 November 1995

---

[1] "*Khaire*" or "*chàire*" is the transliteration of the Greek word χαῖρε.
[2] Latin for "cause of our joy" (cf. *Litaniæ lauretanæ* [Litany of the Blessed Virgin Mary], p. 238).

7
MARY SHOWS US GOD'S RESPECT FOR WOMEN

1.1 The theological and spiritual aspects of the Church's teaching on Mary, which have been amply developed in our century, have recently acquired a new importance from the sociological and pastoral standpoint, due also to a clearer understanding of woman's role in the Christian community and in society, as we see in many significant interventions of the Magisterium.

1.2 The message to women addressed by the Fathers at the conclusion of the Second Vatican Council on 8 December 1965 are well known:

"But the hour is coming, in fact has come, when the vocation of woman is being achieved in its fullness, the hour in which woman acquires in the world an influence, an effect and a power never hitherto achieved" (*Enchiridion Vat.*, 1, 307).[1]

1.3 I confirmed these affirmations a few years later in the Apostolic Letter *Mulieris dignitatem*: "The dignity and the vocation of women—a subject of constant human and Christian reflection—have gained exceptional prominence in recent years" (n. 1).[2]

1.4 The role and dignity of woman have been particularly championed in this century by the feminist movement, which has sought to react, sometimes in forceful ways, against everything in the past and present that has hindered the full appreciation and development of the feminine personality as well as her participation in the many expressions of social and political life.

1.5 These demands were in large part legitimate and contributed to building up a more balanced view of the feminine question in the contemporary world. The Church, especially in recent times, has paid special attention to these demands, encouraged by the fact that the figure of Mary, if seen in the light of her Gospel life, is a valid response to woman's desire for emancipation: Mary is the only human person who eminently fulfils God's plan of love for humanity.

2.1 This plan is already manifest in the Old Testament, with the creation narrative that introduces the first couple created in the image of God himself: "So God created man in his own image, in the image of God he created him; male and

---

[1] Saint Paul VI, *Address to Women* ("*Aux femmes*") at the Close of the Second Vatican Ecumenical Council (8 December 1965): *Enchiridion Vaticanum*, 1, 307; *AAS* 58 (1966), 13-14.

[2] "*Mulieris dignitatem et vocationem humana et christiana meditatio, quæ constanter huic studuit argumento, recentioribus annis maximi fecit momenti*" (Sanctus Ioannes Paulus II, Ep. ap. *Mulieris dignitatem* (15 augusti 1988), 1: *AAS* 80 (1988), p. 1653).

female he created them" (*Gn* 1:27).[1] Thus woman, no less than man, bears God's image in herself. This means that, since her appearance on the earth as a result of the divine action, she too is appreciated: "And God saw everything that he had made, and behold, it was very good" (*Gn* 1:31).[2] According to this view, the difference between man and woman does not imply the inferiority of the latter nor her inequality, but is a new element which enriches God's plan, and is "very good".

2.2 However, God's intention goes well beyond what is revealed in the book of Genesis. In fact, in Mary God created a feminine personality which greatly surpasses the ordinary condition of woman as it appears in the creation of Eve. Mary's unique excellence in the world of grace and her perfection are fruits of the particular divine benevolence which seeks to raise everyone, men and women, to the moral perfection and holiness which are proper to the adopted children of God. Mary is "blessed among women"; however, every woman shares in some way in her sublime dignity in the divine plan.

3.1 The remarkable gift to the Mother of the Lord not only testifies to what we could call God's respect for woman, but also emphasises the profound regard in God's plans for her irreplaceable role in human history.

3.2 Women need to discover this divine esteem in order to be ever more aware of their lofty dignity. The historical and social situations which caused the reaction of feminism were marked by a lack of appreciation of woman's worth; frequently she was relegated to a second-rate or even marginal role. This did not allow her to express fully the wealth of intelligence and wisdom contained in her femininity. Indeed, throughout history women have not infrequently suffered from scant esteem for their abilities, and sometimes even scorn and unjust prejudice. This is a state of affairs that, despite important changes, unfortunately continues even today in many nations and in many parts of the world.

4.1 The figure of Mary shows that God has such esteem for woman that any form of discrimination lacks a theoretical basis.

4.2 The marvellous work which the Creator achieved in Mary gives men and women the possibility to discover dimensions of their condition which before were not sufficiently perceived. In beholding the Mother of the Lord, women will be able to understand better their dignity and the greatness of

[1] "*Et creavit Deus hominem ad imaginem suam; ad imaginem Dei creavit illum; masculum et feminam creavit eos*" (*Gen* 1, 27).

[2] "*Viditque Deus cuncta, quæ fecit, et ecce erant valde bona. Et factum est vespere et mane, dies sextus*" (*Gen* 1, 31).

their mission. But men too, in the light of the Virgin Mother, will be able to acquire a fuller and more balanced view of their identity, of the family and of society.

4.3 Attentive consideration of the figure of Mary, as she is presented to us in Sacred Scripture as read in faith by the Church, is still more necessary in view of the disparagement she sometimes receives from certain feminist currents. The Virgin of Nazareth has, in some cases, been presented as the symbol of the female personality imprisoned in a narrow, confining domesticity.

4.4 Mary, on the contrary, is the model of the full development of woman's vocation, since, despite the objective limits imposed by her social condition, she exercised a vast influence on the destiny of humanity and the transformation of society.

5.1 Moreover Marian doctrine can shed light on the multiple ways in which the life of grace promotes woman's spiritual beauty. In view of the shameful exploitation that sometimes makes woman an object without dignity, destined for the satisfaction of base passions, Mary reaffirms the sublime meaning of feminine beauty, a gift and reflection of God's beauty.

5.2 It is true that feminine perfection, as it was fully realised in Mary, can at first sight seem to be an exceptional case and impossible to imitate, a model too lofty for imitation. In fact, the unique holiness of her who from the very first moment received the privilege of the Immaculate Conception is sometimes considered unreachably distant.

5.3 However, far from being a restraint on the way of following the Lord, Mary's exalted holiness is, on the contrary, destined in God's plan to encourage all Christians to open themselves to the sanctifying power of the grace of God, for whom nothing is impossible. Therefore in Mary all are called to put total trust in the divine omnipotence, which transforms hearts, guiding them towards full receptivity to his providential plan of love.

29 November 1995

8
MARY SHEDS LIGHT ON THE ROLE OF WOMEN

1.1 As I have already explained in the preceding catecheses, the role entrusted to Mary by the divine plan of salvation sheds light on the vocation of woman in the life of the Church and society by defining its difference in relation to man. The model represented by Mary clearly shows what is specific to the feminine personality.

1.2 In recent times some trends in the feminist movement, in order to advance women's emancipation, have sought to make her like man in every way. However, the divine intention manifested in creation, though desiring woman to be man's equal in dignity and worth, at the same time clearly affirms her diversity and specific features. Woman's identity cannot consist in being a copy of man, since she is endowed with her own qualities and prerogatives, which give her a particular uniqueness that is always to be fostered and encouraged.

1.3 These prerogatives and particular features of the feminine personality attained their full development in Mary. The fullness of divine grace actually fostered in her all the natural abilities typical of woman.

1.4 Mary's role in the work of salvation is totally dependent on Christ's. It is a unique function, required by the fulfilment of the mystery of the Incarnation: Mary's motherhood was necessary to give the world its Saviour, the true Son of God, but also perfectly man.

1.5 The importance of woman's co-operation in the coming of Christ is emphasised by the initiative of God, who, through the angel, communicates his plan of salvation to the Virgin of Nazareth so that she can consciously and freely co-operate by giving her own generous consent.

1.6 Here the loftiest model of woman's collaboration in the Redemption of man—every man—is fulfilled; this model represents the transcendent reference point for every affirmation of woman's role and function in history.

2.1 In carrying out this sublime form of co-operation, Mary also shows the style in which woman must concretely express her mission.

2.2 With regard to the angel's message, the Virgin makes no proud demands nor does she seek to satisfy personal ambitions. Luke presents her to us as wanting only to offer her humble service with total and trusting acceptance of the divine plan of salvation. This is the meaning of her response: "Behold, I am the handmaid of the Lord; let it be to me according to your word" (*Lk* 1:38).[1]

2.3 It is not a question of a purely passive acceptance, since her consent is given only after she has expressed the difficulty that arose from her intent to remain a virgin, inspired by her will to belong more completely to the Lord.

2.4 Having received the angel's response, Mary immediately expresses her readiness, maintaining an attitude of humble service.

2.5 It is the humble, valuable service that so many women, following Mary's example, have offered and continue to offer in the Church for the growth of Christ's kingdom.

3.1 The figure of Mary reminds women today of the value of motherhood. In the contemporary world the appropriate and balanced importance is not always given to this value. In some cases, the need for women to work in order to provide for the needs of their family and an erroneous concept of freedom, which sees child-care as a hindrance to woman's autonomy and opportunities, have obscured the significance of motherhood for the development of the feminine personality. On the contrary, in other cases the biological aspect of childbirth becomes so important as to overshadow the other significant opportunities woman has for expressing her innate vocation to being a mother.

3.2 In Mary we have been given to understand the true meaning of motherhood, which attains its loftiest dimension in the divine plan of salvation. For her, being a mother not only endows her feminine personality, directed towards the gift of life, with its full development, but also represents an answer of faith to woman's own vocation which assumes its truest value only in the light of God's covenant (cf. *Mulieris dignitatem*, n. 19).

4.1 In looking attentively at Mary, we also discover in her the model of virginity lived for the kingdom.

4.2 The Virgin *par excellence*, in her heart she grew in her desire to live in this state in order to achieve an ever deeper intimacy with God.

4.3 For women called to virginal chastity, Mary reveals the lofty meaning of so special a vocation and thus draws attention to the spiritual fruitfulness which it produces in the divine plan: a higher order of motherhood, a motherhood according to the Spirit (cf. *Mulieris dignitatem*, n. 21).

---

[1] "*Ecce ancilla Domini; fiat mihi secundum verbum tuum*" (*Lc* 1, 38).

4.4 Mary's maternal heart, open to all human misfortune, also reminds women that the development of the feminine personality calls for a commitment to charity. More sensitive to the values of the heart, woman shows a high capacity for personal self-giving.

4.5 To all in our age who offer selfish models for affirming the feminine personality, the luminous and holy figure of the Lord's Mother shows how only by self-giving and self-forgetfulness towards others is it possible to attain authentic fulfilment of the divine plan for one's own life.

4.6 Mary's presence therefore encourages sentiments of mercy and solidarity in women for situations of human distress and arouses a desire to alleviate the pain of those who suffer: the poor, the sick and all in need of help.

4.7 In virtue of her special bond with Mary, woman has often in the course of history represented God's closeness to the expectations of goodness and tenderness of a humanity wounded by hatred and sin, by sowing in the world seeds of a civilisation that can respond to violence with love.

6 December 1995

9
THE SECOND VATICAN COUNCIL'S TEACHING ON MARY

1.1 Today I would like to reflect on the particular presence of the Mother of the Church at what was certainly the most important ecclesial event of our century; the Second Vatican Ecumenical Council, opened by Pope John XXIII[1] on the morning of 11 October 1962 and closed by Pope Paul VI[2] on 8 December 1965.

1.2 An extraordinary Marian tone actually marked the Council from its induction. In the Apostolic Letter *Celebrandi Concilii Œcumenici*, my venerable predecessor, the Servant of God John XXIII, had already recommended recourse to the powerful intercession of Mary, "Mother of grace and heavenly patroness of the Council" (11 April 1961, *AAS* 53 [1961] 242).[3]

1.3 Subsequently, in 1962, on the feast of the Purification of Mary, Pope John set the opening of the Council for 11 October, explaining that he had chosen this date in memory of the great Council of Ephesus, which precisely on that date had proclaimed Mary *Theotókos*, Mother of God (*Motu proprio "Concilium"*, *AAS* 54 [1962] 67-68). Later, in his opening address, the Pope entrusted the Council itself to the "Help of Christians, Help of Bishops", imploring her motherly assistance for the successful outcome of the Council's work (*AAS* 54 [1962] 795).[4]

1.4 The Council Fathers also turned their thoughts expressly to Mary in of their message to the world at the opening of the Council's sessions, saying, "We successors of the Apostles, joined together in prayer with Mary, the Mother of Jesus, form one apostolic body" (*Acta Synodalia* I, I, 254), thus linking themselves, in communion with Mary, to the early Church awaiting the Holy Spirit (cf. *Acts* 1:14).

2.1 At the second session of the Council, it was proposed that the treatment of the Blessed Virgin Mary be put into the Constitution on the Church. This initiative, although expressly recommended by the Theological Commission, prompted a variety of opinions.

---

[1] Pope Saint John XXIII (1881–1963), born Angelo Giuseppe Roncalli, was elected the 261st Bishop of Rome on 28 October 1958. He convened the Second Vatican Council (1962–1965), but did not live to see its completion. He was beatified by Saint John Paul II in 2000 and canonized by Pope Francis in 2014. His feast day is 11 October.

[2] Pope Saint Paul VI (1897–1978), born Giovanni Battista Enrico Antonio Maria Montini, was elected the 262nd Bishop of Rome on 21 June 1963. He was beatified on 19 October 2014 and canonized on 14 October 2018. His feast day is 29 May in the Roman Rite and 30 May in the Ambrosian Rite.

[3] "*Mater gratiæ et Concilii patrona cælestis*" (Sanctus Ioannes XXIII, Ep. ap. *Celebrandi Concilii Œcumenici* (11 aprilis 1961): *AAS* 53 (1961), p. 242).

[4] "*Auxilium Christianorum, Auxilium Episcoporum*" (Sanctus Ioannes XXIII, *Allocutio in sollemni SS. Concilii Inauguratione* (11 octobris 1962): *AAS* 54 (1962), p. 795).

2.2 Some, who considered this proposal inadequate for emphasising the very special mission of Jesus' Mother in the Church, maintained that only a separate document could express Mary's dignity, pre-eminence, exceptional holiness and unique role in the Redemption accomplished by the Son. Furthermore, regarding Mary as above the Church in a certain way, they were afraid that the decision to put the Marian teaching in the treatment of the Church would not sufficiently emphasise Mary's privileges and would reduce her role to the level of other members of the Church (*Acta Synodalia*, II, III, 338-342).

2.3 Others, however, spoke in favour of the Theological Commission's proposal to put the doctrinal treatment of Mary and the Church in a single document. According to them, these realities could not be separated at the Council which, in aiming to rediscover the identity and mission of the People of God, had to show its close connection with her who is the type and exemplar of the Church in her virginity and motherhood. Indeed, as an eminent member of the ecclesial community, the Blessed Virgin has a special place in the Church's doctrine. Furthermore, by stressing the link between Mary and the Church, Christians of the Reformation could better understand of the Marian teaching presented by the Council (*Acta Synodalia*, II, III, 343-345).

2.4 The Council Fathers, moved by the same love for Mary, thus tended, in their expression of different doctrinal positions, to favour various aspects of her person. Some reflected on Mary primarily in her relationship to Christ, others considered her more as a member of the Church.

3.1 After an intense doctrinal discussion attentive to the dignity of the Mother of God and to her particular presence in the Church's life, it was decided that the treatment of Mary would be situated in the Council's document on the Church (cf. *Acta Synodalia*, II, III, 627).

3.2 The new schema on the Blessed Virgin, drafted so as to be included in the Dogmatic Constitution on the Church, shows real doctrinal progress. The stress placed on Mary's faith and a more systematic concern to base Marian doctrine on Scripture are significant and useful elements for enriching the piety and esteem of the Christian people for the Blessed Mother of God.

3.3 Moreover, with the passing of time the danger of reductionism, feared by some Fathers, proved to be unfounded: Mary's mission and privileges were amply reaffirmed: her co-operation in the divine plan of salvation was highlighted; the harmony of this co-operation with Christ's unique mediation appeared were evident.

3.4 For the first time, the conciliar Magisterium offered the Church a doctrinal exposition of Mary's role in Christ's redemptive work and in the life of the Church.

3.5 Thus, we must consider the Council Fathers' choice, which proved very fruitful for later doctrinal work, to have been a truly providential decision.

4.1 During the Council sessions, many Fathers wished further to enrich Marian doctrine with other statements on Mary's role in the work of salvation. The particular context in which Vatican II's Mariological debate took place did not allow those wishes, although substantial and widespread, to be accepted, but the Council's entire discussion of Mary remains vigorous and balanced, and the topics themselves, though not fully defined, received significant attention in the overall treatment.

4.2 Thus, the hesitation of some Fathers regarding the title of Mediatrix[1] did not prevent the Council from using this title once, and from stating in other terms Mary's mediating role from her consent to the Angel's message to her motherhood in the order of grace (cf. *Lumen gentium*, n. 62). Furthermore, the Council asserts her co-operation "in a wholly singular way" in the work of restoring supernatural life to souls (*ibid*., n. 61). Lastly, even if it avoided using the title "Mother of the Church", the text of *Lumen gentium* clearly underscores the Church's veneration for Mary as a most loving Mother.

4.3 The entire exposition in the eighth chapter of the Dogmatic Constitution on the Church clearly shows that terminological precautions did not prevent a very rich and positive presentation of basic doctrine, an expression of faith and love for her whom the Church acknowledges as Mother and Model.

4.4 On the other hand, the Fathers' differing points of view, as they emerged during the conciliar debate, turned out to be providential, because, on the basis of their harmonious relationship, they have afforded the faith and devotion of the Christian people a more complete and balanced presentation of the marvellous identity of the Lord's Mother and of her exceptional role in the work of Redemption.

13 December 1995

---

[1] The Blessed Virgin Mary is the *Mediatrix of All Graces* in her aspect of dispenser of the graces bestowed on mankind by the Holy Spirit through the merits of the crucified Christ. Having cooperated in the Incarnation and the Redemption by her motherhood and by her sufferings at the foot of the cross, our Lady merits to cooperate as a channel for the graces flowing therefrom (cf. Donald Attwater, *A Catholic Dictionary* (1958), p. 316).
There is a growing movement of clergy, religious, and lay faithful that are petitioning His Holiness the Pope to use papal infallibility to proclaim *ex cathedra* the Blessed Virgin Mary as both Co-Redemptrix and Mediatrix of All Graces. If this happens, this would be the fifth Marian dogma. The four Marian dogmas are: [1] the Mother of God or *Theotókos* (First Council of Ephesus, 431), [2] the Perpetual Virginity of the Blessed Virgin Mary (Second Council of Constantinople, 553), [3] the Immaculate Conception of the Blessed Virgin Mary (Blessed Pius IX, 1854), and [4] the Assumption of the Blessed Virgin Mary (Venerable Pius XII, 1950).

10
THE PURPOSE AND METHOD OF EXPOSURE OF MARIAN DOCTRINE

1.1 Following the Dogmatic Constitution *Lumen gentium*, which in Chapter 8 "set forth painstakingly both the role of the Blessed Virgin in the mystery of the Incarnate Word and the Mystical Body, and the duties of the redeemed towards the Mother of God", in this catechesis I would like to offer a basic summary of the Church's faith in Mary, while reaffirming with the Council that I do not intend "to give a complete doctrine on Mary", nor "to decide those questions which the work of theologians has not yet fully clarified" (*Lumen gentium*, n. 54).[1]

1.2 It is my intention first of all to describe "the role of the Blessed Virgin in the mystery of the Incarnate Word and the Mystical Body" (*ibid.*),[2] by referring to data from Scripture and the Apostolic Tradition, and taking into account the doctrinal development that has taken place in the Church up to our day.

1.3 Moreover, since Mary's role in the history of salvation is closely linked to the mystery of Christ and the Church, I will not lose sight of these essential reference points which, by offering Marian doctrine the proper context, enable us to discover its vast and inexhaustible riches.

1.4 Exploring the mystery of the Lord's Mother is truly vast and has occupied many Pastors and theologians down the centuries. Some, in their endeavour to point out the central aspects of Mariology, have sometimes treated it together with Christology or ecclesiology. However, taking into account her relationship with all the mysteries of faith, Mary deserves a specific treatment which highlights her person and role in the history of salvation, in the light of the Bible and of ecclesiastical tradition.

2.1 It also seems useful, following the Council's directives, to explain accurately "the duties of the redeemed towards the Mother of God, who is Mother of Christ and Mother of men, and most of all of those who believe" (*ibid.*).[3]

2.2 Indeed, the part assigned to Mary by the divine plan of salvation requires of Christians not only acceptance and attention, but also concrete choices which express in life the Gospel attitudes of her who goes before the Church in faith

[1] "*Atque quæstiones labore theologorum nondum ad plenam lucem perductas dirimere*" (CONCILIUM VATICANUM II, Const. dogm. de Ecclesia, *Lumen gentium*, 54: *AAS* 57 (1965), p. 59).
[2] "*Illustrare sedulo intendit tum munus Beatæ Virginis in mysterio Incarnati Verbi et Corporis Mystici*" (IBID.).
[3] "*Tum hominum redemptorum officia erga Deiparam, matrem Christi et matrem hominum, maxime fidelium*" (IBID.).

and holiness. The Mother of the Lord is thus destined to exercise a special influence on believers' way of praying. The Church's liturgy itself recognises her singular place in the devotion and life of every believer.

2.3 It is necessary to emphasise that Marian teaching and devotion are not the fruit of sentimentality. The mystery of Mary is a revealed truth which imposes itself on the intellect of believers and requires of those in the Church who have the task of studying and teaching a method of doctrinal reflection no less rigorous than that used in all theology.

2.4 Moreover, Jesus himself had invited his contemporaries not to be led by enthusiasm in considering his Mother, recognising in Mary especially the one who is blessed because she listens to the word of God and keeps it (cf. *Lk* 11:28).

2.5 Not only affection but particularly the light of the Spirit must guide us in understanding the Mother of Jesus and her contribution to the work of salvation.

3.1 With regard to the measure and balance to be maintained in both Marian doctrine and devotion, the Council strongly urges theologians and preachers of the divine word "to be careful to refrain… from all false exaggeration" (*Lumen gentium*, n. 67).

3.2 This exaggeration comes from those who adopt a maximalist attitude, which seeks to extend systematically to Mary the prerogatives of Christ and all the charisms of the Church.

3.3 Instead, it is always necessary in Marian doctrine to safeguard the infinite difference existing between the human person of Mary and the divine person of Jesus. To attribute the "maximum" to Mary cannot become a norm of Mariology, which must make constant reference to the testimony of Revelation regarding God's gifts to the Virgin on account of her sublime mission.

3.4 Likewise, the Council exhorts theologians and preachers to "refrain… from too summary an attitude" (*ibid.*), that is, from the danger of a minimalism that can be manifest in doctrinal positions, in exegetical interpretations and in acts of devotion which tend to reduce and almost deny Mary's importance in the history of salvation, her perpetual virginity and her holiness.

3.5 Such extreme positions should always be avoided through a consistent and sincere fidelity to revealed truth as expressed in Scripture and in the Apostolic Tradition.

4.1 The Council itself offers us a criterion for discerning authentic Marian doctrine: Mary "occupies a place in the Church which is the highest after Christ and also closest to us" (*Lumen gentium*, n. 54).[1]

4.2 The *highest* place: we must discover this lofty position granted to Mary in the mystery of salvation. However, it is a question of a vocation totally in relationship to Christ.

4.3 The place *closest to us*: our life is profoundly influenced by Mary's example and intercession. Nonetheless we must ask ourselves about our effort to be close to her. The entire teaching of salvation history invites us to look to the Virgin. Christian asceticism in every age invites us to think of her as a model of perfect adherence to the Lord's will. The chosen model of holiness, Mary guides the steps of believers on their journey to heaven.

4.4 Through her closeness to the events of our daily history, Mary sustains us in trials; she encourages us in difficulty, always pointing out to us the goal of eternal salvation. Thus her role as Mother is seen ever more clearly: Mother of her Son Jesus, tender and vigilant Mother to each one of us, to whom, from the Cross, the Redeemer entrusted her, that we might welcome her as children in faith.

3 January 1996

---

[1] "*In Sancta Ecclesia locum occupat post Christum altissimum nobisque maxime propinquum*" (Concilium Vaticanum II, Const. dogm. de Ecclesia, *Lumen gentium*, 54: *AAS* 57 (1965), p. 59).

11
MARY IN THE TRINITARIAN PERSPECTIVE

1.1 The eighth chapter of the Constitution *Lumen gentium* shows in the *mystery of Christ* the absolutely necessary reference to Marian doctrine. In this regard, the first words of the Introduction are significant: "Wishing in his supreme goodness and wisdom to effect the redemption of the world, 'when the fullness of time came, God sent his Son, born of a woman... that we might receive the adoption of sons' (*Gal* 4:4-5)" (*Lumen gentium*, n. 52).[1] This son is the Messiah awaited by the people of the Old Covenant, sent by the Father at a decisive moment of history, the "fullness of time" (*Gal* 4:4), which coincides with his birth in our world from a woman. She who brought the eternal Son of God to humanity can never be separated from him who is found at the centre of the divine plan carried out in history.

1.2 The primacy of Christ is shown forth in the Church, his Mystical Body: in her "the faithful are joined to Christ the Head and are in communion with all his saints" (cf. *Lumen gentium*, n. 52). It is Christ who draws all men to himself. Since in her maternal role she is closely united with her Son, Mary helps direct the gaze and heart of believers towards him.

1.3 She is the way that leads to Christ: indeed, she who "at the message of the angel received the Word of God in her heart and in her body" (*Lumen gentium*, n. 53)[2] shows us how to receive into our lives the Son come down from heaven, teaching us to make Jesus the centre and the supreme "law" of our existence.

2.1 Mary also helps us discover, at the origin of the whole work of salvation, the sovereign action of the *Father* who calls men to become sons in the one Son. Recalling the very beautiful expressions of the Letter to the Ephesians: "But God, who is rich in mercy, out of the great love with which he loved us, even when we were dead through our trespasses, made us alive together with Christ" (*Eph* 2:4-5),[3] the Council gives God the title "most merciful": the Son "born of a woman" is thus seen as the fruit of the Father's mercy and enables us to understand better how this Woman is the "mother of mercy".

2.2 In the same context, the Council also calls God "most wise", suggesting a particular attention to the close link between Mary and the divine wisdom, which in its mysterious plan willed the Virgin's motherhood.

---

[1] "*Benignissimus et sapientissimus Deus, mundi redemptionem complere volens, 'ubi venit plenitudo temporis, misit Filium suum factum ex muliere,... ut adoptionem filiorum reciperemus'* (*Gal* 4, 4-5)" (Concilium Vaticanum II, Const. dogm. de Ecclesia, *Lumen gentium*, 52: *AAS* 57 (1965), p. 58).
[2] "*Angelo nuntiante Verbum Dei corde et corpore suscepit*" (Ibid., 53: *AAS* 57 (1965), p. 58).
[3] "*Deus autem, qui dives est in misericordia, propter nimiam caritatem suam, qua dilexit nos, et cum essemus mortui peccatis, convivificavit nos Christo*" (*Eph* 2, 4-5).

3.1 The Council's text also reminds us of the unique bond uniting Mary with the Holy Spirit, using the words of the Nicene-Constantinopolitan Creed which we recite in the Eucharistic liturgy: "For us men and for our salvation he came down from heaven, and by the Holy Spirit was incarnate of the Virgin Mary, and became man."[1]

3.2 In expressing the unchanging faith of the Church, the Council reminds us that the marvellous incarnation of the Son took place in the Virgin Mary's womb without man's co-operation, by the power of the Holy Spirit.

3.3 The introduction to the eighth chapter of *Lumen gentium* thus shows in a Trinitarian perspective an essential dimension of Marian doctrine. Everything in fact comes from the will of the Father, who has sent his Son into the world, revealing him to men and establishing him as the Head of the Church and the centre of history. This is a plan that was fulfilled by the Incarnation, the work of the Holy Spirit, but with the essential co-operation of a woman, the Virgin Mary, who thus became an integral part in the economy of communicating the Trinity to mankind.

4.1 Mary's threefold relationship with the divine Persons is confirmed in precise words and with a description of the characteristic relationship which links the Mother of the Lord to the Church: "She is endowed with the high office and dignity of the Mother of the Son of God, and therefore she is also the beloved daughter of the Father and the temple of the Holy Spirit" (*Lumen gentium*, n. 53).[2]

4.2 Mary's fundamental dignity is that of being "Mother of the Son", which is expressed in Christian doctrine and devotion with the title "Mother of God".

4.3 This is a surprising term, which shows the humility of God's only-begotten Son in his Incarnation and, in connection with it, the most high privilege granted a creature who was called to give him birth in the flesh.

4.4 Mother of the Son, Mary is the "beloved daughter of the Father" in a unique way. She has been granted an utterly special likeness between her motherhood and the divine fatherhood.

4.5 And again: every Christian is a "temple of the Holy Spirit", according to the Apostle Paul's expression (*1 Cor* 6:19).[3] But this assertion takes on an

---

[1] "*Qui propter nos hómines et propter nostram salútem descéndit de cœlis. Et incarnátus est de Spíritu Sancto ex María Vírgine, et homo factus est*" (*Symbolum Nicænum-Constantinopolitanum*: *DS* 150).
[2] "*Hoc summo munere ac dignitate ditatur ut sit Genitrix Dei Filii, ideoque prædilecta filia Patris necnon sacrarium Spiritus Sancti*" (Concilium Vaticanum II, Const. dogm. de Ecclesia, *Lumen gentium*, 53: *AAS* 57 (1965), pp. 58-59).
[3] "*Templum est Spiritus Sancti*" (*1 Cor* 6, 19).

extraordinary meaning in Mary: in her the relationship with the Holy Spirit is enriched with a spousal dimension. I recalled this in the Encyclical *Redemptoris Mater*: "The Holy Spirit had already come down upon her, and she became his faithful spouse at the Annunciation, welcoming the Word of the true God..." (n. 26).[1]

5.1 Mary's privileged relationship with the Trinity therefore confers on her a dignity which far surpasses that of every other creature. The Council recalls this explicitly: because of this "gift of sublime grace" Mary "far surpasses all creatures" (*Lumen gentium*, n. 53).[2] However, this most high dignity does not hinder Mary's solidarity with each of us. The Constitution *Lumen gentium* goes on to say: "But, being of the race of Adam, she is at the same time also united to all those who are to be saved" and she has been "redeemed, in a more exalted fashion, by reason of the merits of her Son" (*ibid.*).[3]

5.2 Here we see the authentic meaning of Mary's privileges and of her extraordinary relationship with the Trinity: their purpose is to enable her to co-operate in the salvation of the human race. The immeasurable greatness of the Lord's Mother therefore remains a gift of God's love for all men. By proclaiming her "blessed" (*Lk* 1:48), generations praise the "great things" (*Lk* 1:49) the Almighty has done in her for humanity, "in remembrance of his mercy" (*Lk* 1:54).[4]

10 January 1996

[1] "*Spiritus enim Sanctus iam in illam descenderat, quæ effecta est in annuntiatione eius sponsa fidelis, Dei veri amplexando Verbum*" (Sanctus Ioannes Paulus II, Litt. enc. *Redemptoris Mater* (25 martii 1987), 26: *AAS* 79 (1987), p. 395).
[2] "*Omnibus aliis creaturis*" (Concilium Vaticanum II, Const. dogm. de Ecclesia, *Lumen gentium*, 53: *AAS* 57 (1965), p. 59).
[3] "*Intuitu meritorum Filii sui sublimiore modo redempta Eique arcto et indissolubili vinculo unita*" (*LG*, n. 53).
[4] "*Recordatus misericordiæ*" (*Lc* 1, 54).

12
MARY IN THE PROTOGOSPEL

1.1 "The books of the Old Testament describe the history of salvation, by which the coming of Christ into the world was slowly prepared. The earliest documents, as they are read in the Church and are understood in the light of a further and full revelation, bring the figure of a woman, Mother of the Redeemer, into a gradually clearer light" (*Lumen gentium*, n. 55).[1]

1.2 With these statements the Second Vatican Council reminds us how the figure of Mary gradually took shape from the very beginning of salvation history. She is already glimpsed in the Old Testament texts but is fully understood only when these "are read in the Church" and understood in the light of the New Testament.

1.3 The Holy Spirit, by inspiring the various human authors, oriented Old Testament Revelation to Christ, who was to come into the world from the Virgin Mary's womb.

2.1 Among the biblical accounts which foretold the Mother of the Redeemer, the Council particularly cites those in which God revealed his plan of salvation after the fall of Adam and Eve. The Lord says to the serpent, the personification of the spirit of evil: "I will put enmity between you and the woman, and between your seed and her seed; he shall bruise your head, and you shall bruise his heel" (*Gn* 3:15).[2]

2.2 These statements, called the "Protogospel", i.e., the first Good News, by Christian tradition since the sixteenth century, enable us to see God's saving will from the very origins of humanity. Indeed according to the sacred author's narrative, the Lord's first reaction to sin was not to punish the guilty but to offer them the hope of salvation and to involve them actively in the work of redemption, showing his great generosity even to those who had offended him.

2.3 The Protogospel's words also reveal the unique destiny of the woman who, although yielding to the serpent's temptation before the man did, in virtue of the divine plan later becomes God's first ally. Eve was the serpent's

---

[1] "*Libri quidem Veteris Testamenti historiam salutis, qua Christi in mundum adventus lento gradu præparatur, describunt. Quæ primæva documenta, qualiter in Ecclesia leguntur et sub luce ulterioris et plenæ revelationis intelliguntur, clarius pedetentim in lucem proferunt figuram mulieris, Matris Redemptoris*" (Concilium Vaticanum II, Const. dogm. de Ecclesia, *Lumen gentium*, 55: *AAS* 57 (1965), p. 59).

[2] "*Inimicitias ponam inter te et mulierem et semen tuum et semen illius; ipsum conteret caput tuum, et tu conteres calcaneum eius*" (*Gen* 3, 15).

accomplice in enticing man to sin. Overturning this situation, God declares that he will make the woman the serpent's enemy.

3.1 Exegetes now agree in recognising that the text of Genesis, according to the original Hebrew, does not attribute action against the serpent directly to the woman, but to her offspring. Nevertheless, the text gives great prominence to the role she will play in the struggle against the tempter: in fact the one who defeats the serpent will be her offspring.

3.2 Who is this woman? The biblical text does not mention her personal name but allows us to glimpse a new woman, desired by God to atone for Eve's fall; in fact, she is called to restore woman's role and dignity, and to contribute to changing humanity's destiny, co-operating through her maternal mission in God's victory over Satan.

4.1 In the light of the New Testament and the Church's tradition, we know that the new woman announced by the Protogospel is Mary, and in "her seed" we recognise her Son, Jesus, who triumphed over Satan's power in the paschal mystery.

4.2 We also observe that in Mary the enmity God put between the serpent and the woman is fulfilled in two ways. God's perfect ally and the devil's enemy, she was completely removed from Satan's domination in the Immaculate Conception, when she was fashioned in grace by the Holy Spirit and preserved from every stain of sin. In addition, associated with her Son's saving work, Mary was fully involved in the fight against the spirit of evil.

4.3 Thus the titles "Immaculate Conception" and "Co-operator of the Redeemer",[1] attributed by the Church's faith to Mary, in order to proclaim her spiritual beauty and her intimate participation in the wonderful work of Redemption, show the lasting antagonism between the serpent and the New Eve.

5.1 Exegetes and theologians claim that the light of the New Eve, Mary, shines from the pages of Genesis onto the whole economy of salvation. In that text they already see the bond between Mary and the Church. Here we point out with joy that the term "woman", used in its generic form in the Genesis text, spurs women especially to join the Virgin of Nazareth and her task in the work of salvation, for they are called to take part in the fight against the spirit of evil.

5.2 Women who, like Eve, could succumb to Satan's seduction, through solidarity with Mary receive superior strength to combat the enemy, becoming God's first allies on the way of salvation.

---

[1] Co-Redemptrix. Cf. Catechesis no. 9, page 47, footnote no. 1.

5.3 God's mysterious alliance with woman can also be seen in a variety of ways in our day: in women's assiduous personal prayer and liturgical devotion, in their catechetical service and in their witness to charity, in the many feminine vocations to the consecrated life, in religious education in the family, etc.

5.4 All these signs are a very concrete fulfilment of the Protogospel's prediction Indeed, by suggesting a universal extension of the word "woman" within and beyond the visible confines of the Church, the Protogospel shows that Mary's unique vocation is inseparable from humanity's vocation and, in particular, from that of every woman, on which light has been shed by the mission of Mary, proclaimed God's first ally against Satan and evil.

24 January 1996

13
ANNOUNCEMENT OF THE MESSIANIC MATERNITY

1.1 In discussing the figure of Mary in the Old Testament, the Council (*Lumen gentium*, n. 55) refers to the well known text of Isaiah, which caught the particular attention of the early Christians: "Behold, a virgin shall conceive and bear a son, and shall call his name Immanuel" (*Is* 7:14).[1]

1.2 During the annunciation of the angel, who invites Joseph to take to himself Mary, his wife, "for that which is conceived in her is of the Holy Spirit", Matthew gives a Christological and Marian significance to the prophecy. In fact, he adds: "All this took place to fulfil what the Lord had spoken by the prophet: 'Behold, a virgin shall conceive and bear a son, and his name shall be called Emmanuel' (which means God with us)" (*Mt* 1:22-23).[2]

2.1 In the Hebrew text this prophecy does not explicitly foretell the virginal birth of Emmanuel: the word used (*almah*), in fact, simply means "a young woman", not necessarily a virgin. Moreover, we know that Jewish tradition did not hold up the idea of perpetual virginity, nor did it ever express the idea of virginal motherhood.

2.2 In the Greek tradition, however, the Hebrew word was translated *parthenos*, "virgin". In this fact, which could seem merely a peculiarity of translation, we must recognise a mysterious orientation given by the Holy Spirit to Isaiah's words in order to prepare for the understanding of the Messiah's extraordinary birth. The translation of the word as "virgin" is explained by the fact that Isaiah's text very solemnly prepares for the announcement of the conception and presents it as a divine sign (*Is* 7:10-14), arousing the expectation of an extraordinary conception. Now, it is not something extraordinary for a young woman to conceive a son after being joined to her husband. However, the prophecy makes no reference to the husband. Such a formulation, then, suggested the interpretation given later in the Greek version.

3.1 In the original context, the prophecy of Isaiah 7:14 was the divine reply to a lack of faith on the part of King Ahaz, who, threatened with an invasion from the armies of the neighbouring kings, sought his own salvation and that of his kingdom in Assyria's protection. In advising him to put his trust solely in God and to reject the dreadful Assyrian intervention, the prophet Isaiah invites him on the Lord's behalf to make an act of faith in God's power: "Ask

[1] "*Ecce, virgo concipiet et pariet filium et vocabit nomen eius Emmanuel*" (*Is* 7, 14).
[2] "*Hoc autem totum factum est, ut adimpleretur id, quod dictum est a Domino per prophetam dicentem: 'Ecce, virgo in utero habebit et pariet filium, et vocabunt nomen eius Emmanuel', quod est interpretatum Nobiscum Deus*" (*Mt* 1, 22-23).

a sign of the LORD your God".[1] At the king's refusal, for he preferred to seek salvation in human aid, the prophet made the famous prediction:

"Hear then, O house of David! Is it too little for you to weary men, that you weary my God also? Therefore the Lord himself will give you a sign. Behold, a virgin shall conceive and bear a son, and shall call his name Immanuel" (*Is* 7:13-14).[2]

3.2 The announcement of the sign of Emmanuel, "God-with-us", implies the promise of God's presence in history, which will find its full meaning in the mystery of the Incarnation of the Word.

4.1 In the announcement of the wondrous birth of Emmanuel, the indication of the woman who conceives and gives birth shows a certain intention to associate the mother with the destiny of the son—a prince destined to establish an ideal kingdom, the "messianic" kingdom—and offers a glimpse of a special divine plan, which highlights the woman's role.

4.2 The sign, in fact, is not only the child, but the extraordinary conception revealed later in the birth itself, a hope-filled event, which stresses the central role of the mother.

4.3 The prophecy of Emmanuel must also be understood in the horizon opened by the promise made to David, a promise we read about in the second book of Samuel. Here the prophet Nathan promises the king God's favour towards his descendent: "He shall build a house for my name, and I will establish the throne of his kingdom forever. I will be his father, and he shall be my son" (*2 Sam* 7:13-14).[3]

4.4 God wants to exercise a paternal role towards David's offspring, a role that will reveal its full, authentic meaning in the New Testament with the Incarnation of the Son of God in the family of David (cf. *Rom* 1:3).

5.1 The same prophet Isaiah, in another very familiar text, confirms the unusual nature of Emmanuel's birth. Here are his words:

"For to us a child is born, to us a son is given; and the government will be upon his shoulder, and he will be called 'Wonderful Counselor, Mighty God, Everlasting Father, Prince of Peace'" (9:5).[4]

---

[1] "*Pete tibi signum a Domino Deo tuo*" (*Is* 7, 10).

[2] "*Audite ergo, domus David; numquid parum vobis est molestos esse hominibus, quia molesti estis et Deo meo? Propter hoc dabit Dominus ipse vobis signum. Ecce, virgo concipiet et pariet filium et vocabit nomen eius Emmanuel*" (*Is* 7, 13-14).

[3] "*Ipse ædificabit domum nomini meo, et stabiliam thronum regni eius usque in sempiternum. Ego ero ei in patrem, et ipse erit mihi in filium*" (*2 Sam* 7, 13-14).

[4] "*Parvulus enim natus est nobis, filius datus est nobis; et factus est principatus super umerum eius; et vocabitur nomen eius admirabilis Consiliarius, Deus fortis, Pater æternitatis, Princeps pacis*" (*Is*

Thus the prophet expresses, in the series of names given the child, the qualities of his royal office: wisdom, might, fatherly kindness, peacemaking.

5.2 The mother is no longer mentioned here, but the exaltation of the son, who brings the people all they can hope for in the messianic kingdom, is also reflected in the woman who conceived him and gave him birth.

6 A famous prophecy of Micah also alludes to the birth of Emmanuel. The prophet says:

"But you, O Bethlehem Ephrathah, who are little to be among the clans of Judah, from you shall come forth for me one who is to be ruler in Israel, whose origin is from of old, from ancient days. Therefore he [the Lord] shall give them up until the time when she who has labor pains has brought forth..." (5:1-2 [2-3]).[1]

These words re-echo the expectation of a birth full of messianic hope, in which once again the mother's role is stressed, the mother explicitly remembered and ennobled by the wondrous event that brings joy and salvation.

7.1 Mary's virginal motherhood was prepared for in a more general way by God's favour to the humble and the poor (cf. *Lumen gentium*, n. 55).

7.2 By their attitude of placing all their trust in the Lord, they anticipated the profound meaning of Mary's virginity. By renouncing the richness of human motherhood, she awaited from God all the fruitfulness of her own life.

7.3 The Old Testament then does not contain a formal announcement of the virginal motherhood, which was fully revealed only by the New Testament. Nevertheless, Isaiah's prophecy (*Is* 7:14) prepares for the revelation of this mystery and was construed so in the Greek translation of the Old Testament. By quoting the prophecy thus translated, Matthew's Gospel proclaims its perfect fulfilment through the conception of Jesus in Mary's virginal womb.

31 January 1996

[1] "*Sed tu, Bethlehem Ephratha, parvulus in milibus Iudæ, ex te mihi egredietur, qui sit dominator in Israel; et egressus eius a temporibus antiquis, a diebus æternitatis. Propter hoc dabit eos usque ad tempus, in quo parturiens pariet...*" (*Mic* 5, 1-2).

14
MOTHERHOOD COMES FROM GOD

1 Motherhood is a gift of God. "I have gotten a man with the help of the LORD" (*Gn* 4:1),[1] Eve exclaims after giving birth to Cain, her first-born son. With these words, the book of Genesis presents the first motherhood in human history as a grace and joy that spring from the Creator's goodness.

2.1 The birth of Isaac is similarly described, at the origin of the chosen people.

2.2 God promises Abraham, who has been deprived of children and is now advanced in years, descendants as numerous as the stars of heaven (cf. *Gn* 15:5). The promise is welcomed by the patriarch with the faith that reveals God's plan to this man: "He believed the LORD; and he reckoned it to him as righteousness" (*Gn* 15:6).[2]

2.3 This promise was confirmed in the words spoken by the Lord on the occasion of the covenant he made with Abraham: "Behold, my covenant is with you, and you shall be the father of a multitude of nations" (*Gn* 17:4).[3]

2.4 Extraordinary and mysterious events emphasise how Sarah's motherhood was primarily the fruit of the mercy of God, who gives life beyond all human expectation: "I will bless her, and moreover I will give you a son by her; I will bless her, and she shall be a mother of nations; kings of peoples shall come from her" (*Gn* 17:15-16).[4]

2.5 Motherhood is presented as a decisive gift of the Lord. The patriarch and his wife will be given a new name to indicate the unexpected and marvellous transformation that God is to work in their life.

3.1 The visit of the three mysterious persons, whom the Fathers of the Church interpreted as a prefiguration of the Trinity, announced the fulfilment of the promise to Abraham more explicitly: "The LORD appeared to him by the Oaks of Mamre, as he sat at the door of his tent in the heat of the day. He lifted up his eyes and looked, and behold, three men stood in front of him" (*Gn* 18:1-2).[5] Abraham objected: "Shall a child be born to a man who is a

---

[1] "*Acquisivi virum per Dominum*" (*Gen* 4, 1).
[2] "*Credidit Domino, et reputatum est ei ad iustitiam*" (*Gen* 15, 6).
[3] "*Ecce pactum meum tecum. Erisque pater multarum gentium*" (*Gen* 17, 4).
[4] "*Et benedicam ei; et ex illa quoque dabo tibi filium. Benedicturus sum eam, eritque in nationes; reges populorum orientur ex ea*" (*Gen* 17, 16).
[5] "*Apparuit autem ei Dominus iuxta Quercus Mambre se denti in ostio tabernaculi sui in ipso fervore diei. Cumque elevasset oculos, apparuerunt ei tres viri stantes prope eum*" (*Gen* 18, 1-2).

hundred years old? Shall Sarah, who is ninety years old, bear a child?" (*Gn* 17:17; cf. 18:11-13).[1] The divine guest replies: "Is anything too hard for the LORD? At the appointed time I will return to you, in the spring, and Sarah shall have a son" (*Gn* 18:14; cf. *Lk* 1:37).[2]

3.2 The narrative stresses the effect of the divine visit, which makes fruitful a conjugal union that had been barren until then. Believing in the promise, Abraham becomes a father against all hope, and "father in the faith" because from his faith "descends" that of the chosen people.

4.1 The Bible relates other stories of women released from sterility and gladdened by the Lord with the gift of motherhood. These are often situations of anguish, which God's intervention transforms into experiences of joy by receiving the heartfelt prayers of those who are humanly without hope. "When Rachel saw that she bore Jacob no children", for example, "she envied her sister; and she said to Jacob, 'Give me children, or I shall die!' Jacob's anger was kindled against Rachel, and he said, 'Am I in the place of God, who has withheld from you the fruit of the womb?'" (*Gn* 30:1-2).[3]

4.2 But the biblical text immediately adds: "Then God remembered Rachel, and God hearkened to her and opened her womb. She conceived and bore a son" (*Gn* 30:22-23).[4] This son, Joseph, would play a very important role for Israel at the time of the migration to Egypt.

4.3 In this as in other narratives, the Bible intends to highlight the marvellous nature of God's intervention in these specific cases by stressing the initial condition of the woman's sterility; however, at the same time, it allows us to grasp the gratuitousness inherent in all motherhood.

5.1 We find a similar process in the account of the birth of Samson. The wife of Manoah, who had never been able to conceive a child, hears the Lord's announcement from the angel: "Behold, you are barren and have no children; but you shall conceive and bear a son" (*Jgs* 13:3).[5] The conception, unexpected and miraculous, announces the great things that the Lord will do through Samson.

---

[1] "*Putasne centenario nascetur filius? Et Sara nonagenaria pariet?*" (*Gen* 17, 17; cf. 18, 11-13).

[2] "*Numquid Domino est quidquam difficile? Revertar ad te hoc eodem tempore, et habebit Sara filium*" (*Gen* 18, 14; cf. *Lc* 1, 37).

[3] "*Cernens autem Rachel quod infecunda esset, invidit sorori et ait marito suo: 'Da mihi liberos, alioquin moriar'. Cui iratus respondit Iacob: 'Num pro Deo ego sum, qui privavit te fructu ventris?'*" (*Gen* 30, 1-2).

[4] "*Recordatus quoque Deus Rachelis exaudivit eam Deus et aperuit vulvam illius. Quæ concepit et peperit filium*" (*Gen* 30, 22-23).

[5] "*Ecce sterilis es et absque liberis, sed concipies et paries filium*" (*Iudic* 13, 3).

5.2 In the case of Hannah, Samson's mother, the special role of prayer is underlined. Hannah suffers the humiliation of being barren but she is full of great trust in God, to whom she turns insistently, that he may help her to overcome this trial. One day, at the temple, she makes a vow:

"O LORD of hosts, if you will indeed look on the affliction of your maidservant, and remember me, and not forget your maidservant, but will give to your maidservant a son, then I will give him to the LORD all the days of his life" (*1 Sm* 1:11).[1]

5.3 Her prayer was answered: "and the LORD remembered her" and "Hannah conceived and bore a son, and she called his name Samuel" (*1 Sm* 1:19-20).[2] Keeping her promise, Hannah offered her son to the Lord:

"For this child I prayed; and the LORD has granted me my petition which I made to him. Therefore I have lent him to the LORD; as long as he lives, he is lent to the LORD" (*1 Sm* 1:27-28).[3]

Given by God to Hannah and then given by Hannah to God, the little Samuel becomes a living bond of communion between Hannah and God.

5.4 Samuel's birth is thus an experience of joy and an occasion for thanksgiving. The first book of Samuel contains a hymn known as Hannah's *Magníficat*, which seems to anticipate Mary's: "My heart exults in the LORD; my strength is exalted in the LORD" (*1 Sm* 2:1).[4]

5.5 The grace of motherhood that God granted to Hannah because of her ceaseless prayers filled her with a new generosity. Samuel's consecration is the grateful response of a mother who, recognising in her child the fruit of God's mercy, returns his gift, entrusting the child she had so longed for to the Lord.

6.1 In the accounts of miraculous motherhood which we have recalled, it is easy to discover the important place the Bible assigns to mothers in the mission of their sons. In Samuel's case, Hannah has a determining role in deciding to give him to the Lord. An equally decisive role is played by another mother, Rebecca, who procures the inheritance for Jacob (*Gn* 27). That maternal intervention, described by the Bible, can be interpreted as the sign of being chosen as an instrument in God's sovereign plan. It is he who chooses the

---

[1] "*Domine exercituum, si respiciens videris afflictionem famulæ tuæ et recordatus mei fueris nec oblitus ancillæ tuæ dederisque servæ tuæ sexum virilem, dabo eum Domino omnes dies vitæ eius* " (*1 Sam* 1, 11).

[2] "*Et recordatus est eius Dominus... concepit Anna et peperit filium vocavitque nomen eius Samuel* " (*1 Sam* 1, 19-20).

[3] "*Pro puero isto oravi, et dedit mihi Dominus petitionem meam, quam postulavi eum. Idcirco et ego commodavi eum Domino; cunctis diebus, quibus vivet, postulatus erit pro Domino*" (*1 Sam* 1, 27-28).

[4] "*Exsultavit cor meum in Do mino, exaltatum est cornu meum in Deo meo*" (*1 Sam* 2, 1).

youngest son, Jacob, to receive the paternal blessing and inheritance, and therefore as the shepherd and leader of his people… It is he who by a free and wise decision, determines and governs each one's destiny (*Wis* 10:10-12).

6.2 The Bible's message regarding motherhood reveals important and ever timely aspects: indeed, it sheds light on the dimension of gratuitousness, which is especially apparent in the case of barren women, God's particular covenant with woman and the special bond between the destiny of the mother and that of the son.

6.3 At the same time, the intervention of God, who, at important moments in the history of his people, causes certain barren women to conceive, prepares for belief in the intervention of God who, in the fullness of time, will make a Virgin fruitful for the Incarnation of his Son.

6 March 1996

15
WOMEN INVOLVED IN THE SALVATION OF THE PEOPLE

1.1 The Old Testament holds up for our admiration some extraordinary women who, impelled by the Spirit of God, share in the struggles and triumphs of Israel or contribute to its salvation. Their presence in the history of the people is neither marginal nor passive: they appear as true protagonists of salvation history. Here are the most significant examples.

1.2 After the crossing of the Red Sea, the sacred text emphasises the initiative of a woman inspired to make this decisive event a festive celebration:

"Then Miriam, the prophetess, the sister of Aaron, took a timbrel in her hand; and all the women went out after her with timbrels and dancing. And Miriam sang to them: 'Sing to the Lord, for he has triumphed gloriously; the horse and his rider he has thrown into the sea'" (*Ex* 15:20-21).[1]

1.3 This mention of feminine enterprise in the context of a celebration stresses not only the importance of woman's role, but also her particular ability for praising and thanking God.

2.1 The action of the prophetess Deborah, at the time of the Judges, is even more important. After ordering the commander of the army to go and gather his men, she guarantees by her presence the success of Israel's army, predicting that another woman, Jael, will kill their enemy's general.

2.2 To celebrate the great victory, Deborah also sings a long canticle praising Jael's action: "Most blessed of women be Jael, ...of tent-dwelling women most blessed" (*Jgs* 5:24).[2] In the New Testament this praise is echoed in the words Elizabeth addresses to Mary on the day of the Visitation: "Blessed are you among women..." (*Lk* 1:42).[3]

2.3 The significant role of women in the salvation of their people, highlighted by the figures of Deborah and Jael, is presented again in the story of another prophetess named Huldah, who lived at the time of King Josiah.

---

[1] "*Sumpsit ergo Maria prophetissa soror Aaron tympanum in manu sua; egressæque sunt omnes mulieres post eam cum tympanis et choris, quibus præcinebat dicens: 'Cantemus Domino, gloriose enim magnificatus est: equum et ascensorem eius deiecit in mare!*'" (*Ex* 15, 20-21).
[2] "*Benedicta præ mulieribus Iahel... præ mulieribus tabernaculi benedicatur!* " (*Iudic* 5, 24).
[3] "*Benedicta tu inter mulieres...*" (*Lc* 1, 42).

2.4 Questioned by the priest Hilkiah, she made prophecies announcing that forgiveness would be shown to the king who feared the divine wrath. Huldah thus becomes a messenger of mercy and peace (cf. *2 Kgs* 22:14-20).

3.1 The books of Judith and Esther, whose purpose is to idealize the positive contribution of woman to the history of the chosen people, present—in a violent cultural context—two women who win victory and salvation for the Israelites.

3.2 The book of Judith, in particular, tells of a fearsome army sent by Nebuchadnezzar to conquer Israel. Led by Holofernes, the enemy army is ready to seize the city of Bethulia, amid the desperation of its inhabitants, who, considering any resistance to be useless, ask their rulers to surrender. But the city's elders, who in the absence of immediate aid declare themselves ready to hand Bethulia over to the enemy, are rebuked by Judith for their lack of faith as she professes her complete trust in the salvation that comes from the Lord.

3.3 After a long invocation to God, she who is a symbol of fidelity to the Lord, of humble prayer and of the intention to remain chaste goes to Holofernes, the proud, idolatrous and dissolute enemy general.

3.4 Left alone with him and before striking him, Judith prays to Yahweh,[1] saying: "Give me strength this day, O Lord God of Israel!" (*Jdt* 13:7).[2] Then, taking Holofernes' sword, she cuts off his head.

3.5 Here too, as in the case of David and Goliath, the Lord used weakness to triumph over strength. On this occasion, however, it was a woman who brought victory: Judith, without being held back by the cowardice and unbelief of the people's rulers, goes to Holofernes and kills him, earning the gratitude and praise of the High Priest and the elders of Jerusalem. The latter exclaimed to the woman who had defeated the enemy:

"You are the exaltation of Jerusalem, you are the great glory of Israel, you are the great pride of our nation! You have done all this singlehanded; you have done great good to Israel, and God is well pleased with it. May the Almighty Lord bless you for ever!" (*Jdt* 15:9-10).[3]

---

[1] *Yahweh* is the English rendering of the Hebrew vocalisation of the Tetragrammaton or Name of God, often replaced in English with LORD. The original Italian text uses *Jahvè*.

[2] "*Confirma me, Domine, Deus Israel, in hoc die*" (*Iudt* 13, 7).

[3] "*Tu exaltatio Ierusalem, tu gloria magna Israel, tu laus magna generis nostri. Fecisti omnia hæc in manu tua, fecisti bona cum Israel, et complacuit in illis Deus. Benedicta esto tu, mulier, apud Deum omnipotentem in æternum tempus*" (*Iudt* 15, 9-10).

4.1 The events narrated in the book of Esther occurred in another very difficult situation for the Jews. In the kingdom of Persia, Haman, the king's superintendent, decrees the extermination of the Jews. To remove the danger, Mordecai, a Jew living in the citadel of Susa, turns to his niece Esther, who lives in the king's palace where she has attained the rank of queen. Contrary to the law in force, she presents herself to the king without being summoned, thus risking the death penalty, and she obtains the revocation of the extermination decree. Haman is executed, Mordecai comes to power and the Jews delivered from menace, thus get the better of their enemies.

4.2 Judith and Esther both risk their lives to win the salvation of their people. The two interventions, however, are quite different: Esther does not kill the enemy but, by playing the role of mediator, intercedes for those who are threatened with destruction.

5.1 This intercessory role is later attributed to another female figure, Abigail, the wife of Nabal, by the first book of Samuel. Here too, it is due to her intervention that salvation is once again achieved.

5.2 She goes to meet David, who has decided to destroy Nabal's family, and asks forgiveness for her husband's sins. Thus she delivers his house from certain destruction (*1 Sm* 25).

5.3 As can be easily noted, the Old Testament tradition frequently emphasises the decisive action of women in the salvation of Israel, especially in the writings closest to the coming of Christ. In this way the Holy Spirit, through the events connected with Old Testament women, sketches with ever greater precision the characteristics of Mary's mission in the work of salvation for the entire human race.

27 March 1996

16
THE MORAL NOBILITY OF WOMAN

1.1 The Old Testament and the Judaic tradition are full of acknowledgements of woman's moral nobility, which is expressed above all in an attitude of trust in the Lord, in prayer to obtain the gift of motherhood and in imploring God for Israel's salvation from the assaults of its enemies. Sometimes, as in Judith's case, this quality is celebrated by the entire community, becoming the object of common admiration.

1.2 Beside the shining examples of the biblical heroines, the negative witnesses of some women are not lacking: such as Delilah who destroys Samson's prophetic ability (*Jgs* 16:4-21), the foreign women who in Solomon's old age turn the king's heart away from the Lord and make him worship other gods (*1 Kgs* 11:1-8), Jezebel who kills all "the prophets of the LORD" (*1 Kgs* 18:13)[1] and has Naboth killed, to give his vineyard to Ahab (*1 Kgs* 21), and Job's wife who insults him in his misfortune and spurs him to rebel (*Jb* 2:9).

1.3 In these cases, the woman's conduct is reminiscent of Eve's. However, the prevailing outlook in the Bible is that inspired by the Protogospel, which sees in woman an ally of God.

2.1 In fact, if foreign women were accused of turning Solomon away from his devotion to the true God, the book of Ruth presents us instead with the most noble figure of a foreign woman: Ruth, the Moabite, an example of piety to her relatives and of sincere and generous humility. Sharing Israel's life and faith, she was to become David's great-grandmother and an ancestor of the Messiah. Matthew, inserting her in Jesus' genealogy (*Mt* 1:5), makes her a sign of universality and a proclamation of God's mercy which extends to all humanity.

2.2 Among Jesus' forebears, the first Evangelist also mentions Tamar, Rahab, and Uriah's wife, three sinful but not wicked women who are listed among the female ancestors of the Messiah, in order to proclaim that divine goodness is greater than sin. Through his grace, God causes their irregular matrimonial situations to contribute to his plans of salvation, thereby also preparing for the future.

---

[1] "*Prophetis Domini*" (*1 Reg* 18, 13).

2.3 Another example of humble dedication, different from Ruth's, is represented by Jephthah's daughter, who agrees to pay for her father's victory over the Ammonites with her own death (*Jgs* 11:34-40). Lamenting her cruel destiny, she does not rebel but gives herself up to death in fulfilment of the thoughtless vow made by her parent in the context of primitive customs that were still prevalent (cf. *Jer* 7:31; *Mi* 6:6-8).

3.1 Although sapiential literature[1] frequently alludes to woman's defects, it perceives in her a hidden treasure: "He who finds a wife finds a good thing, and obtains favour from the LORD" (*Prov* 18:22),[2] says the book of Proverbs, expressing convinced appreciation of the feminine figure, a precious gift of the Lord.

3.2 At the end of the same book the portrait of the ideal woman is sketched. Far from representing an unattainable model, she is a concrete image born from the experience of women of great value: "A good wife who can find? She is far more precious than jewels..." (*Prov* 31:10).[3]

3.3 Sapiential literature sees in woman's fidelity to the divine covenant the culmination of her abilities and the greatest source of admiration. Indeed, although she can sometimes disappoint, woman transcends all expectations when her heart is faithful to God: "Charm is deceitful, and beauty is vain, but a woman who fears the LORD is to be praised" (*Prov* 31:30).[4]

4.1 In this context, the book of the Maccabees, in the story of the mother of the seven brothers martyred during Antiochus Epiphanes' persecution, holds up to us the most admirable example of nobility in trial.

4.2 After describing the death of the seven brothers, the sacred author adds: "The mother was especially admirable and worthy of honourable memory. Though she saw her seven sons perish within a single day, she bore it with good courage because of her hope in the Lord. She encouraged each of them in the language of their fathers. Filled with a noble spirit, she fired her woman's reasoning with a man's courage", thus expressing her hope in a future resurrection:

[1] "Sapiential literature" refers to the seven sapiential or wisdom books of the Bible: the book of Job (*liber Iob*), the book of the Psalms (*liber Psalmorum*), the book of the Proverbs (*liber Proverbiorum*), the book of Ecclesiastes (*liber Ecclesiastes*), the Song of Songs of Solomon (*Canticum Canticorum*), the Wisdom of Solomon (*liber Sapientiæ*), and the book of Sirach or Ecclesiasticus (*liber Ecclesiasticus*).
[2] "*Qui invenit mulierem bonam, invenit bonum et hausit gratiam a Domino*" (*Prov* 18, 22).
[3] "*Mulierem fortem quis inveniet? Longe super gemmas pretium eius*" (*Prov* 31, 10).
[4] "*Fallax gratia et vana est pulchritudo; mulier timens Dominum ipsa laudabitur*" (*Prov* 31, 30).

"Therefore the Creator of the world, who shaped the beginning of man and devised the origin of all things, will in his mercy give life and breath back to you again, since you now forget yourselves for the sake of his laws" (*2 Mc* 7:20-23).[1]

4.3 Urging her seventh son to submit to death rather than disobey the divine law, the mother expresses her faith in the work of God who creates all things from nothing:

"I beg you, my child, to look at the heaven and the earth and see everything that is in them, and recognise that God did not make them out of things that existed. Thus also mankind comes into being. Do not fear this butcher, but prove worthy of your brothers. Accept death, so that in God's mercy I may get you back again with your brothers" (*2 Mc* 7:28-29).[2]

4.3 She then gives herself up to a bloody death, after suffering torture of the heart seven times, witnessing to steadfast faith, boundless hope and heroic courage.

4.4 In these figures of woman, in whom the marvels of divine grace are manifest, we glimpse the one who will be the greatest: Mary, Mother of the Lord.

10 April 1996

---

[1] "*Supra modum autem mater mirabilis et bona memoria digna, quæ pereuntes septem filios sub unius diei tempore conspiciens bono animo ferebat propter spem, quam in Dominum habebat. Singulos illorum hortabatur voce patria, forti repleta sensu et femineam cogitationem masculino excitans animo... sed enim mundi creator, qui formavit hominis nativitatem quique omnium invenit originem, et spiritum et vitam vobis iterum cum misericordia reddet, sicut nunc vosmetipsos despicitis propter leges eius*" (*2 Mac* 7, 20-21, 23).

[2] "*Peto, nate, ut aspicias ad cælum et terram et quæ in ipsis sunt, universa videns intellegas quia non ex his, quæ erant, fecit illa Deus; et hominum genus ita fit. Ne timeas carnificem istum, sed dignus fratribus tuis effectus suscipe mortem, ut in illa miseratione cum fratribus tuis te recipiam*" (*2 Mac* 7, 28-29).

17
THE DAUGHTER OF SION

1.1 The Bible often uses the expression "daughter of Sion"[1] to indicate the inhabitants of the city of Jerusalem, of which Mount Son is historically and religiously the most significant (cf. *Mi* 4:10-13; *Zep* 3:14-18; *Zec* 2:14; 9:9-10).

1.2 This feminine personalization facilitates the spousal interpretation of the loving relationship between God and Israel, frequently described with the terms "betrothed" or "wife".

1.3 Salvation history is the story of God's love, but often too of human infidelity. The Word of the Lord frequently reprimands the wife-people who break the marital Covenant established with God: "Surely, as a faithless wife leaves her husband, so have you been faithless to me, O house of Israel" (*Jer* 3:20),[2] and invites the children of Israel to plead with their mother: "Plead with your mother, plead—for she is not my wife, and I am not her husband" (*Hos* 2:2).[3]

1.4 What is the sin of infidelity that stains Israel, Yahweh's "wife"? It consists above all in idolatry: according to the sacred text, in the Lord's eyes recourse to idols by his chosen people is equivalent to adultery.

2.1 The prophet Hosea develops, with strong and dramatic images, the theme of the spousal Covenant between God and his people and of their betrayal: his own personal experience becomes an eloquent symbol of it. Indeed, at the birth of his children he is ordered: "Call her name Not pitied, for I will no more have pity on the house of Israel, to forgive them at all", and again: "Call his name Not my people, for you are not my people and I am not your God" (*Hos* 1:6, 9).[4]

2.2 The Lord's rebuke and the disappointing experience of worshiping idols makes the faithless wife return to her senses and, repentant, she will say: "I will go and return to my first husband, for it was better with me then than now" (*Hos* 2:7).[5] But God himself wishes to re-establish the Covenant, and

[1] "*Filia Sion*".
[2] "*Sed, quomodo contemnit mulier amatorem suum, sic contempsistis me, domus Israel*" (*Ier* 3, 20).
[3] "*Contendite adversum matrem vestram; contendite, quoniam ipsa non uxor mea, et ego non vir eius*" (*Os* 2, 2 [4]).
[4] "*Voca nomen eius 'Absque misericordia', quia non addam ultra misereri domui Israel, ut ignoscam eis... Voca nomen eius 'Non populus meus', quia vos non populus meus, et ego 'Non sum' vobis*" (*Os* 1, 6. 9).
[5] "*Vadam et revertar ad virum meum priorem, quia bene mihi erat tunc magis quam nunc*" (*Os* 2, 7 [9]).

then his word becomes memory, mercy and tenderness: "Therefore, behold, I will allure her, and bring her into the wilderness, and speak tenderly to her" (*Hos* 2:14).[1] The wilderness, in fact, is the place where God made his definitive Covenant with his people after their deliverance from slavery.

2.3 Through these images of love, which portray the difficult relationship between God and Israel, the prophet illustrates the great tragedy of sin, the unhappiness of the way of infidelity and the efforts of divine love to speak to human hearts and bring them back to the Covenant.

3.1 Despite the problems of the moment, through the mouth of the prophet God announces a more perfect Covenant for the future:

"And in that day, says the LORD, you will call me, 'My husband', and no longer will you call me, 'My Baal'… And I will espouse you for ever; I will espouse you in righteousness and in justice, in steadfast love, and in mercy. I will espouse you in faithfulness; and you shall know the LORD" (*Hos* 2:16, 19-20).[2]

3.2 The Lord is not discouraged by human weakness but responds to human infidelities by proposing a more stable and intimate union:

"And I will sow him for myself in the land. And I will have pity on Not pitied, and I will say to Not my people, 'You are my people'; and he shall say, 'You are my God'" (*Hos* 2:23).[3]

3.3 The same prospect of a new Covenant is presented again by Jeremiah to the people in exile:

"'At that time, says the LORD, I will be the God of all the families of Israel, and they shall be my people'. Thus says the LORD: 'The people who survived the sword found grace in the wilderness; when Israel sought for rest, the LORD appeared to him from afar. I have loved you with an everlasting love; therefore I have continued my faithfulness to you. Again I will build you, and you shall be built, O virgin Israel!'" (*Jer* 31:1-4).[4]

---

[1] "*Propter hoc ecce ego lactabo eam et ducam eam in solitudinem et loquar ad cor eius*" (*Os* 2, 14 [16]).

[2] "*Et erit: in die illa, ait Dominus, vocabis me: 'Vir meus' et non vocabis me ultra: 'Baal meus'… Et sponsabo te mihi in sempiternum; et sponsabo te mihi in iustitia et iudicio et in misericordia et miserationibus*" (*Os* 2, 16. 19-20 [18. 21-22).

[3] "*Et seminabo eam mihi in terram et miserebor eius, quæ fuit 'Absque misericordia'; et dicam 'Non populo meo': 'Populus meus tu'; et ipse dicet: 'Deus meus es tu'*" (*Os* 2, 23 [25-26]).

[4] "'*In tempore illo, dicit Dominus, ero Deus universis cognationibus Israel, et ipsi erunt mihi in populum'. Hæc dicit Dominus: 'Invenit gratiam in deserto populus, qui remanserat a gladio; vadet ad requiem suam Israel'. De longe Dominus apparuit mihi: 'In caritate perpetua dilexi te; ideo attraxi te in misericordia. Rursumque ædificabo te, et ædificaberis, virgo Israel*'" (*Ier* 31, 1-4).

3.4 Despite the people's infidelity, God's eternal love is always ready to re-establish the pact of love and to offer a salvation beyond all expectation.

4.1 Ezekiel and Isaiah also mention the image of the unfaithful woman who is forgiven. Through Ezekiel the Lord tells his wife: "Yet I will remember my covenant with you in the days of your youth, and I will establish with you an everlasting covenant" (*Ez* 16:60).[1]

4.2 The book of Isaiah quotes an oracle filled with tenderness:

"For your Maker is your husband... For a brief moment I forsook you, but with great compassion I will gather you. In overflowing wrath for a moment I hid my face from you, but with everlasting love I will have compassion on you, says the LORD, your Redeemer" (*Is* 54:5, 7-8).[2]

4.3 That promise to the daughter of Sion is a new and faithful love, a magnificent hope which overcomes the abandonment of the faithless wife:

"Say to the daughter of Sion: 'Behold, your salvation comes; behold, his reward is with him, and his recompense before him'. And they shall be called The holy people, The redeemed of the LORD; and you shall be called Sought out, a city not forsaken" (*Is* 62:11-12).[3]

4.4 The prophet explains:

"You shall no more be termed Forsaken, and your land shall no more be termed Desolate; but you shall be called My delight is in her, and your land Married; for the LORD delights in you, and your land shall be married. For as a young man marries a virgin, so shall your sons marry you, and as the bridegroom rejoices over the bride, so shall your God rejoice over you" (*Is* 62:4-5).[4]

4.5 Images and attitudes of love, which the Canticle of Canticles summarises in the statement: "I am my beloved's and my beloved is mine" (*Sg* 6:3).[5] Thus

[1] "*Et recordabor ego pacti mei tecum in diebus adulescentiæ tuæ et suscitabo tibi pactum sempiternum*" (*Ez* 16, 60).

[2] "*Qui enim fecit te, erit sponsus tuus... Ad punctum in modico dereliqui te et in miserationibus magnis congregabo te. In momento indignationis abscondi faciem meam parumper a te et in misericordia sempiterna misertus sum tui, dixit redemptor tuus Dominus*" (*Is* 54, 5. 7-8).

[3] "*Dicite filiæ Sion: Ecce salus tua venit, ecce merces eius cum eo, et præmium eius coram illo. Et vocabunt eos Populus sanctus, Redempti a Domino; tu autem vocaberis Quæsita, Civitas non derelicta*" (*Is* 62, 11-12).

[4] "*Non vocaberis ultra Derelicta, et terra tua non vocabitur amplius Desolata; sed vocaberis Beneplacitum meum in ea, et terra tua Nupta, quia complacuit Domino in te, et terra tua erit nupta. Nam ut iuvenis uxorem ducit virginem, ita ducent te filii tui; ut gaudet sponsus super sponsam, ita gaudebit super te Deus tuus*" (*Is* 62, 4-5).

[5] "*Ego dilecto meo, et dilectus meus mihi*" (*Cant* 6, 3).

the relationship between Yahweh and his people is presented again in ideal terms.

5.1 When she listened to the reading of the prophecies, Mary must have thought of this perspective, which nourished messianic hope in her heart.

5.2 The rebukes addressed to the unfaithful people must have inspired in her a more ardent commitment of fidelity to the Covenant, opening her spirit to the proposal of a definitive spousal communion with the Lord in grace and love. From this new Covenant would come the salvation of the whole world.

24 April 1996

18
THE NEW DAUGHTER OF SION

1.1 At the time of the Annunciation, Mary, the "exalted daughter of Sion" (*Lumen gentium*, n. 55),[1] is greeted by the angel as the representative of humanity, called to give her own consent to the Incarnation of the Son of God.

1.2 The first word the angel addresses to her is an invitation to joy: *chàire*[2] that is, "rejoice". The Greek term has been translated in Latin with *Ave*, a simple expression of greeting which does not seem to correspond fully to the divine messenger's intentions and the context in which the meeting takes place.

1.3 Of course, *chàire* was also a form of greeting frequently used by the Greeks, but the extraordinary circumstances in which it is uttered have nothing to do with the atmosphere of a habitual meeting. In fact, we must not forget that the angel is aware of bringing an announcement that is unique in human history: thus a simple, normal greeting would be out of place. Instead, the reference to the original meaning of the expression *chàire*, which is "rejoice", seems more suitable for this exceptional occasion.

1.4 As the Greek Fathers in particular constantly pointed out, citing various prophetic oracles, the invitation to joy is especially appropriate for the announcement of the Messiah's coming.

2.1 Our thoughts turn first of all to the prophet Zephaniah. The text of the Annunciation shows a significant parallelism with his oracle: "Sing aloud, O daughter of Sion; shout, O Israel! Rejoice and exult with all your heart, O daughter of Jerusalem!" (*Zep* 3:14).[3] There is the invitation to joy: "Rejoice and exult with all your heart" (v. 14).[4] Mention is made of the Lord's presence: "The King of Israel, the LORD, is in your midst" (v. 15).[5] There is the exhortation not to be afraid: "Do not fear, O Sion, let not your hands grow weak" (v. 16).[6] Finally, there is the promise of God's saving intervention: "The LORD, your God is in your midst, a warrior who gives victory" (v. 17).[7] The comparisons are so numerous and regular that they lead one to recognise Mary as the new "daughter of Sion", who has full reason to rejoice because God has decided to fulfil his plan of salvation.

---

[1] "*Præcelsa Filia Sion*" (CONCILIUM VATICANUM II, Const. dogm. de Ecclesia, *Lumen gentium*, 55: *AAS* 57 (1965), p. 60).
[2] "*Khaîre*" or " *Chàire*" is the transliteration of the Greek word χαῖρε.
[3] "*Lauda, filia Sion; iubilate, Israel! Lætare et exsulta in omni corde, filia Ierusalem!*" (*Soph* 3, 14).
[4] "*Lætare et exsulta in omni corde*" (*Soph* 3, 14).
[5] "*Rex Israel, Dominus, in medio tui, non timebis malum ultra*" (*Soph* 3, 15).
[6] "*Noli timere, Sion; ne dissolvantur manus tuæ!*" (*Soph* 3, 16).
[7] "*Dominus Deus tuus in medio tui, fortis ipse salvabit*" (*Soph* 3, 17).

2.2 A similar invitation to joy, even if it is in a different context, comes from Joel's prophecy: "Fear not, O land; be glad and rejoice, for the LORD has done great things! ...You shall know that I am in the midst of Israel" (*Jl* 2:21, 27).[1]

3.1 Also significant is the oracle of Zechariah, cited in connection with Jesus' entry into Jerusalem (*Mt* 21:5; *Jn* 12:15). In it the reason for joy is seen in the coming of the Messianic king:

"Rejoice greatly, O daughter of Sion! Shout aloud, O daughter of Jerusalem! Behold, your king comes to you; triumphant and victorious is he, humble... and he shall command peace to the nations" (*Zec* 9:9-10).[2]

3.2 Finally, the announcement of joy to the new Sion springs, in the book of Isaiah, from its numerous posterity, a sign of divine blessing:

"Sing O barren one, who did not bear; break forth into singing and cry aloud, you who have not had labour pains! For the children of the desolate one will be more than the children of her that is married, says the LORD" (*Is* 54:1).[3]

3.3 The three reasons for the invitation to joy: God's saving presence among his people, the coming of the messianic king and gratuitous and superabundant fruitfulness, find their fulfilment in Mary. They justify the pregnant meaning attributed by Tradition to the angel's greeting. By inviting her to give her assent to the fulfilment of the messianic promise and announcing to her the most high dignity of being Mother of the Lord, the angel could not but invite her to rejoice. Indeed, as the Council reminds us:

"After a long period of waiting the times are fulfilled in her, the exalted daughter of Sion, and the new plan of salvation is established, when the Son of God has taken human nature from her, that he might in the mysteries of his flesh free man from sin" (*Lumen gentium*, n. 55).[4]

4.1 The account of the Annunciation allows us to recognise in Mary the new "daughter of Sion", invited by God to deep joy. It expresses her extraordinary role as mother of the Messiah, indeed, as mother of the Son of God. The

---

[1] "*Noli timere, terra; exsulta et lætare, quoniam magna Dominus operatus est... Et scietis quia in medio Israel ego sum*" (*Ioel* 2, 21. 27).

[2] "*Exsulta satis, filia Sion; iubila, filia Ierusalem. Ecce rex tuus venit tibi iustus et salvator ipse, pauper... et loquetur pacem gentibus*" (*Zac* 9, 9-10).

[3] "*Exsulta, sterilis, quæ non peperisti, lætare, gaude, quæ non parturisti, quoniam multi sunt filii desertæ magis quam filii nuptæ, dicit Dominus*" (*Is* 54, 1).

[4] "*Cum Ipsa tandem præcelsa Filia Sion, post diuturnam exspectationem promissionis, complentur tempora et nova instauratur œconomia, quando Filius Dei humanam naturam ex ea assumpsit, ut mysteriis carnis suæ hominem a peccato liberaret*" (CONCILIUM VATICANUM II, Const. dogm. de Ecclesia, *Lumen gentium*, 55: *AAS* 57 (1965), p. 60).

Virgin accepts the message on behalf of the people of David, but we can say that she accepts it on behalf of all humanity, because the Old Testament extended the role of the Davidic Messiah to all nations (cf. *Ps* 2:8; 71 [72]:8). In the divine intention, the announcement addressed to her looks to universal salvation.

4.2 To confirm this universal perspective of God's plan, we can recall several Old and New Testament texts which compare salvation to a great feast for all peoples on Mount Sion (cf. *Is* 25:6f.) and which announce the final banquet of God's kingdom (cf. *Mt* 22:1-10).

4.3 As "daughter of Sion", Mary is the Virgin of the Covenant which God establishes with all humanity. Mary's representational role in this event is clear. And it is significant that it is a woman who carries out this function.

5.1 As the new "daughter of Sion", Mary in fact is particularly suited to entering into the spousal Covenant with God. More and better than any member of the Chosen People, she can offer the Lord the true heart of a Bride.

5.2 With Mary, "daughter of Sion" is not merely a collective subject, but a person who represents humanity and, at the moment of the Annunciation, she responds to the proposal of divine love with her own spousal love. Thus she welcomes in a quite special way the joy foretold by the prophecies, a joy which reaches its peak here in the fulfilment of God's plan.

1 May 1996

19
"FULL OF GRACE"

1.1 In the account of the Annunciation, the first word of the Angel's greeting, "Rejoice", is an invitation to joy which recalls the oracles of the Old Testament addressed to the "daughter of Sion". We pointed this out in our previous catecheses and also explained the reasons for this invitation: God's presence among his people, the coming of the messianic king and maternal fruitfulness. These reasons are fulfilled in Mary.

The Angel Gabriel, addressing the Virgin of Nazareth after the greeting, *chàire,*[1] "rejoice", calls her *kecharitoméne,*[2] "full of grace". The words of the Greek text, *chàire* and *kecharitoméne*, are deeply interconnected: Mary is invited to rejoice primarily because God loves her and has filled her with grace in view of her divine motherhood!

The Church's faith and the experience of the saints teach us that grace is a source of joy, and that true joy comes from God. In Mary, as in Christians, the divine gift produces deep joy.

2.1 *Kecharitoméne:* this term addressed to Mary seems to be the proper way to describe the woman destined to become the mother of Jesus. *Lumen gentium* appropriately recalls this when it affirms: "The Virgin of Nazareth is hailed by the heralding angel, by divine command, as 'full of grace'" (*Lumen gentium*, n. 56).[3]

The fact that the heavenly messenger addresses her in this way enhances the value of the angelic greeting: it is a manifestation of God's mysterious saving plan in Mary's regard. As I wrote in the Encyclical *Redemptoris Mater*: "'The fullness of grace' indicates all the supernatural munificence from which Mary benefits by being chosen and destined to be the Mother of Christ" (n. 9).[4]

"Full of grace" is the name Mary possesses in the eyes of God. Indeed, the angel, according to the Evangelist Luke's account, uses this expression even before he speaks the name "Mary", and thus emphasises the predominant aspect which the Lord perceived in the Virgin of Nazareth's personality.

---

[1] "*Khaîre*" or " *Chàire*" is the transliteration of the Greek word χαῖρε.

[2] "*Kecharitoméne*" is the transliteration of the Greek word κεχαριτωμένη.

[3] "*Nazarethana Virgo ab Angelo nuntiante, Dei mandato, ut 'gratia plena' salutatur*" (CONCILIUM VATICANUM II, Const. dogm. de Ecclesia, *Lumen gentium*, 56: *AAS* 57 [1965]).

[4] "*Sed simul 'plenitudo gratiæ' totam largitionem supernaturalem indicat, qua Maria fruitur, eo quod electa et constituta est, ut Christi Mater esset*" (SANCTUS IOANNES PAULUS II, Litt. enc. *Redemptoris Mater* (25 martii 1987), 9: *AAS* 79 (1987), p. 371).

The expression "full of grace" is the translation of the Greek word *kecharitoméne*, which is a passive participle. Therefore to render more exactly the nuance of the Greek word one should not say merely "full of grace", but "*made* full of grace", or even "*filled* with grace", which would clearly indicate that this was a gift given by God to the Blessed Virgin. This term, in the form of a perfect participle, enhances the image of a perfect and lasting grace which implies fullness. The same verb, in the sense of "to bestow grace", is used in the Letter to the Ephesians to indicate the abundance of grace granted to us by the Father in his beloved Son (*Eph* 1:6), and which Mary receives as the first fruits of Redemption (cf. *Redemptoris Mater*, n. 10).

3.1 In the Virgin's case, God's action certainly seems surprising. Mary has no human claim to receiving the announcement of the Messiah's coming. She is not the high priest, official representative of the Hebrew religion, nor even a man, but a young woman without any influence in the society of her time. In addition, she is a native of Nazareth, a village which is never mentioned in the Old Testament. It must not have enjoyed a good reputation, as Nathanael's question, recorded in John's Gospel, makes clear: "Can anything good come out of Nazareth?" (*Jn* 1:46).[1]

The extraordinary and gratuitous nature of God's intervention becomes even clearer in comparison with Luke's text, which recounts what happened to Zechariah. The latter's priestly status is highlighted as well as his exemplary life, which make him and his wife Elizabeth models of Old Testament righteousness: they walked "blameless in all the commandments and ordinances of the Lord" (*Lk* 1:6).[2]

But we are not informed of Mary's origins either: the expression "of the house of David" (*Lk* 1:27)[3] in fact refers only to Joseph. No mention is made then of Mary's behaviour. With this literary choice, Luke stresses that everything in Mary derives from a sovereign grace. All that is granted to her is not due to any claim of merit, but only to God's free and gratuitous choice.

4.1 In so doing, the Evangelist does not of course intend to downplay the outstanding personal value of the Blessed Virgin. Rather, he wishes to present Mary as the pure fruit of God's goodwill: he has so taken possession of her as to make her, according to the title used by the Angel, "full of grace". The abundance of grace itself is the basis of Mary's hidden spiritual richness.

---

[1] "*A Nazareth potest aliquid boni esse?*" (*Io* 1, 46).
[2] "*In omnibus mandatis et iustificationibus Domini*" (*Lc* 1, 6).
[3] "*De domo David*" (*Lc* 1, 27).

In the Old Testament, Yahweh expresses the superabundance of his love in many ways and on many occasions. At the dawn of the New Testament, the gratuitousness of God's mercy reaches the highest degree in Mary. In her, God's predilection, shown to the chosen people and in particular to the humble and the poor, reaches its culmination.

Nourished by the Word of the Lord and the experience of the saints, the Church urges believers to keep their gaze fixed on the Mother of the Redeemer and to consider themselves, like her, loved by God. She invites them to share our Lady's humility and poverty, so that, after her example and through her intercession, they may persevere in the grace of God who sanctifies and transforms hearts.

8 May 1996

20
THE PERFECT HOLINESS OF MARY

1.1 Mary, "full of grace", has been recognised by the Church as "all holy and free from every stain of sin", "enriched from the first instant of her conception with the splendour of an entirely unique holiness" (*Lumen gentium*, n. 56).[1]

1.2 This recognition required a long process of doctrinal reflection, which finally led to the solemn proclamation of the dogma of the Immaculate Conception.

1.3 The title "*made* full of grace", addressed by the angel to Mary at the Annunciation, refers to the exceptional divine favour shown to the young woman of Nazareth in view of the motherhood which was announced, but it indicates more directly the effect of divine grace in Mary; Mary was inwardly and permanently imbued with grace and thus sanctified. The title *kecharitoméne* has a very rich meaning and the Holy Spirit has never ceased deepening the Church's understanding of it.

2.1 In the preceding catechesis I pointed out that in the angel's greeting the expression "full of grace" serves almost as a name: it is Mary's name in the eyes of God. In Semitic usage, a name expresses the reality of the persons and things to which it refers. As a result, the title "full of grace" shows the deepest dimension of the young woman of Nazareth's personality: fashioned by grace and the object of divine favour to the point that she can be defined by this special predilection.

2.2 The Council recalls that the Church Fathers alluded to this truth when they called Mary the "all-holy one", affirming at the same time that she was "fashioned as it were by the Holy Spirit and formed as a new creature" (*Lumen gentium*, n. 56).[2]

2.3 Grace, understood in the sense of "sanctifying grace" which produces personal holiness, brought about the new creation in Mary, making her fully conformed to God's plan.

3.1 Doctrinal reflection could thus attribute to Mary a perfection of holiness that, in order to be complete, had necessarily to include the beginning of her life.

3.2 Bishop Theoteknos of Livias in Palestine, who lived between 550 and 650, seems to have moved in the direction of this original purity. In presenting

---

[1] "*Omni peccati labe immunem... Singularis prorsus sanctitatis splendoribus a primo instante suæ conceptionis ditata*" (CONCILIUM VATICANUM II, Const. dogm. de Ecclesia, *Lumen gentium*, 56: *AAS* 57 (1965), p. 60).

[2] "*Totam sanctam... quasi a Spiritu Sancto plasmatam novamque creaturam formatam*" (IBID.).

Mary as "holy and all-fair", "pure and stainless", he referred to her birth in these words: "She is born like the cherubim, she who is of a pure, immaculate clay" (*Panegyric for the feast of the Assumption*, 5-6).

3.3 This last expression, recalling the creation of the first man, fashioned of a clay not stained by sin, attributes the same characteristics to Mary's birth: the Virgin's origin was also "pure and immaculate", that is, without any sin. The comparison with the cherubim also emphasises the outstanding holiness that characterised Mary's life from the very beginning of her existence.

3.4 Theoteknos' assertion marks a significant stage in the theological reflection on the mystery of the Lord's Mother. The Greek and Eastern Fathers had acknowledged a purification brought about by grace in Mary, either before the Incarnation (Saint Gregory Nazianzen,[1] *Oratio* 38, 16) or at the very moment of the Incarnation (Saint Ephrem,[2] Severian of Gabala,[3] James of Sarug[4]). Theoteknos of Livias seems to have required of Mary an absolute purity from the beginning of her life. Indeed, she who was destined to become the Saviour's Mother had to have had a perfectly holy, completely stainless origin.

4.1 In the eighth century, Andrew of Crete[5] is the first theologian to see a new creation in Mary's birth. This is how he reasons:

"Today humanity, in all the radiance of her immaculate nobility, receives its ancient beauty. The shame of sin had darkened the splendour and attraction of human nature; but when the Mother of the Fair One *par excellence* is born, this nature regains in her person its ancient privileges and is fashioned according toperfect model truly worthy of God… The reform of our nature begins today and the aged world, subjected to a wholly divine transformation, receives the first fruits of the second creation" (*Serm. I on the Birth of Mary*).[6]

---

[1] Saint Gregory of Nazianzus or Nanzianzen (ca. 329–389/390) was a Patriarch of Constantinople and one of the three Cappadocian Fathers (the brothers Saint Basil the Great and Saint Gregory of Nyssa being the other two). His feast day is 2 January; 25 January in the East.

[2] Saint Ephrem (Ephræm) the Syrian (ca. 306–373) was a layman, poet, and theologian and is a Doctor of the Church. His feast day is 18 June.

[3] Severian of Gabala (ca. 380-408) was Bishop of Gabala in Syria and an adversary of Saint John Chrysostom, condemning him at the Synod of the Oak, a provincial synod held in July of 403, which deposed Saint John Chrysostom as Patriarch of Constantinople.

[4] Saint James of Sarug (Serug) or Jacob of Serugh (ca. 451-521) was a Syrian poet and theologian and is known as "the Flute of the Spirit".

[5] Saint Andrew of Crete or of Jerusalem (ca. 650–712, 726, or 740) was the 21st Archbishop of Crete, theologian, homilist, and hymnographer. His feast day is 17 July (4 July in the Julian Calendar)

[6] "*Hodie pura hominum ingenuitas, primæ a Deo creationis munus recipit, et ad seipsam revertitur: quemque speciei decorem obscuravit vitiosa ignobilitas, hunc natura natæ matri eius qui speciosus est adhærens, optimam divinissimamque fictionem suscipit: efficiturque fictio reparatio absoluta: reparatio autem, deificatio: illaque, in antiquum efformatio... Hodie reformari incipit natura, mundusque veteratus deiformem omnino reformationem accipiens, secundæ a Deo fictionis initia sucipit*" (SANCTUS ANDREAS CRETENSIS, *Orationes*, oratio I, In Nativitatem B. Mariæ: *PG* 97, 811).

4.2 Then, taking up again the image of the primordial clay, he states: "The Virgin's body is ground which God has tilled, the first fruits of Adam's soil divinised by Christ, the image truly like the former beauty, the clay kneaded by the divine Artist" (*Serm. I on the Dormition of Mary*).[1]

4.3 Mary's pure and Immaculate Conception is thus seen as the beginning of the new creation. It is a question of a personal privilege granted to the woman chosen to be Christ's Mother, who ushers in the time of abundant grace willed by God for all humanity.

4.4 This doctrine, taken up again in the eighth century by Saint Germanus of Constantinople[2] and Saint John Damascene,[3] sheds light on the value of Mary's original holiness, presented as the beginning of the world's Redemption.

4.5 In this way the Church's tradition assimilates and makes explicit the authentic meaning of the title "full of grace" given by the angel to the Blessed Virgin. Mary is full of sanctifying grace and is so from the first moment of her existence. This grace, according to the Letter to the Ephesians (1:6),[4] is bestowed in Christ on all believers. Mary's original holiness represents the unsurpassable model of the gift and the distribution of Christ's grace in the world.

15 May 1996

[1] "*Corpus, inquam, pretiosum virginitatis monile, præcellens cælum, Deo culta terra, delibatio massæ humani ex Adam generis in Christo deitate donatæ, simillima principis speciei atque decoris repræsentatio*" (Sanctus Andreas Cretensis, *Orationes*, oratio XII, In Dormitionem S. Mariæ: *PG* 97, 1067).

[2] Saint Germanus (Germanos) I of Constantinople was appointed Patriarch of Constantinople from 715 until 730; feast day: 12 May.

[3] Saint John Damascene or John of Damascus (ca. 676-749), "Doctor of the Assumption", was a monk, priest, hymnographer, and apologist. He was proclaimed a Doctor of the Church in 1890 by Pope Leo XIII and his feast day is 4 December in the Ordinary Form of the Roman Rite, 27 March in the Extraordinary Form.

[4] "To the praise of his glorious grace which he freely bestowed on us in the Beloved [*In laudem gloriæ gratiæ suæ, in qua gratificavit nos in Dilecto*]" (*Eph* 1:6).

21
THE IMMACULATE CONCEPTION

1.1 In the doctrinal reflection of the Eastern Church, the expression "full of grace", as we saw in the preceding catecheses, has been interpreted since the sixth century as a unique holiness which Mary enjoys throughout her existence. She thus initiates the new creation.

1.2 Along with Luke's account of the Annunciation, Tradition and the Magisterium have seen in the so-called Protoevangelium (*Gn* 3:15) a scriptural source for the truth of Mary's Immaculate Conception. On the basis of the ancient Latin version: "She will crush your head",[1] this text inspired many depictions of the *Immaculata*[2] crushing the serpent under her feet.

1.3 On an earlier occasion[3] we recalled that this version does not agree with the Hebrew text, in which it is not the woman but her offspring, her descendant, who will bruise the serpent's head. This text then does not attribute the victory over Satan to Mary but to her Son. Nevertheless, since the biblical concept establishes a profound solidarity between the parent and the offspring, the depiction of the Immaculata crushing the serpent, not by her own power but through the grace of her Son, is consistent with the original meaning of the passage.

2.1 The same biblical text also proclaims the enmity between the woman and her offspring on the one hand, and the serpent and his offspring on the other. This is a hostility expressly established by God, which has a unique importance, if we consider the problem of the Virgin's personal holiness. In order to be the irreconcilable enemy of the serpent and his offspring, Mary had to be free from all power of sin, and to be so from the first moment of her existence.

2.2 In this regard, the Encyclical *Fulgens corona*, published by Pope Pius XII in 1953 to commemorate the centenary of the definition of the dogma of the Immaculate Conception, reasons thus:

"If at a given moment the Blessed Virgin Mary had been left without divine grace, because she was defiled at her conception by the hereditary stain of sin, between her and the serpent there would no longer have been—at least during this period of time, however brief—that eternal enmity spoken of in the earliest tradition up to the definition of the Immaculate Conception, but rather a certain enslavement" (*AAS* 45 [1953], 579).[4]

---

[1] *Genesis* 3:15 — "*Ipsa conteret caput tuum*" (*Vulgata Clementina*, 1592); "She shall crush thy head" (*Douay-Rheims*, 1582). "*Ipsum conteret caput tuum*" (*Nova-Vulgata*, 1979); "He shall bruise your head" (*Revised Standard Version, First Catholic Edition*, 1966).

[2] *Immaculata* is Latin for "Immaculate One".

[3] Cf. catechesis no. 12, p. 54.

[4] "*Si aliquando Beata Virgo Maria, utpote hereditaria peccati labe in suo conceptu inquinata, divinæ*

2.3 The absolute hostility put between the woman and the devil thus demands in Mary the Immaculate Conception, that is, a total absence of sin, from the very beginning of her life. The Son of Mary won the definitive victory over Satan and enabled his Mother to receive its benefits in advance by preserving her from sin. As a result, the Son granted her the power to resist the devil, thus achieving in the mystery of the Immaculate Conception the most notable effect of his redeeming work.

3.1 By drawing our attention to Mary's special holiness and her complete removal from Satan's influence, the title "full of grace" and the *Protoevangelium* enable us to perceive, in the unique privilege the Lord granted to Mary, the beginning of a new order which is the result of friendship with God and which, as a consequence, entails a profound enmity between the serpent and men.

3.2 The twelfth chapter of the Apocalypse, which speaks of the "woman clothed with the sun" (12:1),[1] is often cited too as biblical testimony on behalf of the Immaculate Conception. Current exegesis agrees in seeing in this woman the community of God's People, giving birth in pain to the risen Messiah. Along with the collective interpretation, however, the text suggests an individual one in the statement: "She brought forth a male child, one who is to rule all the nations with a rod of iron" (12:5).[2] With this reference to childbirth, it is acknowledged that the woman clothed with the sun is in a certain sense identified with Mary, the woman who gave birth to the messiah. The woman-community is actually described with the features of the woman-Mother of Jesus.

3.3 Identified by her motherhood, the woman "was with child and she cried out in her pangs of birth, in anguish for her delivery" (12:2).[3] This note refers to the Mother of Jesus at the Cross (cf. *Jn* 19:25), where she shares in anguish for the delivery of the community of disciples with a soul pierced by the sword (cf. *Lk* 2:35). Despite her sufferings, she is "clothed with the sun"—that is, she reflects the divine splendour—and appears as a "great sign"[4] of God's spousal relationship with his people.

3.4 These images, although not directly indicating the privilege of the Immaculate Conception, can be interpreted as an expression of the Father's loving care which surrounds Mary with the grace of Christ and the splendour of the Spirit.

gratiæ evasisset expers, eo saltem, etsi brevissimo, temporis vestigio, inter ipsam et serpentem non ea sempiterna, de qua inde a privæva 'traditione' usque ad definitionem sollemnem Conceptionis Immaculatæ Virginis fit mentio, inimicitia intercessisset, sed potius quædam subiectio" (Pius XII, Litt. enc. *Fulgens corona* (8 septembris 1953), 7: *AAS* 45 (1953), p. 579).

[1] "*Mulier amicta sole*" (*Ap* 12, 1).

[2] "*Et peperit filium, masculum, qui recturus est omnes gentes in virga ferrea*" (*Ap* 12, 5).

[3] "*In utero habens, et clamat parturiens et cruciatur, ut pariat*" (*Ap* 12, 2).

[4] "*Signum magnum*" (*Ap* 12, 1).

3.5 Finally, the Apocalypse invites us more particularly to recognise the ecclesial dimension of Mary's personality: the woman clothed with the sun represents the Church's holiness, which is fully realised in the Holy Virgin by virtue of a singular grace.

4.1 These scriptural assertions, to which Tradition and the Magisterium refer in order to ground the doctrine of the Immaculate Conception, would seem to contradict the biblical texts which affirm the universality of sin.

4.2 The Old Testament speaks of a sinful contamination which affects everyone "born of woman" (*Ps* 50 [51]:7; *Jb* 14:2). In the New Testament, Paul states that, as a result of Adam's sin, "all men sinned", and that "one man's trespass led to condemnation for all men" (*Rom* 5:12, 18).[1] Therefore, as the *Catechism of the Catholic Church*[2] recalls, original sin "affected human nature", which is thus found "in a fallen state". Sin is therefore transmitted "by propagation to all mankind, that is, by the transmission of a human nature deprived of original holiness and justice" (n. 404).[3] Paul however admits an exception to this universal law: Christ, he "who knew no sin" (*2 Cor* 5:21),[4] and was thus able, "where sin increased" (*Rom* 5:20),[5] to make grace abound all the more.

4.3 These assertions do not necessarily lead to the conclusion that Mary was involved in sinful humanity. The parallel, established by Paul between Adam and Christ, is completed by that between Eve and Mary: the role of woman, important in the drama of sin, is equally so in the Redemption of mankind.

4.4 Saint Irenaeus[6] presents Mary as the new Eve, who by her faith and obedience compensated for the disbelief and disobedience of Eve. Such a role in the economy of salvation requires the absence of sin. It was fitting that like Christ, the new Adam, Mary too, the new Eve did not know sin and was thus capable of co-operating in the Redemption.

4.5 Sin, which washes over humanity like a torrent, halts before the Redeemer and his faithful Collaborator. With a substantial difference: Christ is all holy by virtue of the grace that in his humanity derives from the divine person; Mary is all holy by virtue of the grace received by the merits of the Saviour.

29 May 1996

---

[1] "*Omnes peccaverunt... per unius delictum in omnes homines in condemnationem*" (*Rom* 5, 12. 18).
[2] The *Catechism of the Catholic Church* (*Catechismus Catholicæ Ecclesiæ*) was promulgated by Pope Saint John Paul II on 11 October 1992, the 30th anniversary of the opening of the Second Vatican Council, with the apostolic constitution *Fidei depositum*. On 15 August 1997, he promulgated the Latin typical edition with the apostolic letter *Lætamur magnopere*.
[3] "*Per propagationem transmittetur, id est per transmissionem naturæ humanæ privatæ originalibus sanctitate et iustitia*" (*Catechismus Catholicæ Ecclesiæ, editio typica* (1997), n. 404).
[4] "*Qui non noverat peccatum*" (*2 Cor* 5, 21).
[5] "*Ubi autem abundavit peccatum*" (*Rom* 5, 20).
[6] Saint Irenaeus (ca. 130-202) was Bishop of Lugdunum in Gaul, which is today Lyons, France. Venerated as a martyr, his feast day is 28 June.

22
THE *IMMACULATA*: REDEEMED THROUGH PRESERVATION

1.1 The doctrine of Mary's perfect holiness from the first moment of her conception met with a certain resistance in the West, on account of Saint Paul's statements about original sin and about the universality of sin, which were taken up again and explained with particular force by Saint Augustine.[1]

1.2 This great doctor of the Church certainly realised that Mary's status as Mother of a completely holy Son required total purity and an extraordinary holiness. This is why, in the controversy with Pelagius,[2] he stressed that Mary's holiness is an exceptional gift of grace and stated in this regard:

"We make an exception for the Blessed Virgin Mary, whom, for the sake of the Lord's honour, I would in no way like to be mentioned in connection with sin. Do we not know why she was granted a greater grace in view of the complete victory over sin, she who merited to conceive and give birth to him who obviously had no sin?" (*De natura et gratia*, n. 42).[3]

1.3 Augustine stressed Mary's perfect holiness and the absence of any personal sin in her because of her lofty dignity as Mother of the Lord. Nonetheless, he could not understand how the affirmation of a total absence of sin at the time of conception could be reconciled with the doctrine of the universality of original sin and the need of redemption for all Adam's descendants. This conclusion was later reached by an ever more penetrating understanding of the Church's faith, explaining how Mary had benefited from Christ's redemptive grace from her conception.

2.1 In the ninth century the feast of Mary's Conception was also introduced in the West, first in southern Italy, in Naples, and then in England.

2.2 Around 1128, a monk of Canterbury, Eadmer,[4] writing the first treatise on the Immaculate Conception, complained that its respective liturgical celebration,

[1] Saint Augustine of Hippo (354–439) was Bishop of Hippo in North Africa and is a Doctor of the Church. His feast day is 28 August.

[2] Pelagius (ca. AD 354 – ca. AD 420 or 440) was an ascetic who denied the doctrine of original sin and was declared a heretic by the Council of Carthage (c. 418).

[3] "*Excepta itaque sancta virgine Maria, de qua propter honorem Domini nullam prorsus cum de peccatis agitur, haberi volo quæstionem: unde enim scimus quid ei plus gratiae collatum fuerit ad vincendum omni ex parte peccatum, quae concipere ac parere meruit, quem constat nullum habuisse peccatum?*" (Sanctus Augustinus, *De natura et gratia*, cap. XXXVI, 42: *PL* 44, 267).

[4] Eadmer (or Edmer) of Canterbury (ca. 1060 – ca. 1124) was an English historian, theologian, and a contemporary biographer of Saint Anselm of Canterbury.

especially pleasing to those "in whom a pure simplicity and most humble devotion to God was found" (*Tract. de conc. B.M.V.*, 1-2),[1] had been set aside or suppressed.

Wishing to promote the restoration of this feast, the devout monk rejected Saint Augustine's objections to the privilege of the Immaculate Conception, based on the doctrine of the transmission of original sin in human generation. He fittingly employed the image of a chestnut "which is conceived, nourished and formed beneath its bur and yet is protected from being pricked by it" (*Tract.* 10). Even beneath the bur of an act of generation which in itself must transmit original sin, Eadmer argues, Mary was preserved from every stain by the explicit will of God who "was obviously able to do this and wanted to do so. Thus if he willed it, he did it" (*ibid.*).[2]

2.3 Despite Eadmer, the great theologians of the thirteenth century made Saint Augustine's difficulties their own, advancing this argument: the Redemption accomplished by Christ would not be universal if the condition of sin were not common to all human beings. And if Mary had not contracted original sin, she could not have been redeemed. Redemption in fact consists in freeing those who are in the state of sin.

3.1 Duns Scotus,[3] following several twelfth century theologians, found the key to overcoming these objections to the doctrine of Mary's Immaculate Conception. He held that Christ, the perfect mediator, exercised the highest act of mediation precisely in Mary, by preserving her from original sin.

3.2 Thus he introduced into theology the concept of Redemption by preservation, according to which Mary was redeemed in an even more wonderful way: not by being freed from sin, but by being preserved from sin.

3.3 The insight of Blessed Duns Scotus, who later became known as "the Doctor of the *Immaculata*", was well received by theologians, especially Franciscans, from the very beginning of the fourteenth century. After Sixtus IV's[4] approval in 1477 of the Mass of the Conception, this doctrine was increasingly accepted in the theological schools.

---

[1] "*In quibus pura simplicitas et humilior in Deum vigebat devotio*" (Eadmerus Cantuariensis, *Tractatus de conceptione sanctæ Mariæ*: *PL* 159, 301).

[2] "*Confert ut inter spinas remota punctione concipiatur, alatur, formetur... potuit plane, et voluit; si igitur voluit, fecit*" (Eadmerus Cantuariensis, *Tractatus de conceptione sanctæ Mariæ*: *PL* 159, 305).

[3] Blessed John (Johannes) Duns Scotus (c. 1266–1308) was a Franciscan and is popularly known as "*Doctor Subtilis* (the Subtle Doctor)". He was beatified on 20 March 1993 by Pope Saint John Paul II and his feast day is 8 November.

[4] Pope Sixtus IV (1414–1484), born Francesco della Rovere, was elected 212th Bishop of Rome on 9 August 1471. He founded the Sistine Chapel and was uncle to the future Pope Julius II (1443–1513).

3.4 This providential development of liturgy and doctrine prepared for the definition of the Marian privilege by the Supreme Magisterium. The latter only occurred many centuries later, and was spurred by a fundamental insight of faith: the Mother of Christ had to be perfectly holy from the very beginning of her life.

4.1 No one fails to see how the affirmation of the exceptional privilege granted to Mary stresses that Christ's redeeming action does not only free us from sin, but also preserves us from it. This dimension of preservation, which in Mary is total, is present in the redemptive intervention by which Christ, in freeing man from sin, also gives him the grace and strength to conquer its influence in his life.

4.2 In this way the dogma of Mary's Immaculate Conception does not obscure but rather helps wonderfully to shed light on the effects in human nature of Christ's redemptive grace.

4.3 Christians look to Mary, the first to be redeemed by Christ and who had the privilege of not being subjected, even for an instant, to the power of evil and sin, as the perfect model and icon of that holiness (cf. *Lumen gentium*, n. 65) which they are called to attain in their life with the help of the Lord's grace.

5 June 1996

23
THE *IMMACULATA*: THE DOGMATIC DEFINITION OF THE PRIVILEGE

1.1 Down the centuries, the conviction that Mary was preserved from every stain of sin from her conception, so that she is to be called all holy, gradually gained ground in the liturgy and theology. At the start of the nineteenth century, this development led to a petition drive for a dogmatic definition of the privilege of the Immaculate Conception.

1.2 Around the middle of the century, with the intention of accepting this request, Pope Pius IX, after consulting the theologians, questioned the Bishops about the opportuneness and the possibility of such a definition, convoking as it were a "council in writing". The result was significant: the vast majority of the 604 Bishops gave a positive response to the question.

1.3 After such an extensive consultation, which emphasised my venerable Predecessor's concern to express the Church's faith in the definition of the dogma, he set about preparing the document with equal care.

1.4 The special commission of theologians set up by Pius IX to determine the revealed doctrine assigned the essential role to ecclesial practice. And this criterion influenced the formulation of the dogma, which preferred expressions taken from the Church's lived experience, from the faith and worship of the Christian people, to scholastic definitions.

1.5 Finally in 1854, with the Bull *Ineffabilis*, Pius IX solemnly proclaimed the dogma of the Immaculate Conception:

"...We declare, pronounce and define that the doctrine which asserts that the Blessed Virgin Mary, from the first moment of her conception, by a singular grace and privilege of almighty God, and in view of the merits of Jesus Christ, Saviour of the human race, was preserved free from every stain of original sin is a doctrine revealed by God and, for this reason, must be firmly and constantly believed by all the faithful" (*DS* 2803).[1]

2.1 The proclamation of the dogma of the Immaculate Conception expresses the essential datum of faith. Pope Alexander VII,[2] in the Bull *Sollicitudo* of 1661,

---

[1] "*Declaramus, pronuntiamus et definimus, doctrinam, quæ tenet, beatissimam Virginem Mariam in primo instanti suæ conceptionis fuisse singulari omnipotentis Dei gratia et privilegio, intuitu meritorum Christi Iesu Salvatoris humani generis, ab omni originalis culpae labe præservatam immunem, esse a Deo revelatam atque idcirco ab omnibus fidelibus firmiter constanterque credendam*" (Beatus Pius IX, Const. ap. *Ineffabilis Deus* (8 decembris 1854): *DS* 2803).

[2] Pope Alexander VII (1599–1667), born Fabio Chigi, was elected the 237th Bishop of Rome on 7 April 1655.

spoke of the preservation of Mary's soul "in its creation and infusion into the body" (*DS* 2017).[1] Pius IX's definition, however, prescinds from all explanations about how the soul is infused into the body and attributes to the person of Mary, at the first moment of her conception, the fact of her being preserved from every stain of original sin.

2.2 The freedom "from every stain of original sin" entails as a positive consequence the total freedom from all sin as well as the proclamation of Mary's perfect holiness, a doctrine to which the dogmatic definition makes a fundamental contribution. In fact, the negative formulation of the Marian privilege, which resulted from the earlier controversies about original sin that arose in the West, must always be complemented by the positive expression of Mary's holiness more explicitly stressed in the Eastern tradition.

2.3 Pius IX's definition refers only to the freedom from original sin and does not explicitly include the freedom from concupiscence. Nevertheless, Mary's complete preservation from every stain of sin also has as a consequence her freedom from concupiscence, a disordered tendency which, according to the Council of Trent,[2] comes from sin and inclines to sin (*DS* 1515).[3]

3.1 Granted "by a singular grace and privilege of almighty God", this preservation from original sin is an absolutely gratuitous divine favour, which Mary received at the first moment of her existence.

3.2 The dogmatic definition does not say that this singular privilege is unique, but lets that be intuited. The affirmation of this uniqueness, however, is explicitly stated in the Encyclical *Fulgens corona* of 1953, where Pope Pius XII speaks of "the very singular privilege which was never granted to another person" (*AAS* 45 [1953], 580),[4] thus excluding the possibility, maintained by some but without foundation, of attributing this privilege also to Saint Joseph.

3.3 The Virgin Mother received the singular grace of being immaculately conceived "in view of the merits of Jesus Christ, Saviour of the human race", that is, of his universal redeeming action.

---

[1] "*In sui creatione et in corpus infusione*" (Alexander VII, Bulla *Sollicitudo omnium ecclesiarum* (8 decembris 1661): *DS* 2017).

[2] The Council of Trent (*Concilium Tridentinum*) was the 19th Ecumenical Council of the Church, held in Trento, Italy, between 1545–1563. It is considered to be one of the most important ecumenical councils due to its sweeping decrees on self-reform and for its dogmatic definitions that clarified virtually every doctrine contested by the Protestant Pseudo-Reformation.

[3] *Enchiridion symbolorum definitionum et declarationum de rebus fidei et morum* [*Compendium of Creeds, Definitions, and Declarations on Matters of Faith and Morals*], Heinrich Joseph Dominicus Denzinger (1819–1883), n. 1515.

[4] "*Itemque hoc singularissimum privilegium, nulli umquam concessum*" (Ven. Pius XII, Litt. enc. *Fulgens corona* (8 septembris 1953), 10: *AAS* 45 (1953), p. 580).

3.4 The text of the dogmatic definition does not expressly declare that Mary was redeemed, but the same Bull *Ineffabilis* states elsewhere that "she was redeemed in the most sublime way". This is the extraordinary truth: Christ was the redeemer of his Mother and carried out his redemptive action in her "in the most perfect way" (*Fulgens corona, AAS* 45 [1953], 581),[1] from the first moment of her existence. The Second Vatican Council proclaimed that the Church "admires and exalts in Mary the most excellent fruit of the Redemption" (*Sacrosanctum Concilium*, n. 103).[2]

4.1 This solemnly proclaimed doctrine is expressly termed a "doctrine revealed by God". Pope Pius IX adds that it must be "firmly and constantly believed by all the faithful". Consequently, whoever does not make this doctrine his own, or maintains an opinion contrary to it, "is shipwrecked in faith' and "separates himself from Catholic unity".[3]

4.2 In proclaiming the truth of this dogma of the Immaculate Conception, my venerable Predecessor was conscious of exercising his power of infallible teaching as the universal Pastor of the Church, which several years later would be solemnly defined at the First Vatican Council.[4] Thus he put his infallible Magisterium into action as a service to the faith of God's People; and it is significant that he did so by defining Mary's privilege.

12 June 1996

[1] "*Perfettissimo quodam modo*" (VEN. PIUS XII, Litt. enc. *Fulgens corona* (8 septembris 1953), 14: *AAS* 45 (1953), p. 581).

[2] "*In qua præcellentem Redemptionis fructum miratur et exaltat*" (CONCILIUM VATICANUM II, Const. de Sacra Liturgia, *Sacrosanctum Concilium*, 103: *AAS* 56 (1964). p. 125).

[3] "*Naufragium circa fidem passos esse et ab unitate Ecclesiæ defecisse*" (BEATUS PIUS IX, Const. ap. *Ineffabilis Deus* (8 decembris 1854): *DS* 2804).

[4] The First Vatican Council (1869–1870) was the 20th Ecumenical Council of the Church, convened by Blessed Pius IX to address contemporary problems such as the rising influence of rationalism, liberalism, and materialism.

24
HOLY THROUGHOUT LIFE

1.1 The definition of the dogma of the Immaculate Conception directly concerns only the first moment of Mary's existence, from when she was "preserved free from every stain of original sin". The papal Magisterium thus wished to define only the truth which had been the subject of controversy down the centuries: *her preservation from original sin*, and was not concerned with defining the lasting holiness of the Lord's Virgin Mother.

1.2 This truth already belongs to the common awareness of the Christian people. It testifies that Mary, free from original sin, was also preserved from all actual sin and that this initial holiness was granted to her in order to fill her entire life.

2.1 The Church has constantly regarded Mary as holy and free from all sin or moral imperfection. The Council of Trent expresses this conviction, affirming that no one "can avoid all sins, even venial sins, throughout his life, unless he is given a special privilege, as the Church holds with regard to the Blessed Virgin" (*DS* 1573).[1] Even the Christian transformed and renewed by grace is not spared the possibility of sinning. Grace does not preserve him from all sin throughout his whole life, unless, as the Council of Trent asserts, a special privilege guarantees this immunity from sin. And this is what happened with Mary.

2.2 The Council of Trent did not wish to define this privilege but stated that the Church vigorously affirms it: "*Tenet*", that is, she firmly holds it. This is a decision which, far from relegating this truth to pious belief or devotional opinion, confirms its nature as a solid doctrine, quite present in the faith of the People of God. Moreover, this conviction is based on the grace attributed to Mary by the angel at the time of the Annunciation. Calling her "full of grace", *kecharitoméne*, the angel acknowledged her as the woman endowed with a lasting perfection and a fullness of sanctity, without shadow of sin or of moral or spiritual imperfection.

3.1 Several early Fathers of the Church, who were not yet convinced of her perfect holiness, attributed imperfections or moral defects to Mary. Some recent authors have taken the same position. However, the Gospel texts cited to justify these opinions provide no basis at all for attributing a sin or even a moral imperfection to the Mother of the Redeemer.

---

[1] "*Posse in tota vita peccata omnia etiam venialia vitare, nisi ex speciali Dei privilegio, quemadmodum de beata Virgine tenet Ecclesia*" (*DS* 1573).

3.2 Jesus' reply to his mother at the age of 12: "How is it that you sought me? Did you not know that I must be in my Father's house?" (*Lk* 2:49),[1] has sometimes been interpreted as a veiled rebuke. A careful reading of the episode, however, shows that Jesus did not rebuke his mother and Joseph for seeking him, since they were responsible for looking after him.

3.3 Coming upon Jesus after an anxious search, Mary asked him only the "why" of his behaviour: "Son, why have you treated us so?" (*Lk* 2:48).[2] And Jesus answers with another "why", refraining from any rebuke and referring to the mystery of his divine sonship.

3.4 Nor can the words he spoke at Cana: "O woman, what have you to do with me? My hour has not yet come" (*Jn* 2:4),[3] be interpreted as a rebuke. Seeing the likely inconvenience which the lack of wine would have caused the bride and groom, Mary speaks to Jesus with simplicity, entrusting the problem to him. Though aware of being the Messiah bound to obey the Father's will alone, he answers the Mother's implicit request. He responds above all to the Virgin's faith and thus performs the first of his miracles, thereby manifesting his glory.

4.1 Later some gave a negative interpretation to the statement Jesus made when, at the beginning of his public life, Mary and his relatives asked to see him. Relating to us Jesus' reply to the one who said to him: "Your mother and your brethren are standing outside, desiring to see you",[4] the Evangelist Luke offers us the interpretive key to the account, which must be understood on the basis of Mary's inner inclinations, which were quite different from those of his "brethren" (cf. *Jn* 7:5). Jesus replied: "My mother and my brethren are those who hear the word of God and do it" (*Lk* 8:21).[5] In the Annunciation account, Luke in fact showed how Mary was the model of listening to the word of God and of generous docility. Interpreted in this perspective, the episode offers great praise of Mary, who perfectly fulfilled the divine plan in her own life. Although Jesus' words are opposed to the brethren's attempt, they exalt Mary's fidelity to the will of God and the greatness of her motherhood, which she lived not only physically but also spiritually.

4.2 In expressing this indirect praise, Jesus uses a particular method: he stresses the nobility of Mary's conduct in the light of more general statements, and shows more clearly the Virgin's solidarity with and closeness to humanity on the difficult way of holiness.

---

[1] "*Quid est quod me quærebatis? Nesciebatis quia in his, quæ Patris mei sunt, oportet me esse?*" (*Lc* 2, 49).
[2] "*Fili, quid fecisti nobis sic?*" (*Lc* 2, 48).
[3] "*Quid mihi et tibi, mulier? Nondum venit hora mea*" (*Io* 2, 4),
[4] "*Mater tua et fratres tui stant foris volentes te videre*" (*Lc* 8, 20).
[5] "*Mater mea et fratres mei hi sunt, qui verbum Dei audiunt et faciunt*" (*Lc* 8, 21).

4.3 Lastly, the words: "Blessed rather are those who hear the word of God and keep it!" (*Lk* 11:28),[1] spoken by Jesus in reply to the woman who had called his Mother blessed, far from putting into doubt Mary's personal perfection, bring out her faithful fulfilment of the word of God: so has the Church understood them, putting this sentence into the liturgical celebrations in Mary's honour. The Gospel text actually suggests that he made this statement to reveal that the highest reason for his Mother's blessedness lies precisely in her intimate union with God and her perfect submission to the divine word.

5.1 The special privilege granted by God to her who is "all holy" leads us to admire the marvels accomplished by grace in her life. It also reminds us that Mary belonged always and completely to the Lord, and that no imperfection harmed her perfect harmony with God.

5.2 Her earthly life was therefore marked by a constant, sublime growth in faith, hope and charity. For believers, Mary is thus the radiant sign of divine Mercy and the sure guide to the loftiest heights of holiness and Gospel perfection.

19 June 1996

[1] "*Quinimmo beati, qui audiunt verbum Dei et custodiunt!*" (*Lc* 11, 28).

25
SHE WHO BELIEVED

1.1 In the Gospel account of the Visitation, Elizabeth, "filled with the Holy Spirit", welcomes Mary to her home and exclaims: "And blessed is she who believed that there would be a fulfilment of what was spoken to her from the Lord" (*Lk* 1:45).[1] This beatitude, the first reported in Luke's Gospel, presents Mary as the one who, by her faith, precedes the Church in fulfilling the spirit of the beatitudes.

1.2 Elizabeth's praise of Mary's faith is reinforced by comparing it to the angel's announcement to Zechariah. A superficial reading of the two announcements might consider Zechariah and Mary as having given similar responses to the divine message: "How shall I know this? For I am an old man, and my wife is advanced in years", Zechariah says; and Mary: "How can this be, since I have no husband?" (*Lk* 1:18, 34).[2] But the profound difference between the interior attitudes of the principals in these two episodes can be seen from the very words of the angel, who rebukes Zechariah for his disbelief, while he gives an immediate reply to Mary's question. Unlike Elizabeth's husband, Mary fully submits to the divine plan and does not condition her consent on the granting of a visible sign.

1.3 The angel, who proposed that she become a mother, is reminded by Mary of her intention to remain a virgin. Believing that the announcement could be fulfilled, she questions the divine messenger only about the manner of its accomplishment, in order better to fulfil God's will, to which she intends to submit with total readiness. "She sought the manner; she did not doubt God's omnipotence", Saint Augustine remarks (*Sermo* 291).[3]

2.1 The context in which the two announcements are made also helps to exalt the excellence of Mary's faith. In Luke's account, we see the more favourable situation of Zechariah and the inadequacy of his response. He receives the angel's announcement in the temple of Jerusalem, at the altar before the "Holy of Holies" (cf. *Ex* 30:6-8); the angel addresses him as he is offering incense, thus, as he is carrying out his priestly duties, at a significant moment in his life; the divine decision is communicated to him in a vision. These particular circumstances favour an easier understanding of the divine authenticity of the message and offer an incentive to accept it promptly.

---

[1] "*Et beata, quæ credidit, quoniam perficientur ea, quæ dicta sunt ei a Domino*" (*Lc* 1, 45).
[2] "*Unde hoc sciam? Ego enim sum senex, et uxor mea processit in diebus suis*" (*Lc* 1, 18); "*Quomodo fiet istud, quoniam virum non cognosco?*" (*Lc* 1, 18. 34).
[3] "*Modum quæsivit, non de Dei omnipotentia dubitavit*" (Sanctus Augustinus, *Sermo CCXCI*, 5: *PL* 38, 1318).

2.2 The announcement to Mary, however, takes place in a simpler, workaday context, without the external elements of sacredness which accompanied the one made to Zechariah. Luke does not indicate the precise place where the Annunciation of the Lord's birth occurred: he reports only that Mary was in Nazareth, a village of little importance, which did not seem predestined for the event. In addition, the Evangelist does not ascribe unusual importance to the moment when the angel appears and does not describe the historical circumstances. In meeting the heavenly messenger, one's attention is focused on the meaning of his words, which demand of Mary intense listening and a pure faith.

2.3 This last consideration allows us to appreciate the greatness of Mary's faith, especially in comparison with the tendency, then as now, to ask insistently for sensible signs in order to believe. In contrast, the Virgin's assent to the divine will is motivated only by her love of God.

3.1 Mary is asked to assent to a much loftier truth than that announced to Zechariah. The latter was invited to believe in a wondrous birth that would take place within a sterile marital union, which God wished to make fruitful: a divine intervention similar to those benefiting several Old Testament women: Sarah (*Gn* 17:15-21; 18:10-14), Rachel (*Gn* 30:22), the mother of Samson (*Jgs* 13:1-7), Hanna, the mother of Samuel (*1 Sm* 1:11-20). In these episodes the gratuitousness of God's gift is particularly emphasised.

3.2 Mary is called to believe in a virginal motherhood, for which the Old Testament mentions no precedent. In fact, the well-known prophecy of Isaiah: "Behold, a virgin shall conceive and bear a son, and shall call his name Immanuel" (7:14),[1] although not excluding such a view, was explicitly interpreted in this sense only after Christ's coming and in the light of the Gospel revelation.

3.3 Mary is asked to assent to a truth never expressed before. She accepts it with a simple yet daring heart. With the question: "How can this be?", she expresses her faith in the divine power to make virginity compatible with her exceptional and unique motherhood.

3.4 By replying: "The Holy Spirit will come upon you, and the power of the Most High will overshadow you" (*Lk* 1:35),[2] the angel offers God's ineffable solution to the question Mary asked. Virginity, which seemed an obstacle, becomes the concrete context in which the Holy Spirit will accomplish in her the conception of the incarnate Son of God. The angel's response opens the way to the Virgin's co-operation with the Holy Spirit in the begetting of Jesus.

---

[1] "*Ecce, virgo concipiet et pariet filium et vocabit nomen eius Emmanuel*" (*Is* 7, 14).
[2] "*Spiritus Sanctus superveniet in te, et virtus Altissimi obumbrabit tibi*" (*Lc* 1, 35).

4.1 The free co-operation of the human person is realised in carrying out the divine plan. By believing in the Lord's word, Mary co-operates in fulfilling the motherhood announced to her.

4.2 The Fathers of the Church often stress this aspect of Jesus' virginal conception. In commenting on the Gospel of the Annunciation, Saint Augustine in particular states: "The angel announces, the Virgin listens, believes and conceives" (*Sermo* 13 *in Nat. Dom.*).[1] And again: "Christ is believed and conceived through faith. The coming of faith first occurs in the Virgin's heart and then fruitfulness comes to the Mother's womb" (*Sermo* 293).[2]

4.3 Mary's act of faith recalls the faith of Abraham, who at the dawn of the Old Covenant, believed in God and thus became the father of a great posterity (cf. *Gn* 15:6; *Redemptoris Mater*, n. 14). At the start of the New Covenant, Mary also exerts a decisive influence with her faith on the fulfilment of the mystery of the Incarnation, the beginning and the synthesis of Jesus' entire redeeming mission.

4.4 The close relationship between faith and salvation, stressed by Jesus in his public life (cf. *Mt* 5:34; 10:52; etc.), helps us also to understand the fundamental role which Mary's faith exercised and continues to exercise in the salvation of the human race.

3 July 1996

---

[1] "*Angelus nuntiat, virgo audit, credit, et concipit*" (SANCTUS AUGUSTINUS, *Sermo CXCVI* [*In Natali Domini XIII*], 1: *PL* 38, 1019).
[2] "*Creditur Christus, et fide concipitur. Fit prius adventus fidei in cor virginis, et sequitur fecunditas in utero matris*" (SANCTUS AUGUSTINUS, *Sermo CCXCIII* [*In Natali Joannis Baptistae*], 1: *PL* 38, 1327).

26
THE VIRGINITY OF MARY, THE TRUTH OF FAITH

1.1 The Church has constantly held that Mary's virginity is a truth of faith, as she has received and reflected on the witness of the Gospels of Luke, of Matthew and probably also of John.

In the episode of the Annunciation, the Evangelist Luke calls Mary a "virgin", referring both to her intention to persevere in virginity, as well as to the divine plan which reconciles this intention with her miraculous motherhood. The affirmation of the virginal conception, due to the action of the Holy Spirit, excludes every hypothesis of natural parthenogenesis and rejects the attempts to explain Luke's account as the development of a Jewish theme or as the derivation of a pagan mythological legend.

1.2 The structure of the Lucan text (cf. *Lk* 1:26-38; 2:19, 51) resists any reductive interpretation. Its coherence does not validly support any mutilation of the terms or expressions which affirm the virginal conception brought about by the Holy Spirit.

2.1 The Evangelist Matthew, reporting the angel's announcement to Joseph, affirms like Luke that the conception was the work "of the Holy Spirit" (cf. *Mt* 1:20)[1] and excluded marital relations.

2.2 Furthermore, Jesus' virginal conception is communicated to Joseph at a later time: for him it is not a question of being invited to give his assent prior to the conception of Mary's Son, the fruit of the supernatural intervention of the Holy Spirit and the co-operation of the mother alone. He is merely asked to accept freely his role as the Virgin's husband and his paternal mission with regard to the child.

2.3 Matthew presents the virginal origins of Jesus as the fulfilment of Isaiah's prophecy. "'Behold, a virgin shall conceive and bear a son, and his name shall be called Emmanuel' (which means, God with us)" (*Mt* 1:23; cf. *Is* 7:14).[2] In this way Matthew leads us to conclude that the virginal conception was the object of reflection in the first Christian community, which understood its conformity to the divine plan of salvation and its connection with the identity of Jesus, "God with us".

---

[1] "*De Spiritu Sancto est*" (*Mt* 1, 20).

[2] "'*Ecce, virgo in utero habebit et pariet filium, et vocabunt nomen eius Emmanuel,' quod est interpretatum Nobiscum Deus*" (*Mt* 1, 23; cf. *Is* 7, 14).

3.1 Unlike Luke and Matthew, Mark's Gospel does not mention Jesus' conception and birth; nonetheless it is worth noting that Mark never mentions Joseph, Mary's husband. Jesus is called "the son of Mary" by the people of Nazareth or in another context, "the Son of God" several times (3:11; 5:7; cf. 1:11; 9:7; 14:61-62; 15:39).

3.2 These facts are in harmony with belief in the mystery of his virginal conception.

This truth, according to a recent exegetical discovery, would be explicitly contained in verse 13 of the Prologue of John's Gospel, which some ancient authoritative authors (for example, Irenaeus and Tertullian) present, not in the usual plural form, but in the singular: "He, who was born, not of blood nor of the will of the flesh nor of the will of man, but of God".[1] This version in the singular would make the Johannine Prologue one of the major attestations of Jesus' virginal conception, placed in the context of the mystery of the Incarnation.

3.2 Paul's paradoxical affirmation: "But when the time had fully come, God sent forth his Son, born of woman... so that we might receive adoption as sons" (*Gal* 4:4-5),[2] paves the way to the question about this Son's personhood, and thus about his virginal birth.

3.3 The uniform Gospel witness testifies how faith in the virginal conception of Jesus was firmly rooted in various milieu of the early Church. This deprives of any foundation several recent interpretations which understand the virginal conception not in a physical or biological sense, but only as symbolic or metaphorical: it would designate Jesus as God's gift to humanity. The same can be said for the opinion advanced by others, that the account of the virginal conception would instead be a *theologoumenon*, that is, a way of expressing a theological doctrine, that of Jesus' divine sonship, or would be a mythological portrayal of him.

3.4 As we have seen, the Gospels contain the explicit affirmation of a virginal conception of the biological order, brought about by the Holy Spirit. The Church made this truth her own, beginning with the very first formulations of the faith (cf. *Catechism of the Catholic Church*, n. 496).

4.1 The faith expressed in the Gospels is confirmed without interruption in later tradition.

---

[1] "*Qui non ex sanguinibus neque ex voluntate carnis neque ex voluntate viri, sed ex Deo nati sunt*" (*Io* 1, 13).

[2] "*At ubi venit plenitudo temporis, misit Deus Filium suum, factum ex muliere... ut adoptionem filiorum reciperemus*" (*Gal* 4, 4-5).

The formulas of faith of the first Christian writers presuppose the assertion of the virginal birth: Aristides, Justin, Irenaeus, and Tertullian are in agreement with Ignatius of Antioch, who proclaims Jesus "truly born of a virgin" (*Smyrn.* 1, 2).[1] These authors mean a real, historical virginal conception of Jesus and are far from affirming a virginity that is only moral or a vague gift of grace manifested in the child's birth.

4.2 The solemn definitions of faith by the Ecumenical Councils and the papal Magisterium, which follow the first brief formulas of faith, are in perfect harmony with this truth. The Council of Chalcedon (451),[2] in its profession of faith, carefully phrased and with its infallibly defined content, affirms that Christ was "begotten... as to his humanity in these last days, for us and for our salvation, by the Virgin Mary, the Mother of God" (*DS* 301).[3] In the same way the Third Council of Constantinople (681)[4] proclaimed that Jesus Christ was "begotten... as to his humanity, by the Holy Spirit and the Virgin Mary, she who is properly and in all truth the Mother of God" (*DS* 555).[5] Other Ecumenical Councils (Constantinople II, Lateran IV and Lyons II) declared Mary "ever-virgin", stressing her perpetual virginity (*DS* 423, 801, 852). These affirmations were taken up by the Second Vatican Council, which highlighted the fact that Mary "through her faith and obedience... gave birth on earth to the very Son of the Father, not through the knowledge of man but by the overshadowing of the Holy Spirit" (*Lumen gentium*, n. 63).[6]

4.3 In addition to the conciliar definitions, there are the definitions of the papal Magisterium concerning the Immaculate Conception of the "Blessed Virgin Mary" (*DS* 2803)[7] and the Assumption of the "Immaculate and Ever-Virgin Mother of God" (*DS* 3903).[8]

---

[1] "*Natum vere ex virgine*" (Sanctus Ignatius Antiochenus, *Epistula ad Smyrnaeos*, 1, 2: *Catechismus Catholicæ Ecclesiæ*, 496; cf. *SC* 10, 154-157).

[2] The Council of Chalcedon was the 4th Ecumenical Council of the Church, held in Chalcedon, now a part of Istanbul in Turkey, between 8 October to 1 November 451 and convoked by Marcian, Emperor of the East Roman or Byzantine Empire (396–457).

[3] "*Genitum... in novissimis autem diebus eundem propter nos et propter nostram salutem ex Maria virgine, Dei genitrice secundum humanitatem*" (*Symbolum Chalcedonense*); cf. *DS* 301 for the original Greek text.

[4] The Third Council of Constantinople was the 6th General Ecumenical Council of the Church, beginning on 7 November 680 and ending in 681. Convened by Byzantine Emperor Constantine IV (c. 652–685) during the reign of Pope Agatho († 681), the council condemned the heresy of Monothelitism.

[5] "*Ante sæcula quidem ex Patre genitum secundum deitatem, in ultimis diebus autem eundem propter nos et propter nostram salutem de Spiritu Sancto et Maria Virgine proprie et veraciter Dei genitrice secundum humanitatem*" (cf. *DS* 555 for the original Greek text).

[6] "*Credens enim et obœdiens, ipsum Filium Patris in terris genuit, et quidem viri nescia, Spiritu Sancto obumbrata*" (Concilium Vaticanum II, Const. dogm. de Ecclesia, *Lumen gentium*, 63: *AAS* 57 (1965), p. 64).

[7] "*Beatissimam Virginem Mariam*" (*DS* 2803).

[8] "*Immaculatam Deiparam semper Virginem Mariam*" (*DS* 3903).

5.1 Although the definitions of the Magisterium, except for those of the Lateran Council of 649, desired by Pope Martin I,[1] do not explain the meaning of the term “virgin”, it is clear that this term is used in its customary sense: the voluntary abstention from sexual acts and the preservation of bodily integrity. However, physical integrity is considered essential to the truth of faith of Jesus’ virginal conception (cf. *Catechism of the Catholic Church*, n. 496).

5.2 The description of Mary as “Holy Ever-Virgin, Immaculate” draws attention to the connection between holiness and virginity. Mary wanted a virginal life, because she was motivated by the desire to give her whole heart to God.

5.3 The expression used in the definition of the Assumption, “the Immaculate, Ever-Virgin Mother of God”, also implies the connection between Mary’s virginity and her motherhood: two prerogatives miraculously combined in the conception of Jesus, true God and true man. Thus Mary’s virginity is intimately linked to her divine motherhood and perfect holiness.

10 July 1996

[1] Pope Saint Martin I († 655) was elected 74th Bishop of Rome in July 649 AD. Also known as Martin the Confessor, he served as an ambassador to Constantinople for Pope Theodore I before succeeding him as Bishop of Rome. He was the only pope during the Eastern Roman domination of the papacy whose election did not receive an imperial mandate from Constantinople. Saint Martin strongly opposed Monothelitism, which led to his arrest by Emperor Constans II. He was taken to Constantinople and ultimately banished to Cherson. Saint Martin is recognized as a martyr and is considered a saint by both the Catholic Church and the Eastern Orthodox Church. He is considered a saint by both the Catholic Church and the Eastern Orthodox Church, and he is the last pope recognized as a martyr.

27
THE PURPOSE OF VIRGINITY

1.1 Mary asks a question of the angel who tells her of Jesus' conception and birth: "How can this be since I do not know man" (*Lk* 1:34).[1] Such a query seems surprising, to say the least, if we call to mind the biblical accounts that relate the announcement of an extraordinary birth to a childless woman. Those cases concerned married women who were naturally sterile, to whom God gave the gift of a child through their normal conjugal life (*1 Sm* 1:19-20), in response to their anguished prayers (cf. *Gn* 15:2; 30:22-23; *1 Sm* 1:10; *Lk* 1:13).

1.2 Mary receives the angel's message in a different situation. She is not a married woman with problems of sterility; by a voluntary choice she intends to remain a virgin. Therefore her intention of virginity, the fruit of her love for the Lord, appears to be an obstacle to the motherhood announced to her.

1.3 At first sight, Mary's words would seem merely to express only her present state of virginity: Mary would affirm that she does not "know" man, that is, that she is a virgin. Nevertheless, the context in which the question is asked: "How can this be?", and the affirmation that follows: "since I do not know man", emphasise both Mary's present virginity and her intention to remain a virgin. The expression she uses, with the verb in the present tense, reveals the permanence and continuity of her state.

2.1 Mentioning this difficulty, Mary does not at all oppose the divine plan, but shows her intention to conform totally to it. Moreover, the girl from Nazareth always lived in full harmony with the divine will and had chosen a virginal life with the intention of pleasing the Lord. In fact, her intention of virginity disposed her to accept God's will "with all her human and feminine 'I', and this response of faith included both perfect co-operation with the 'grace of God that precedes and assists' and perfect openness to the action of the Holy Spirit" (*Redemptoris Mater*, n. 13).[2]

2.2 To some, Mary's words and intentions appear improbable, since in the Jewish world virginity was considered neither a value nor an ideal to be pursued. The same Old Testament writings confirm this in several well-known episodes and expressions. In the book of Judges, for example, Jephthah's daughter who, having to face death while still young and unmarried, bewails her virginity, that is, she laments that she has been unable to marry (*Jgs* 11:38).

[1] "*Quomodo fiet istud, quoniam virum non cognosco?*" (*Lc* 1, 34).

[2] "*Respondit igitur tota sua persona humana, teminea; qua fidei responsione continebantur perfecta cooperatio cum « gratia, quae praevenit et succurrit », et perfecta inclinatio ad actionem Spiritus Sancti*" (SANCTUS IOANNES PAULUS II, Litt. enc. *Redemptoris Mater* (25 martii 1987), 13: *AAS* 79 [1987]).

Marriage, moreover, by virtue of the divine command, "Be fruitful and multiply" (*Gn* 1:28),[1] is considered woman's natural vocation which involves the joys and sufferings that go with motherhood.

3.1 In order better to understand the context in which Mary's decision came to maturity it is necessary to remember that in the period immediately preceding the beginning of the Christian era, a certain positive attitude to virginity began to appear in some Jewish circles. For example, the Essenes, of whom many important historical testimonies have been found at Qumran, lived in celibacy or restricted the use of marriage because of community life and the search for greater intimacy with God.

3.2 Furthermore, in Egypt there was a community of women who, associated with the Essene spirituality, observed continence. These women, the Therapeutae, belonging to a sect described by Philo of Alexandria (*De vita contemplativa*, 21-90), were dedicated to contemplation and sought wisdom.

3.3 It does not seem that Mary ever knew about these Jewish religious groups which practised the ideal of celibacy and virginity. But the fact that John the Baptist probably lived a celibate life and that in the community of his disciples it was held in high esteem would support the supposition that Mary's choice of virginity belonged to this new cultural and religious context.

4.1 However, the extraordinary case of the Virgin of Nazareth must not lead us into the error of tying her inner dispositions completely to the mentality of her surroundings, thereby eliminating the uniqueness of the mystery that came to pass in her. In particular, we must not forget that, from the very beginning of her life, Mary received a wondrous grace, recognised by the angel at the moment of the Annunciation. "Full of grace" (*Lk* 1:28),[2] Mary was enriched with a perfection of holiness that, according to the Church's interpretation, goes back to the very first moment of her existence: the unique privilege of the Immaculate Conception influenced the whole development of the young woman of Nazareth's spiritual life.

4.2 Thus it should be maintained that Mary was guided to the ideal of virginity by an exceptional inspiration of that same Holy Spirit who, in the course of the Church's history, will spur many women to the way of virginal consecration.

4.3 The singular presence of grace in Mary's life leads to the conclusion that the young girl was committed to virginity. Filled with the Lord's exceptional gifts from the beginning of her life, she was oriented to a total gift of self—body and soul—to God, in the offering of herself as a virgin.

---

[1] "*Crescite et multiplicamini*" (*Gen* 1, 28).
[2] "*Gratia plena*" (*Lc* 1, 28).

4.4 In addition, her aspiration to the virginal life was in harmony with that "poverty" before God which the Old Testament holds in high esteem. Fully committing herself to this path, Mary also gives up motherhood, woman's personal treasure, so deeply appreciated in Israel. Thus she "stands out among the poor and humble of the Lord, who confidently hope for and receive salvation from him" (*Lumen gentium*, n. 55).[1] However, presenting herself to God as poor and aiming only at spiritual fruitfulness, the fruit of divine love, at the moment of the Annunciation, Mary discovers that the Lord has transformed her poverty into riches: she will be the Virgin Mother of the Son of the Most High. Later she will also discover that her motherhood is destined to extend to all men, whom the Son came to save (cf. *Catechism of the Catholic Church*, n. 501).

24 July 1996

[1] "*Ipsa præcellit inter humiles ac pauperes Domini, qui salutem cum fiducia ab Eo sperant et accipiunt*" (Concilium Vaticanum II, Const. dogm. de Ecclesia, *Lumen gentium*, 55: *AAS* 57 (1965), pp. 59-60).

28
THE VALUE OF THE VIRGINAL CONCEPTION OF JESUS

1.1 In his saving plan, God wanted his only Son to be born of a virgin. This divine decision calls for a profound relationship between Mary's virginity and the Incarnation of the Word.

"The eyes of faith can discover in the context of the whole of Revelation the mysterious reasons why God in his saving plan wanted his Son to be born of a virgin. These reasons touch both on the person of Christ and his redemptive mission, and on the welcome Mary gave that mission on behalf of all men" (*Catechism of the Catholic Church*, n. 502).[1]

1.2 The virginal conception, by excluding human fatherhood, affirms that Jesus' only father is the heavenly Father and that the Son's being born in time reflects his eternal birth: the Father, who begot the Son in eternity, also begets him in time as a man.

2.1 The account of the Annunciation emphasises his state as "Son of God", the result of God's intervention in his conception.

"The Holy Spirit will come upon you, and the power of the Most High will overshadow you; therefore the child to be born will be called holy, the Son of God" (*Lk* 1:35).[2]

2.2 He who is born of Mary is already Son of God by virtue of his eternal birth; his virginal birth, brought about by the Most High, shows that he is Son of God even in his humanity.

2.3 The revelation of his eternal birth in his virginal birth is also suggested by the passages in the Prologue of John's Gospel which relate the manifestation of the invisible God to the work of the "the only-begotten Son, who is in the bosom of the Father" (1:18),[3] by his coming in the flesh:

"And the Word became flesh and dwelt among us, full of grace and truth; we have beheld his glory, glory as of the only-begotten Son from the Father" (*Jn* 1:14).[4]

---

[1] "*Intuitus fidei, in connexione cum Revelationis complexu, arcanas potest detegere rationes, propter quas Deus, in Suo consilio salvifico, voluit Filium Suum e Virgine nasci. Hæ rationes tam ad Personam et redemptricem Christi missionem quam ad huius missionis ex parte Mariæ pro omnibus hominibus referuntur acceptationem*" (*Catechismus Catholicæ Ecclesiæ, editio typica 1997*, n. 502).

[2] "*Spiritus Sanctus superveniet in te, et virtus Altissimi obumbrabit tibi: ideoque et quod nascetur sanctum, vocabitur Filius Dei*" (*Lc* 1, 35).

[3] "*Unigenitus Deus, qui est in sinum Patris*" (*Io* 1, 18),

[4] "*Et Verbum caro factum est et habitavit in nobis; et vidimus gloriam eius, gloriam quasi Unigeniti a Patre, plenum gratiæ et veritatis*" (*Io* 1, 14).

2.4 In recounting the birth of Jesus, Luke and Matthew also speak of the role of the Holy Spirit. The latter is not the father of the Child. Jesus is the Son of the Eternal Father alone (cf. *Lk* 1:32-35), who through the Spirit is at work in the world and begets the Word in his human nature. Indeed, at the Annunciation the angel calls the Spirit "the power of the Most High" (*Lk* 1:35), in harmony with the Old Testament, which presents him as the divine energy at work in human life, making it capable of marvellous deeds. Manifesting itself to the supreme degree in the mystery of the Incarnation, this power, which in the Trinitarian life of God is Love, has the task of giving humanity the Incarnate Word.

3.1 The Holy Spirit, in particular, is the person who communicates divine riches to men and makes them sharers in God's life. He, who in the mystery of the Trinity is the unity of the Father and the Son, unites humanity with God by bringing about the virginal birth of Jesus.

3.2 The mystery of the Incarnation also highlights the incomparable greatness of Mary's virginal motherhood: the conception of Jesus is the fruit of her generous co-operation with the action of the Spirit of Love, the source of all fruitfulness.

3.3 In the divine plan of salvation, the virginal conception is therefore an announcement of the new creation: by the work of the Holy Spirit, he who will be the new Adam is begotten in Mary. As the *Catechism of the Catholic Church* states: "Jesus is conceived by the Holy Spirit in the Virgin Mary's womb because he is the New Adam who inaugurates the new creation" (n. 504).[1]

3.4 The role of Mary's virginal motherhood shines forth in the mystery of this new creation. Calling Christ "the firstborn of the Virgin" (*Ad Haer.*, 3, 16, 4), Saint Irenaeus recalls that after Jesus many others are born of the Virgin, in the sense that they receive the new life of Christ.

"Jesus is Mary's only Son, but her spiritual motherhood extends to all men whom indeed he came to save: the Son whom she brought forth is he whom God placed as the first-born among many brethren, that is, the faithful in whose generation and formation she co-operates with a mother's love" (*Catechism of the Catholic Church*, n. 501).[2]

---

[1] "*Iesus de Spiritu Sancto in sinu Virginis Mariæ conceptus est, quia est* novus Adam, *qui creationem novam inaugurat*" (*Catechismus Catholicæ Ecclesiæ, editio typica 1997*, n. 504).

[2] "*Iesus est unicus Mariæ Filius. Sed spiritualis Mariæ maternitas ad omnes extenditur homines, ad quos Ille venit salvandos: « Filium autem peperit, quem Deus posuit primogenitum in multis fratribus* (*Rom* 8, 29), *fidelibus nempe, ad quos gignendos et educandos materno amore cooperatur* »" (*Ibid.*, n. 501).

4.1 The communication of the new life is the transmission of divine sonship. Here we can recall the perspective opened up by John in the Prologue of his Gospel: he who was begotten by God gives all believers the power to become children of God (cf. *Jn* 1:12-13). The virginal birth allows the extension of the divine fatherhood: men are made the adoptive children of God in him who is Son of the Virgin and of the Father.

4.2 Contemplating the mystery of the virgin birth thus enables us to realise that God chose a Virgin Mother for his Son to offer his fatherly love more generously to humanity.

31 July 1996

29
MARY, MODEL OF VIRGINITY

1.1 The intention to remain a virgin, apparent in Mary's words at the moment of the Annunciation, has traditionally been considered the beginning and the inspiration of Christian virginity in the Church.

1.2 Saint Augustine does not see in this resolution the fulfilment of a divine precept, but a vow freely taken. In this way it was possible to present Mary as an example to "holy virgins" throughout the Church's history. Mary "dedicated her virginity to God when she did not yet know whom she would conceive, so that the imitation of heavenly life in the earthly, mortal body would come about through a vow, not a precept, through a choice of love and not through the need to serve" (*De Sancta Virg.*, IV, *PL* 40:398).[1]

1.3 The Angel does not ask Mary to remain a virgin; it is Mary who freely reveals her intention of virginity. The choice of love that leads her to consecrate herself totally to the Lord by a life of virginity is found in this commitment.

1.4 In stressing the spontaneity of Mary's decision, we must not forget that God's initiative is at the root of every vocation. By choosing the life of virginity, the young girl of Nazareth was responding to an interior call, that is, to an inspiration of the Holy Spirit that enlightened her about the meaning and value of the virginal gift of herself. No one can accept this gift without feeling called or without receiving from the Holy Spirit the necessary light and strength.

2.1 Although Saint Augustine uses the word "vow" to show those he calls "holy virgins" the first example of their state of life, the Gospel does not testify that Mary had expressly made a vow, which is the form of consecration and offering of one's life to God which has been in use since the early centuries of the Church. From the Gospel we learn that Mary made a personal decision to remain a virgin, offering her heart to the Lord. She wants to be his faithful bride, fulfilling her vocation as the "daughter of Sion". By her decision however she becomes the archetype of all those in the Church who have chosen to serve the Lord with an undivided heart in virginity.

2.2 Neither the Gospels nor any other New Testament writings tell us when Mary made the decision to remain a virgin. However it is clearly apparent from her question to the angel at the time of the Annunciation that she had come to a very firm decision. Mary does not hesitate to express her desire to preserve

---

[1] "*Virginitatem Dei dicavit, cum adhuc quid esset conceptura nesciret, ut in terreno mortalique corpore cælestis vitæ imitatio voto fieret, non præcepto; amore eligendi, non necessitate serviendi*" (Sanctus Augustinus, *De sancta virginitate*, cap. IV: *PL* 40, 398).

her virginity even in view of the proposed motherhood, showing that her intention had matured over a long period.

2.3 Indeed, Mary's choice of virginity was not made in the unforeseeable prospect of becoming the Mother of God, but developed in her consciousness before the Annunciation. We can suppose that this inclination was always present in her heart: the grace which prepared her for virginal motherhood certainly influenced the whole growth of her personality, while the Holy Spirit did not fail to inspire in her, from her earliest years, the desire for total union with God.

3.1 The marvels God still works today in the hearts and lives of so many young people were first realised in Mary's soul. Even in our world, so distracted by the attractions of a frequently superficial and consumerist culture, many adolescents accept the invitation that comes from Mary's example and consecrate their youth to the Lord and to the service of their brothers and sisters.

3.2 This decision is the choice of greater values, rather than the renunciation of human values. In this regard, in his Apostolic Exhortation *Marialis cultus* my venerable predecessor Paul VI emphasises how anyone who looks at the witness of the Gospel with an open mind "will appreciate that Mary's choice of the state of virginity... was not a rejection of any of the values of the married state but a courageous choice which she made in order to consecrate herself totally to the love of God" (n. 37).[1]

3.3 In short, the choice of the virginal state is motivated by full adherence to Christ.

This is particularly obvious in Mary. Although before the Annunciation she is not conscious of it, the Holy Spirit inspires her virginal consecration in view of Christ: she remains a virgin to welcome the Messiah and Saviour with her whole being. The virginity begun in Mary thus reveals its own Christocentric dimension, essential also for virginity lived in the Church, which finds its sublime model in the Mother of Christ. If her personal virginity, linked to the divine motherhood, remains an exceptional fact, it gives light and meaning to every gift of virginity.

4.1 How many young women in the Church's history, as they contemplate the nobility and beauty of the virginal heart of the Lord's Mother, have felt encouraged to respond generously to God's call by embracing the ideal

---

[1] "*Recogitabit deinde Mariam, cum virginitatis statum sebi elegisset... nequaquam matrimonii bona ac dignitatem respuisse, verum libere et animose egisse, ut se tota Dei amori devoveret*" (SANCTUS PAULUS VI, Adh. ap. *Marialis cultus* (2 februarii 1974), 37: *AAS* 66 (1974), p. 148).

of virginity! "Precisely such virginity", as I recalled in the Encyclical *Redemptoris Mater*, "after the example of the Virgin of Nazareth, is the source of a special spiritual fruitfulness: it is the source of motherhood in the Holy Spirit" (n. 43).[1]

4.2 Mary's virginal life inspires in the entire Christian people esteem for the gift of virginity and the desire that it should increase in the Church as a sign of God's primacy over all reality and as a prophetic anticipation of the life to come. Together let us thank the Lord for those who still today generously consecrate their lives in virginity to the service of the kingdom of God.

4.3 At the same time, while in various regions evangelised long ago hedonism and consumerism seem to dissuade many young people from embracing the consecrated life, we must incessantly ask God through Mary's intercession for a new flowering of religious vocations. Thus the face of Christ's Mother, reflected in the many virgins who strive to follow the divine Master, will continue to be the sign of God's mercy and tenderness for humanity.

7 August 1996

[1] "*Hæc ipsa virginitas, exemplo Virginis Nazarethanæ, fons est peculiaris fecunditatis spiritualis: scilicet est tons maternitatis in* Spiritu Sancto" (SANCTUS IOANNES PAULUS II, Litt. enc. *Redemptoris Mater* (25 martii 1987), 43: *AAS* 79 (1987), p. 420).

30
MARY AND JOSEPH LIVED THE GIFT OF VIRGINITY

1.1 In presenting Mary as a "virgin", the Gospel of Luke adds that she was "betrothed to a man whose name was Joseph, of the house of David" (1:27).[1] These two pieces of information at first sight seem contradictory.

1.2 It should be noted that the Greek word used in this passage does not indicate the situation of a woman who has contracted marriage and therefore lives in the marital state, but that of betrothal. Unlike what occurs in modern cultures, however, the ancient Jewish custom of betrothal provided for a contract and normally had definitive value: it actually introduced the betrothed to the marital state, even if the marriage was brought to full completion only when the young man took the girl to his home.

1.3 At the time of the Annunciation, Mary thus had the status of one betrothed. We can wonder why she would accept betrothal, since she had the intention of remaining a virgin forever. Luke is aware of this difficulty, but merely notes the situation without offering any explanation. The fact that the Evangelist, while stressing Mary's intention of virginity, also presents her as Joseph's spouse, is a sign of the historical reliability of the two pieces of information.

2.1 It may be presumed that at the time of their betrothal there was an understanding between Joseph and Mary about the plan to live as a virgin. Moreover, the Holy Spirit, who had inspired Mary to choose virginity in view of the mystery of the Incarnation and who wanted the latter to come about in a family setting suited to the Child's growth, was quite able to instil in Joseph the ideal of virginity as well.

2.2 The angel of the Lord appeared in a dream and said to him: "Joseph, son of David, do not fear to take Mary your wife, for that which is conceived in her is of the Holy Spirit" (*Mt* 1:20).[2] Thus he received confirmation that he was called to live his marriage in a completely special way. Through virginal communion with the woman chosen to give birth to Jesus, God calls him to co-operate in carrying out his plan of salvation.

2.3 The type of marriage to which the Holy Spirit led Mary and Joseph can only be understood in the context of the saving plan and of a lofty spirituality. The concrete realisation of the mystery of the Incarnation called for a virgin birth which would highlight the divine sonship and, at the same time, for a family that could provide for the normal development of the Child's personality.

---

[1] "*Desponsatam viro, cui nomen erat Ioseph de domo David*" (*Lc* 1, 27).
[2] "*Ioseph fili David, noli timere accipere Mariam coniugem tuam. Quod enim in ea natum est, de Spiritu Sancto est*" (*Mt* 1, 20).

2.4 Precisely in view of their contribution to the mystery of the Incarnation of the Word, Joseph and Mary received the grace of living both the charism of virginity and the gift of marriage. Mary and Joseph's communion of virginal love, although a special case linked with the concrete realisation of the mystery of the Incarnation, was nevertheless a true marriage (cf. Apostolic Exhortation *Redemptoris custos*, n. 7).

2.5 The difficulty of accepting the sublime mystery of their spousal communion has led some, since the second century, to think of Joseph as advanced in age and to consider him Mary's guardian more than her husband. It is instead a case of supposing that he was not an elderly man at the time, but that his interior perfection, the fruit of grace, led him to live his spousal relationship with Mary with virginal affection.

3.1 Joseph's co-operation in the mystery of the Incarnation also includes exercising the role of Jesus' father. The angel acknowledged this function of his when he appeared in a dream and invited him to name the Child: "She will bear a son, and you shall call his name Jesus, for he will save his people from their sins" (*Mt* 1:21).[1]

3.2 While excluding physical generation, Joseph's fatherhood was something real, not apparent. Distinguishing between father and the one who begets, an ancient monograph on Mary's virginity—the *De Margarita* (fourth century)—states that "the commitments assumed by the Virgin and by Joseph as husband and wife made it possible for him to be called by this name (father); a father, however, who did not beget". Joseph thus carried out the role of Jesus' father, exercising an authority to which the Redeemer was freely "obedient" (*Lk* 2:51),[2] contributing to his upbringing and teaching him the carpenter's trade.

3.3 Christians have always acknowledged Joseph as the one who lived in intimate communion with Mary and Jesus, concluding that also in death he enjoyed their affectionate, consoling presence. From this constant Christian tradition, in many places a special devotion has grown to the Holy Family and, in it, to Saint Joseph, Guardian of the Redeemer. As everyone knows, Pope Leo XIII[3] entrusted the entire Church to his protection.

21 August 1996

[1] "*Pariet autem filium, et vocabis nomen eius Iesum: ipse enim salvum faciet populum suum a peccatis eorum*" (*Mt* 1, 21).

[2] "*Subditus*" (*Lc* 2, 51).

[3] Pope Leo XIII (1810–1903), born Count Vincenzo Gioacchino Raffaele Luigi Pecci, was elected the 257th Bishop of Rome on 20 February 1878. He reigned until the age of 93.

31
THE CHURCH PRESENTS MARY AS EVER-VIRGIN

1.1 The Church has always professed her belief in the perpetual virginity of Mary. The most ancient texts, when referring to the conception of Jesus, call Mary simply "virgin", inferring that they considered this quality a permanent fact with regard to her whole life.

1.2 The early Christians expressed this conviction of faith in the Greek term *aeiparthenos*—"ever virgin"—created to describe Mary's person in a unique and effective manner, and to express in a single word the Church's belief in her perpetual virginity. We find it used in the second symbol of faith composed by Saint Epiphanius in the year 374, in relation to the Incarnation: the Son of God "was incarnate, that is, he was generated in a perfect way by Mary, the ever blessed virgin, through the Holy Spirit" (*Ancoratus*, 119, 5; *DS* 44).[1]

1.3 The expression "ever virgin" was taken up by the Second Council of Constantinople (553), which affirms: the Word of God, "incarnate of the holy and glorious Mother of God and *ever virgin* Mary, was born of her" (*DS* 422).[2] This doctrine is confirmed by two other Ecumenical Councils, the Fourth Lateran Council (1215) (*DS* 801) and the Second Council of Lyons (1274) (*DS* 852), and by the text of the definition of the dogma of the Assumption (1950) (*DS* 3903) in which Mary's perpetual virginity is adopted as one of the reasons why she was taken up in body and soul to heavenly glory.

2.1 In a brief formula, the Church traditionally presents Mary as "virgin *before*, *during* and *after* giving birth",[3] affirming, by indicating these three moments, that she never ceased to be a virgin.

2.2 Of the three, the affirmation of her virginity "before giving birth" is, undoubtedly, the most important, because it refers to Jesus' conception and directly touches the very mystery of the Incarnation. From the beginning it has been constantly present in the Church's belief.

2.3 Her virginity "during and after giving birth", although implicit in the title virgin already attributed to Mary from the Church's earliest days, became the object of deep doctrinal study since some began explicitly to cast doubts on it.

---

[1] "*Et incarnatus est, hoc est, ex Maria semper virgine per Spiritum sanctum perfecte genitus*" (SANCTUS EPIPHANIUS, *Ancoratus*, CXX, 5: *PG* 43, 234; cf. *DS* 44 for the original Greek text).

[2] "*Et incarnatus de sancta gloriosa Dei Genitrice et* semper Virgine *Maria, natus est ex ipsa*" (*DS* 422).

[3] "*Ante partum, in partu, et post partum*" (cf. BENEDICTUS HENRICUS MERKELBACH, OP., *Mariologia* (1939), p. 217, n. 115).

Pope Saint Hormisdas[1] explains that "the Son of God became Son of man, born in time in the manner of a man, opening his mother's womb to birth [cf. *Lk* 2:23] and, through God's power, not dissolving his mother's virginity" (*DS* 368).[2] This doctrine was confirmed by the Second Vatican Council, which states that the firstborn Son of Mary "did not diminish his Mother's virginal integrity but sanctified it" (*Lumen gentium*, n. 57).[3] As regards her virginity after the birth, it must first of all be pointed out that there are no reasons for thinking that the will to remain a virgin, which Mary expressed at the moment of the Annunciation (cf. *Lk* 1:34) was then changed. Moreover, the immediate meaning of the words: "Woman, behold, your son!", "Behold, your mother" (*Jn* 19:26),[4] which Jesus addressed to Mary and to his favourite disciple from the Cross, imply that Mary had no other children.

2.4 Those who deny her virginity after the birth thought they had found a convincing argument in the term "firstborn", attributed to Jesus in the Gospel (*Lk* 2:7),[5] almost as though this word implied that Mary had borne other children after Jesus. But the word "firstborn" literally means "a child not preceded by another" and, in itself, makes no reference to the existence of other children. Moreover, the Evangelist stresses this characteristic of the Child, since certain obligations proper to Jewish law were linked to the birth of the firstborn son, independently of whether the mother might have given birth to other children. Thus every only son was subject to these prescriptions because he was "begotten first" (cf. *Lk* 2:23).

3.1 According to some, Mary's virginity after the birth is denied by the Gospel texts which record the existence of four "brothers of Jesus": James, Joseph, Simon and Judas (*Mt* 13:55-56; *Mk* 6:3), and of several sisters.

3.2 It should be recalled that no specific term exists in Hebrew and Aramaic to express the word "cousin", and that the terms "brother" and "sister", therefore had a far broader meaning which included several degrees of relationship. In fact, the phrase "brothers of Jesus" indicates "the children" of a Mary who was a disciple of Christ (cf. *Mt* 27:56) and who is significantly described as "the other Mary" (*Mt* 28:1).[6] "They are close relations of Jesus, according to an Old Testament expression" (*Catechism of the Catholic Church*, n. 500).[7]

---

[1] Pope Saint Hormisdas († 523) was a widower and elected the 52nd Bishop of Rome on 20 July 514. His son was the future Pope Saint Silverius († 537).

[2] "*Ut qui ante tempora erat Filius Dei, fieret Filius hominis et nasceretur ex tempore hominis more, matris vulvam natus aperiens et virginitatem matris deitatis virtute non solvens*" (*DS* 368).

[3] "*Virginalem eius integritatem non minuit sed sacravit*" (CONCILIUM VATICANUM II, Const. dogm. de Ecclesia, *Lumen gentium*, 57: *AAS* 57 (1965), p. 61).

[4] "*Mulier, ecce filius tuus… Ecce mater tua*" (*Io* 19, 26-27).

[5] "*Primogenitum*" (*Lc* 2, 7).

[6] "*Altera Maria*" (*Mt* 28, 1); "*Maria Cleophæ*" [Mary of Cleophas] (*Io* 19, 25).

[7] "*Agitur de proximis propinquis secundum quamdam notam Veteris Testamenti expressionem* (cf. *Gn* 13, 8; 14, 16; 29, 15; etc.)" (*Catechismus Catholicæ Ecclesiæ, editio typica 1997*, n. 500); cf. catechesis n. 1, p. 21, note 2.

3.3 Mary Most Holy is thus the "ever virgin". Her prerogative is the consequence of her divine motherhood which totally consecrated her to Christ's mission of redemption.

28 August 1996

32
MARY OFFERS A SUBLIME MODEL OF SERVICE

1.1 Mary's words at the Annunciation "Behold, I am the handmaid of the Lord; let it be to me according to your word" (*Lk* 1:38),[1] indicate an attitude characteristic of Jewish piety. At the beginning of the Old Covenant, Moses, in response to the Lord's call, proclaims himself his servant (cf. *Ex* 4:10; 14:31). With the coming of the New Covenant, Mary also responds to God with an act of free submission and conscious abandonment to his will, showing her complete availability to be the "handmaid of the Lord".

1.2 In the Old Testament, the qualification "servant" of God links all those who are called to exercise a mission for the sake of the Chosen People: Abraham (*Gn* 26:24), Isaac (*Gn* 24:14) Jacob (*Ex* 32:13; *Ez* 37:25), Joshua (*Jos* 24:29), David (*2 Sam* 7, 8, etc.). Prophets and priests, who have been entrusted with the task of forming the people in the faithful service of the Lord, are also servants. The book of the prophet Isaiah exalts, in the docility of the "suffering Servant", a model of fidelity to God in the hope of redemption for the sins of the many (cf. *Is* 42:53). Some women also offer examples of fidelity, such as Queen Esther who, before interceding for the salvation of the Jews, addresses a prayer to God, calling herself many times "your servant" (*Est* 4:17).

2 Mary, "full of grace", by proclaiming herself "handmaid of the Lord" intends to commit herself to fulfil personally and in a perfect manner the service God expects of all his people. The words: "Behold, I am the handmaid of the Lord", foretell the One who will say of himself: "For the Son of man also came not to be served but to serve, and to give his life as a ransom for many" (*Mk* 10:45: cf. *Mt* 20:28).[2] Thus the Holy Spirit brings about a harmony of intimate dispositions between the Mother and the Son, which will allow Mary to assume fully her maternal role to Jesus, as she accompanies him in his mission as Servant. In Jesus' life the will to serve is constant and surprising: as Son of God, he could rightly have demanded to be served. Attributing to himself the title "Son of Man", whom, according to the book of Daniel, "all peoples, nations, and languages should serve" (*Dn* 7:14),[3] he could have claimed mastery over others. Instead, combating the mentality of the time which was expressed in the disciples' ambition for the first places (cf. *Mk* 9:34) and in Peter's protest during the washing of the feet (cf. *Jn* 13:6), Jesus does not want to be served, but desires to serve to the point of totally giving his life in the work of redemption.

---

[1] "*Ecce ancilla Domini; fiat mihi secundum verbum tuum*" (*Lc* 1, 38).

[2] "*Nam et Filius hominis non venit, ut ministraretur ei, sed ut ministraret et daret animam suam redemptionem pro multis*" (*Mk* 10, 45: cf. *Mt* 20, 28).

[3] "*Omnes populi, tribus et linguæ ipsi servierunt*" (*Dan* 7, 14).

3.1 Furthermore, Mary, although aware of the lofty dignity conferred upon her at the angel's announcement, spontaneously declares herself "the handmaid of the Lord". In this commitment of service she also includes the intention to serve her neighbour, as the link between the episodes of the Annunciation and the Visitation show: informed by the angel of Elizabeth's pregnancy, Mary sets out "with haste" (*Lk* 1:39) for Judah, with total availability to help her relative prepare for the birth. She thus offers Christians of all times a sublime model of service.

3.2 The words: "Let it be to me according to your word" (*Lk* 1:38), show in her who declared herself handmaid of the Lord, a total obedience to God's will.

3.3 The optative *genoito,* "let it be done", used by Luke, expresses not only acceptance but staunch assumption of the divine plan, making it her own with the involvement of all her personal resources.

4.1 By conforming to the divine will, Mary anticipates and makes her own the attitude of Christ who, according to the Letter to the Hebrews, coming into the world, says: "Sacrifice and offerings you did not desire, but a body you prepared for me… Then I said… 'Behold, I come to do your will, O God'" (*Heb* 10:5-7; *Ps* 39 [40]:7-9).[1]

4.2 Mary's docility likewise announces and prefigures that expressed by Jesus in the course of his public life until Calvary. Christ would say: "My food is to do the will of him who sent me, and to accomplish his work" (*Jn* 4:34).[2] On these same lines, Mary makes the Father's will the inspiring principle of her whole life, seeking in it the necessary strength to fulfil the mission entrusted to her.

4.3 If at the moment of the Annunciation, Mary does not yet know of the sacrifice which will mark Christ's mission, Simeon's prophecy will enable her to glimpse her Son's tragic destiny (cf. *Lk* 3:34-35). The Virgin will be associated with him in intimate sharing. With her total obedience to God's will, Mary is ready to live all that divine love may plan for her life, even to the "sword" that will pierce her soul.

4 September 1996

[1] "*Hostiam et oblationem noluisti, corpus autem aptasti mihi… Tunc dixi: Ecce venio… Deus, voluntatem tuam*" (*Hebr* 10, 5-7; *Ps* 39 [40], 7-9).
[2] "*Meus cibus est, ut faciam voluntatem eius, qui misit me, et ut perficiam opus eius*" (*Io* 4, 34).

33
MARY, THE NEW EVE, FREELY OBEYED GOD

1.1 Commenting on the episode of the Annunciation, the Second Vatican Council gives special emphasis to the value of Mary's assent to the divine messenger's words. Unlike what occurs in similar biblical accounts, it is expressly awaited by the angel:

"The Father of mercies willed that the Incarnation should be preceded by assent on the part of the predestined mother, so that just as a woman had a share in bringing about death, so also a woman should contribute to life" (*Lumen gentium*, n. 56).[1]

1.2 *Lumen gentium* recalls the contrast between Eve's behaviour and that of Mary, described by Saint Irenaeus:

"Just as the former—that is, Eve—was seduced by the words of an angel so that she turned away from God by disobeying his word, so the latter—Mary—received the good news from an angel's announcement in such a way as to give birth to God by obeying his word; and as the former was seduced so that she disobeyed God, the latter let herself be convinced to obey God, and so the Virgin Mary became the advocate of the virgin Eve. And as the human race was subjected to death by a virgin, it was liberated by a Virgin; a virgin's disobedience was thus counterbalanced by a Virgin's obedience..." (*Adv. Haer.*, V, 19, 1).[2]

2.1 In stating her total "yes" to the divine plan, Mary is completely free before God. At the same time, she feels personally responsible for humanity, whose future was linked with her reply.

2.2 God puts the destiny of all mankind in a young woman's hands. Mary's "yes" is the premise for fulfilling the plan which God in his love had prepared for the world's salvation.

---

[1] "*Voluit autem misericordiarum Pater, ut acceptatio prædestinatæ matris incarnationem præcederet, ut sic, quemadmodum femina contulit ad mortem, ita etiam femina conferret ad vitam*" (Concilium Vaticanum II, Const. dogm. de Ecclesia, *Lumen gentium*, 56: *AAS* 57 (1965), p. 60).

[2] "*Quemadmodum enim illa per angeli sermonem seducta est, ut effugeret Deum, prævaricata verbum eius; ita et hæc per angelicum sermonem evangelizata est, ut portaret Deum, obediens eius verbo. Et si ea inobedierat Deo; sed hæc suasa est obedire Deo, uti virginis Evae Virgo Maria fieret advocata. Et quemadmodum astrictum est morti genus humanum per Virginem, salvatur per Virginem æqua lance disposita, virginalis inobedientia, per virginalem obedientiam*" (Sanctus Irenæus Lugdunensis, *Adversus hæreses*, lib. V, cap. 19, 1: *PG* 1, 1175-1176).

2.3 The *Catechism of the Catholic Church* briefly and effectively summarises the decisive value for all humanity of Mary's free consent to the divine plan of salvation.

"The Virgin Mary 'cooperated through free faith and obedience in human salvation'. She uttered her yes 'in the name of all human nature'. By her obedience she became the New Eve, mother of the living" (n. 511).[1]

3.1 By her conduct, Mary reminds each of us of our serious responsibility to accept God's plan for our lives. In total obedience to the saving will of God expressed in the angel's words, she becomes a model for those whom the Lord proclaims blessed, because they "hear the word of God and keep it" (*Lk* 11:28). Jesus, in answering the woman in the crowd who proclaimed his mother blessed, discloses the true reason for Mary's blessedness: her adherence to God's will, which led her to accept the divine motherhood.

3.2 In the Encyclical *Redemptoris Mater*, I pointed out that the new spiritual motherhood of which Jesus speaks is primarily concerned with her. Indeed,

"Is not Mary the first of 'those who hear the word of God and do it'? And therefore does not the blessing uttered by Jesus in response to the woman in the crowd refer primarily to her?" (n. 20).[2]

In a certain sense therefore Mary is proclaimed the first disciple of her Son (cf. *ibid.*) and, by her example, invites all believers to respond generously to the Lord's grace.

4.1 The Second Vatican Council explains Mary's total dedication to the person and work of Christ:

"She devoted herself totally, as a handmaid of the Lord, to the person and work of her Son, under and with him, serving the mystery of redemption, by the grace of almighty God" (*Lumen gentium*, n. 56).[3]

4.2 For Mary, dedication to the person and work of Jesus means intimate union with her Son, motherly involvement in nurturing his human growth and co-operation with his work of salvation.

---

[1] "*Maria Virgo « libera fide et obœdientia humanæ saluti » est cooperata. Illa assensum suum, « loco totius humanæ naturæ », pronuntiavit. Illa est facta, sua obœdientia, nova Eva, Mater viventium*" (*Catechismus Catholicæ Ecclesiæ, editio typica 1997*, n. 511).

[2] "*Nonne enim* Maria prima eminet inter eos « qui verbum Dei audiunt et faciunt »? *Nonne igitur illam imprimis respicit ea benedictio, quam enuntiavit Iesus, cum mulieris ignotæ vocibus respondit?*" (Sanctus Ioannes Paulus II, Litt. enc. *Redemptoris Mater* (25 martii 1987), 20: *AAS* 79 (1987), p. 386).

[3] "*Semetipsam ut Domini ancillam personæ et operi Filii sui totaliter devovit, sub Ipso et cum Ipso, omnipotentis Dei gratia*" (Concilium Vaticanum II, Const. dogm. de Ecclesia, *Lumen gentium*, 56: *AAS* 57 (1965), p. 60).

4.3 Mary carries out this last aspect of her dedication to Jesus "under him", that is, in a condition of subordination, which is the fruit of grace. However this is true co-operation, because it is realised "with him" and, beginning with the Annunciation, it involves active participation in the work of redemption. "Rightly, therefore", the Second Vatican Council observes, "the Fathers see Mary not merely as passively engaged by God, but as freely co-operating in the work of man's salvation through faith and obedience. For, as Saint Irenaeus says, she 'being obedient, became the cause of salvation for herself and for the whole human race (*Adv. Haer.* III, 22, 4)'" (*ibid.*).[1]

4.4 Mary, associated with Christ's victory over the sin of our first parents, appears as the true "mother of the living" (*ibid.*). Her motherhood, freely accepted in obedience to the divine plan, becomes a source of life for all humanity.

18 September 1996

[1] "*Merito igitur SS. Patres Mariam non mere passive a Deo adhibitam, sed libera fide et obœdientia humanæ saluti cooperantem censent. Ipsa enim, ut ait S. Irenæus, « obœdiens et sibi et universo generi humano causa facta est salutis »* (S. IRENÆUS, *Adv. Hær.* III, 22, 4: *PG* 7, 959A).

34
THE VISITATION IS A PRELUDE TO THE MISSION OF CHRIST

1.1 In the Visitation episode, Saint Luke shows how the grace of the Incarnation, after filling Mary, brings salvation and joy to Elizabeth's house. The Saviour of men, carried in his Mother's womb, pours out the Holy Spirit, revealing himself from the very start of his coming into the world.

1.2 In describing Mary's departure for Judea, the Evangelist uses the verb *anístemi*,[1] which means "to arise", "to start moving". Considering that this verb is used in the Gospels to indicate Jesus' Resurrection (*Mk* 8:31; 9:9, 31; *Lk* 24:7, 46) or physical actions that imply a spiritual effort (*Lk* 5:27-28; 15:18, 20), we can suppose that Luke wishes to stress with this expression the vigorous zeal which led Mary, under the inspiration of the Holy Spirit, to give the world its Saviour.

2.1 The Gospel text also reports that Mary made the journey "with haste" (*Lk* 1:39).

Even the note "into the hill country" (*Lk* 1:39),[2] in the Lucan context, appears to be much more than a simple topographical indication, since it calls to mind the messenger of good news described in the book of Isaiah: "How beautiful upon the mountains are the feet of him who brings good tidings, who publishes peace, who brings good tidings of good, who publishes salvation, who says to Sion: 'Your God reigns'" (*Is* 52:7).[3]

2.2 Like Saint Paul, who recognises the fulfilment of this prophetic text in the preaching of the Gospel (*Rom* 10:15), Saint Luke also seems to invite us to see Mary as the first "evangelist", who spreads the "good news", initiating the missionary journeys of her divine Son.

2.3 Lastly, the direction of the Blessed Virgin's journey is particularly significant: it will be from Galilee to Judea, like Jesus' missionary journey (cf. 9:51).

2.4 Mary's visit to Elizabeth, in fact, is a prelude to Jesus' mission and, in cooperating from the beginning of her motherhood in the Son's redeeming work, she becomes the model for those in the Church who set out to bring Christ's light and joy to the people of every time and place.

---

[1] *Anístemi* is the transliteration of the Greek word ἀνίστημι.

[2] "*Exsurgens autem Maria in diebus illis abiit in montana cum festinatione in civitatem Iudæ*" (*Lc* 1, 39); "In those days Mary arose and went with haste into the hill country, to a city of Judah" (*Lk* 1:39).

[3] "*Quam pulchri super montes pedes annuntiantis, prædicantis pacem, annuntiantis bonum, prædicantis salutem, dicentis Sion: 'Regnavit Deus tuus!'*" (*Is* 52, 7).

3.1 The meeting with Elizabeth has the character of a joyous saving event that goes beyond the spontaneous feelings of family sentiment. Where the embarrassment of disbelief seems to be expressed in Zechariah's muteness, Mary bursts out with the joy of her quick and ready faith: "She entered the house of Zechariah and greeted Elizabeth" (*Lk* 1:40).[1]

3.2 Saint Luke relates that "when Elizabeth heard the greeting of Mary, the child leaped in her womb" (*Lk* 1:41).[2] Mary's greeting caused Elizabeth's son to leap for joy: Jesus' entrance into Elizabeth's house, at Mary's doing, brought the unborn prophet that gladness which the Old Testament foretells as a sign of the Messiah's presence.

3.3 At Mary's greeting, messianic joy comes over Elizabeth too and "filled with the Holy Spirit... she exclaimed with a loud cry, 'Blessed are you among women, and blessed is the fruit of your womb!'" (*Lk* 1:41-42).[3]

3.4 By a higher light, she understands Mary's greatness: more than Jael and Judith, who prefigured her in the Old Testament, she is blessed among women because of the fruit of her womb, Jesus, the Messiah.

4.1 Elizabeth's exclamation, made "with a loud cry", shows a true religious enthusiasm, which continues to be echoed on the lips of believers in the prayer *Ave Maria*, as the Church's song of praise for the great works accomplished by the Most High in the Mother of his Son.

4.2 In proclaiming her "blessed among women", Elizabeth points to Mary's faith as the reason for her blessedness: "And blessed is she who believed that there would be a fulfilment of what was spoken to her from the Lord" (*Lk* 1:45).[4] Mary's greatness and joy arise from the fact the she is the one who believes.

4.3 In view of Mary's excellence, Elizabeth also understands what an honour her visit is for her: "And why is this granted me, that the mother of my Lord should come to me?" (*Lk* 1:43).[5] With the expression "my Lord", Elizabeth recognises the royal, indeed messianic, dignity of Mary's Son. In the Old Testament this expression was in fact used to address the king (cf. *1 Kgs* 1:13, 20, 21 etc.) and to speak of the Messiah King (*Ps* 10:1). The angel had said

---

[1] "*Intravit in domum Zachariæ et salutavit Elisabeth*" (*Lc* 1, 40).
[2] "*Et factum est, ut audivit salutationem Mariæ Elisabeth, exsultavit infans in utero eius*" (*Lc* 1, 41).
[3] "*Repleta est Spiritu Sancto... exclamavit voce magna et dixit: 'Benedicta tu inter mulieres, et benedictus fructus ventris tui'*" (*Lc* 1, 41-42).
[4] "*Et beata, quæ credidit, quoniam perficientur ea, quæ dicta sunt ei a Domino*" (*Lc* 1, 45).
[5] "*Et unde hoc mihi, ut veniat mater Domini mei ad me?*" (*Lc* 1, 43).

of Jesus: "The Lord God will give to him the throne of his father David" (*Lk* 1:32).[1] "Filled with the Holy Spirit", Elizabeth has the same insight. Later, the paschal glorification of Christ will reveal the sense in which this title is to be understood, that is, a transcendent sense (cf. *Jn* 20:28; *Acts* 2:34-36).

4.4 With her admiring exclamation, Elizabeth invites us to appreciate all that the Virgin's presence brings as a gift to the life of every believer.

4.5 In the Visitation, the Virgin brings Christ to the Baptist's mother, the Christ who pours out the Holy Spirit. This role of Mediatrix is brought out by Elizabeth's very words: "For behold, when the voice of your greeting came to my ears, the child in my womb leaped for joy" (*Lk* 1:44).[2] By the gift of the Holy Spirit, Mary's presence serves as a prelude to Pentecost, confirming a co-operation which, having begun with the Incarnation, is destined to be expressed in the whole work of divine salvation.

2 October 1996

[1] "*Dabit illi Dominus Deus sedem David patris eius*" (*Lc* 1, 32).
[2] "*Ecce enim ut facta est vox salutationis tuæ in auribus meis, exsultavit in gaudio infans in utero meo*" (*Lc* 1, 44).

35
MARY SINGS THE PRAISES OF GOD'S MERCY

1.1 Inspired by the Old Testament tradition, with the song of the *Magníficat* Mary celebrates the marvels God worked in her. This song is the Virgin's response to the mystery of the Annunciation: the angel had invited her to rejoice and Mary now expresses the exultation of her spirit in God her Saviour. Her joy flows from the personal experience of God's looking with kindness upon her, a poor creature with no historical influence.

1.2 The word *Magníficat*, the Latin version of a Greek word with the same meaning, celebrates the greatness of God, who reveals his omnipotence through the angel's message, surpassing the expectations and hopes of the people of the Covenant, and even the noblest aspirations of the human soul.

1.3 In the presence of the powerful and merciful Lord, Mary expresses her own sense of lowliness: "My soul magnifies the Lord, and my spirit rejoices in God my Savior, for he has regarded the low estate of his handmaiden" (*Lk* 1:47-48).[1] The Greek word *tapeínosis*[2] is probably borrowed from the song of Hannah, Samuel's mother. It calls attention to the "humiliation" and "misery" of a barren woman (cf. *1 Sam* 1:11), who confides her pain to the Lord. With a similar expression, Mary makes known her situation of poverty and her awareness of being little before God, who by a free decision looked upon her, a humble girl from Nazareth and called her to become the Mother of the Messiah.

2 The words "henceforth all generations will call me blessed" (*Lk* 1:48)[3] arise from the fact that Elizabeth was the first to proclaim Mary "blessed" (*Lk* 1:45). Not without daring, the song predicts that this same proclamation will be extended and increased with relentless momentum. At the same time, it testifies to the special veneration for the Mother of Jesus which has been present in the Christian community from the very first century. The *Magníficat* is the first fruit of the various forms of devotion, passed on from one generation to the next, in which the Church has expressed her love for the Virgin of Nazareth.

3.1 "For he who is mighty has done great things for me, and holy is his name. And his mercy is on those who fear him from generation to generation" (*Lk* 1:49-50).[4]

---

[1] "*Magnificat anima mea Dominum, et exsultavit spiritus meus in Deo salvatore meo, quia respexit humilitatem ancillæ suæ* [Μεγαλύνει ή ψυχή μου τὸν κύριον, καὶ ἠγαλλίασεν τὸ πνεῦμά μου ἐπὶ τῷ θεῷ τῷ σωτῆρί μου]" (*Lc* 1, 46-48).

[2] *Tapeínosis* is the transliteration for the Greek word ταπείνωσις.

[3] "*Enim ex hoc beatam me dicent omnes generationes*" (*Lc* 1, 48).

[4] "*Quia fecit mihi magna, qui potens est, et sanctum nomen eius, et misericordia eius in progenies et progenies timentibus eum*" (*Lc* 1, 49-50).

3.2 What are the "great things" that the Almighty accomplished in Mary? The expression recurs in the Old Testament to indicate the deliverance of the people of Israel from Egypt or Babylon. In the *Magníficat*, it refers to the mysterious event of Jesus' virginal conception, which occurred in Nazareth after the angel's announcement.

3.3 In the *Magníficat*, a truly theological song because it reveals the experience Mary had of God's looking upon her, God is not only the *Almighty* to whom nothing is impossible, as Gabriel had declared (cf. *Lk* 1:37), but also the *Merciful*, capable of tenderness and fidelity towards every human being.

4.1 "He has shown strength with his arm, he has scattered the proud in the imagination of their hearts, he has put down the mighty from their thrones, and exalted those of low degree; he has filled the hungry with good things, and the rich he has sent empty away" (*Lk* 1:51-53).[1]

4.2 With her wise reading of history, Mary leads us to discover the criteria of God's mysterious action. Overturning the judgements of the world, he comes to the aid of the poor and lowly, to the detriment of the rich and powerful, and in a surprising way he fills with good things the humble who entrust their lives to him (cf. *Redemptoris Mater*, n. 37).

4.3 While these words of the song show us Mary as a concrete and sublime model, they give us to understand that it is especially humility of heart which attracts God's kindness.

5.1 Lastly, the song exalts the fulfilment of God's promises and his fidelity to the chosen people: "He has helped his servant Israel, in remembrance of his mercy, as he spoke to our fathers, to Abraham and to his posterity for ever" (*Lk* 1:54-55).[2]

5.2 Filled with divine gifts, Mary does not limit her vision to her own personal case, but realises how these gifts show forth God's mercy towards all his people. In her, God fulfils his promises with a superabundance of fidelity and generosity.

5.3 Inspired by the Old Testament and by the spirituality of the daughter of Sion, the *Magníficat* surpasses the prophetic texts on which it is based, revealing in her who is "full of grace" the beginning of a divine intervention which far exceeds Israel's messianic hopes: the holy mystery of the Incarnation of the Word.

6 November 1996

[1] "*Fecit potentiam in brachio suo, dispersit superbos mente cordis sui; deposuit potentes de sede et exaltavit humiles; esurientes implevit bonis et divites dimisit inanes*" (*Lc* 1, 51-53).
[2] "*Suscepit Israel puerum suum, recordatus misericordiæ, sicut locutus est ad patres nostros, Abraham et semini eius in sæcula*" (*Lc* 1, 54-55).

36
THE NATIVITY SHOWS MARY'S CLOSENESS TO JESUS

1.1 In the story of Jesus' birth, the Evangelist Luke recounts several facts that help us better understand the meaning of the event.

1.2 He first mentions the census ordered by Caesar Augustus,[1] which obliges Joseph, "of the house and lineage of David", and Mary his wife to go "to the city of David, which is called Bethlehem" (*Lk* 2:4).[2]

1.3 In informing us about the circumstances in which the journey and birth take place, the Evangelist presents us with a situation of hardship and poverty, which lets us glimpse some basic characteristics of the messianic kingdom: a kingdom without earthly honours or powers, which belongs to him who, in his public life, will say of himself: "But the Son of man has nowhere to lay his head" (*Lk* 9:58).[3]

2.1 Luke's account contains a few seemingly unimportant notes, which are meant to arouse in the reader a better understanding of the mystery of the Nativity and the sentiments of her who gave birth to the Son of God.

2.2 The description of the birth, recounted in simple fashion, presents Mary as intensely participating in what was taking place in her: "She gave birth to her first-born son and wrapped him in swaddling clothes, and laid him in a manger…" (*Lk* 2:7).[4] The Virgin's action is the result of her complete willingness to co-operate in God's plan, already expressed at the Annunciation in her "let it be to me according to your word" (*Lk* 1:38).[5]

2.3 Mary experiences childbirth in a condition of extreme poverty: she cannot give the Son of God even what mothers usually offer a newborn baby; instead, she has to lay him "in a manger", an improvised cradle which contrasts with the dignity of the "Son of the Most High".

3.1 The Gospel notes that "there was no place for them in the inn" (*Lk* 2:7).[6] This statement, recalling the text in John's Prologue: "His own people received him not" (*Jn* 1:11),[7] foretells as it were the many refusals Jesus will meet with

---

[1] Gaius Julius Caesar Augustus (63 BC–14 AD), 1st Emperor of the Roman Empire.
[2] "*De domo et familia David*"…"*civitate Nazareth in Iudæam in civitatem David, quæ vocatur Bethlehem*" (*Lc* 2, 4).
[3] "*Filius autem hominis non habet, ubi caput reclinet*" (*Lc* 9, 58).
[4] "*Peperit filium suum primogenitum; et pannis eum involvit et reclinavit eum in præsepio*" (*Lc* 2, 7).
[5] "*Fiat mihi secundum verbum tuum*" (*Lc* 1, 38).
[6] "*Quia non erat eis locus in deversorio*" (*Lc* 2, 7).
[7] "*Sui eum non receperunt*" (*Io* 1, 11).

during his earthly life. The phrase "for them" joins the Son and the Mother in this rejection, and shows how Mary is already associated with her Son's destiny of suffering and shares in his redeeming mission.

3.2 Rejected by "his own", Jesus is welcomed by the shepherds, rough men of ill repute, but chosen by God as the first to receive the good news of the Saviour's birth. The message the Angel gives them is an invitation to rejoice: "Behold, I bring you good news of a great joy which will come to all the people" (*Lk* 2:10),[1] along with a request to overcome all fear: "Be not afraid".[2]

3.3 Indeed, as it was for Mary at the time of the Annunciation, so too for them the news of Jesus' birth represents the great sign of God's goodwill towards men. In the divine Redeemer, contemplated in the poverty of a Bethlehem cave, we can see an invitation to approach with confidence the One who is the hope of humanity.

3.4 The angels' song: "Glory to God in the highest, and on earth peace among men with whom he is pleased!", which can also be translated as "men of goodwill" (*Lk* 2:14),[3] reveals to the shepherds what Mary had expressed in her *Magníficat:* Jesus' birth is the sign of God's merciful love, which is especially shown towards the poor and humble.

4.1 The shepherds respond enthusiastically and promptly to the angel's invitation: "Let us go over to Bethlehem and see this thing that has happened, which the Lord has made known to us" (*Lk* 2:15).[4]

4.2 They did not search in vain: "And they… found Mary and Joseph, and the babe" (*Lk* 2:16).[5] To them, as the Council recalls, "the Mother of God joyfully showed her first-born Son" (*Lumen gentium*, n. 57).[6] It was the defining moment of their lives.

4.3 The shepherds' spontaneous desire to make known what "had been told them concerning this child" (*Lk* 2:17),[7] after the wondrous experience of meeting the Mother and her Son, suggests to evangelisers in every age the importance

---

[1] "*Ecce enim evangelizo vobis gaudium magnum, quod erit omni populo*" (*Lc* 2, 10).

[2] "*Nolite timere*".

[3] "*Gloria in altissimis Deo, et super terram pax in hominibus bonæ voluntatis*" (*Lc* 2, 14). The Sacred Liturgy uses the translation "*Glória in excélsis Deo et in terra pax homínibus bonæ voluntátis* [Glory to God in the highest, and on earth peace to people of good will]" (*Missale Romanum, editio typica tertia emendata 2008, Ordo Missæ*, n. 8).

[4] "*Transeamus usque Bethlehem et videamus hoc verbum, quod factum est, quod Dominus ostendit nobis*" (*Lc* 2, 15).

[5] "*Et invenerunt Mariam et Ioseph et infantem*" (*Lc* 2, 16).

[6] "*In nativitate vero, cum Deipara Filium suum primogenitum, qui virginalem eius integritatem non minuit sed sacravit, pastoribus et Magis lætabunda ostendit*" (Concilium Vaticanum II, Const. dogm. de Ecclesia, *Lumen gentium*, 57: *AAS* 57 (1965), p. 61).

[7] "*Quod dictum erat illis de puero hoc*" (*Lc* 2, 17).

and, even more, the necessity of a deep spiritual relationship with Mary, in order to know Jesus better and to become the joyful proclaimers of his Gospel of salvation.

4.4 With regard to these extraordinary events, Luke tells us that Mary "kept all these things, pondering them in her heart" (*Lk* 2:19).[1] While the shepherds passed from fear to wonder and praise, the Virgin, because of her faith, kept alive the memory of the events involving her Son, and deepened her understanding of them by reflecting on them in her heart, that is, in the inmost core of her person. In this way she suggests that another mother, the Church, should foster the gift and task of contemplation and theological reflection, in order better to accept the mystery of salvation, to understand it more thoroughly and to proclaim it with renewed effort to the people of every age.

20 November 1996

[1] "*Conservabat omnia verba hæc conferens in corde suo*" (*Lc* 2, 19).

37
THE CHURCH PROCLAIMS MARY AS THE MOTHER OF GOD

1.1 Contemplation of the mystery of the Saviour's birth has led Christian people not only to invoke the Blessed Virgin as the Mother of Jesus, but also to recognise her as Mother of God. This truth was already confirmed and perceived as belonging to the Church's heritage of faith from the early centuries of the Christian era, until it was solemnly proclaimed at the Council of Ephesus in 431.

1.2 In the first Christian community, as the disciples became more aware that Jesus is the Son of God, it became ever clearer that Mary is the *Theotókos*, the Mother of God. This is a title which does not appear explicitly in the Gospel texts, but in them the "Mother of Jesus" is mentioned and it is affirmed that Jesus is God (*Jn* 20:28; cf. 5:18; 10:30, 33). Mary is in any case presented as the Mother of Emmanuel, which means "God with us" (cf. *Mt* 1:22-23).

1.3 Already in the third century, as can be deduced from an ancient written witness, the Christians of Egypt addressed this prayer to Mary: "We fly to thy patronage, O holy Mother of God: despise not our petitions in our necessities, but deliver us from all evil, O glorious and blessed Virgin" (from the *Liturgy of the Hours*).[1] The expression *Theotókos* appears explicitly for the first time in this ancient witness.

1.4 In pagan mythology, it often happened that a certain goddess would be presented as the mother of some god. For example, the supreme god, Zeus, had the goddess Rhea as his mother. This context perhaps helped Christians to use the title *Theotókos*, "Mother of God", for the Mother of Jesus. It should nevertheless be noted that this title did not exist but was created by Christians to express a belief which had nothing to do with pagan mythology, belief in the virginal conception in Mary's womb of the One who had always been the eternal Word of God.

2.1 By the fourth century, the term *Theotókos* was frequently used in the East and West. Devotion and theology refer more and more to this term, which had by now become part of the Church's patrimony of faith.

2.2 One can therefore understand the great protest movement that arose in the fifth century when Nestorius[2] cast doubt on the correctness of the title

---

[1] The *Sub tuum præsídium* (We fly to your patronage) is used at Compline, particularly during Ordinary Time after Pentecost (*Tempus per annum post Pentecosten*); cf. Appendix of Marian Prayers, page 232.
[2] Nestorius (ca. 386–ca. 451) was Archbishop of Constantinople and condemned at the First Council of Ephesus.

"Mother of God". In fact, being inclined to hold that Mary was only the mother of the man Jesus, he maintained that "Mother of Christ" was the only doctrinally correct expression. Nestorius was led to make this error by his difficulty in admitting the unity of Christ's person and by his erroneous interpretation of the distinction between the two natures—divine and human—present in him.

2.3 In 431 the Council of Ephesus condemned his theses and, in affirming the subsistence of the divine and human natures in the one person of the Son, proclaimed Mary the Mother of God.

3.1 Now, the difficulties and objections raised by Nestorius offer us the opportunity to make several useful reflections for correctly understanding and interpreting this title. The expression *Theotókos*, which literally means, "she who has begotten God", can at first sight seem surprising; in fact it raises the question as to how it is possible for a human creature to give birth to God. The answer of the Church's faith is clear: Mary's divine motherhood refers only to the human begetting of the Son of God but not, however, to his divine birth. The Son of God was eternally begotten of God the Father, and is consubstantial with him. Mary, of course, has no part in this eternal birth. However, the Son of God assumed our human nature 2,000 years ago and was conceived by and born of Mary.

3.2 In proclaiming Mary "Mother of God", the Church thus intends to affirm that she is the "Mother of the Incarnate Word, who is God". Her motherhood does not, therefore, extend to all the Trinity, but only to the Second Person, the Son, who, in becoming incarnate, took his human nature from her.

3.3 Motherhood is a relationship of person to person: a mother is not only mother of the body or of the physical creature born of her womb, but of the person she begets. Thus having given birth, according to his human nature, to the person of Jesus, who is a divine person, Mary is the Mother of God.

4.1 In proclaiming Mary "Mother of God", the Church in a single phrase professes her belief regarding the Son and the Mother. This union was already seen at the Council of Ephesus; in defining Mary's divine motherhood, the Fathers intended to emphasise their belief in the divinity of Christ. Despite ancient and recent objections about the appropriateness of recognising Mary by this title, Christians of all times, by correctly interpreting the meaning of this motherhood, have made it a privileged expression of their faith in the divinity of Christ and their love for the Blessed Virgin.

4.2 On the one hand, the Church recognises the *Theotókos* as guaranteeing the reality of the Incarnation because—as Saint Augustine says—"if the Mother were fictitious, the flesh would also be fictitious... and the scars of the Resurrection" (*Tract. in Ev. Ioannis*, 8, 6-7).[1] On the other hand, she also contemplates with wonder and celebrates with veneration the immense greatness conferred on Mary by the One who wanted to be her Son. The expression "Mother of God" refers to the Word of God, who in the Incarnation assumed the lowliness of the human condition in order to raise man to divine sonship. But in the light of the sublime dignity conferred on the Virgin of Nazareth, this title also proclaims the nobility of woman and her loftiest vocation. God in fact treats Mary as a free and responsible person and does not bring about the Incarnation of his Son until after he has obtained her consent.

4.3 Following the example of the ancient Christians of Egypt, let the faithful entrust themselves to her who, being the Mother of God, can obtain from her divine Son the grace of deliverance from evil and of eternal salvation.

27 November 1996

[1] "*Si enim falsa mater, falsa caro, falsa mors, falsa vulnera passionis, falsae cicatrices resurrectionis; non veritas credentes in eum, sed potius falsitas liberabit* [For if He had a false mother, false flesh, false death, false wounds in His death, false scars in His resurrection, then it will not be the truth, but rather falsehood, that shall make free those that believe in Him]" (Sanctus Augustinus, *In evangelium Ioannis tractatus*, tract. VIII, 7: *PL* 35, 1454).

38
TEACHER OF THE SON OF GOD

1.1 Although occurring by the work of the Holy Spirit and a Virgin Mother, the birth of Jesus, like that of all human beings, went through the phases of conception, gestation and delivery. In addition, Mary's motherhood was not limited to the biological process of giving birth, but as it happens with every other mother, she also made an essential contribution to her son's growth and development.

1.2 A mother is not only a woman who gives birth to a child, but one who brings him up and teaches him; indeed, we might well say that, according to God's plan, the educational task is the natural extension of procreation.

1.3 Mary is the *Theotókos*, not only because she conceived and gave birth to the Son of God, but also because she accompanied him in his human growth.

2.1 We might think that, since Jesus possessed in himself the fullness of divinity, he had no need of teachers. But the mystery of the Incarnation reveals to us that the Son of God came into the world in a human condition similar to us in all things except sin (cf. *Heb* 4:15). As is the case with every human being, Jesus' growth, from infancy to adulthood (cf. *Lk* 2:40), also needed his parents' educational activity.

2.2 The Gospel of Luke, particularly attentive to the childhood period, says that at Nazareth Jesus was obedient to Joseph and Mary (cf. *Lk* 2:51). This dependence shows us that Jesus was receptive, open to the teaching of his mother and Joseph, who also carried out their task by virtue of the docility he constantly showed.

3.1 The special gifts which God had showered on Mary made her particularly suited to her task as mother and teacher. In the concrete circumstances of everyday life, Jesus could find in her a model to follow and imitate and an example of perfect love for God and for his brothers and sisters.

3.2 Along with Mary's motherly presence, Jesus could count on the paternal figure of Joseph, a just man (cf. *Mt* 1:19), who provided the necessary balance in the educational activity. Carrying out his role as father, Joseph co-operated with his wife in making the home in Nazareth an environment favourable to the growth and personal maturity of the Saviour of humanity. By later introducing him to the hard work of the carpenter, Joseph enabled Jesus to be involved in the world of work and social life.

4.1 The few elements that the Gospel offers do not allow us to know and fully appreciate the ways in which Mary taught her divine Son. Certainly she, together with Joseph, introduced Jesus to the rites and prescriptions of Moses, to prayer to the God of the Covenant by using the Psalms, to the history of the people of Israel centred on the Exodus from Egypt. From her and Joseph Jesus learned to attend the synagogue and to make the annual pilgrimage to Jerusalem for the Passover.

4.2 Looking at the results, we can certainly conclude that Mary's teaching was deep and effective, and found very fertile soil in Jesus' human psychology.

5.1 Mary's educational task with regard to such a unique son presents several special features in comparison with the role of other mothers. She only provided favourable conditions for the development of the potential and essential values for growth, already present in the Son. For example, the absence of any form of sin in Jesus demanded a constantly positive orientation from Mary, which excluded any form of corrective intervention. Furthermore, although it was his mother who introduced Jesus to the culture and traditions of the people of Israel, it was he, from the time of his finding in the temple, who would reveal his full awareness of being the Son of God, sent to spread the truth in the world and exclusively follow the Father's will. From being her Son's "teacher", Mary thus becomes the humble disciple of the divine Master to whom she had given birth.

5.2 The importance of the Virgin Mother's task remains: from his infancy to adulthood, she helped her Son Jesus to grow "in wisdom and in stature, and in favour with God and man" (*Lk* 2:52),[1] and to prepare for his mission.

5.3 Mary and Joseph can therefore be seen as models for all educators. They sustain them in the great difficulties that the family encounters today, and show them the way to their children's precise and effective formation.

5.4 Their educational experience is a sure reference point for Christian parents who are called, in ever more complex and difficult conditions, to devote themselves to the service of the integral development of their children's personality, so that they will live lives worthy of man and corresponding to God's plan.

4 December 1996

[1] "*Sapientia et œtate et gratia apud Deum et homines*" (*Lc* 2, 52).

39
THE PRESENTATION OF JESUS IN THE TEMPLE

1.1 In the episode of the Presentation of Jesus in the temple, Saint Luke emphasises Jesus' messianic destiny. The immediate purpose of the Holy Family's journey from Bethlehem to Jerusalem according to the Lucan text was to fulfil the law:

"And when the time came for their purification according to the law of Moses, they brought him up to Jerusalem to present him to the Lord (as it is written in the law of the Lord, 'Every male that opens the womb shall be called holy to the Lord'), and to offer a sacrifice according to what is said in the law of the Lord, 'a pair of turtledoves, or two young pigeon'" (*Lk* 2:22-24).[1]

1.2 With this act, Mary and Joseph show their intention of faithfully obeying God's will, rejecting every kind of privilege. Their coming to the temple in Jerusalem has the significance of a consecration to God in the place where he is present.

1.3 Obliged by her poverty to offer turtledoves or pigeons, Mary in fact gives the true Lamb who would redeem humanity, thus anticipating what was prefigured in the ritual offerings of the old law.

2.1 While the law required the purification after birth of the mother alone, Luke speaks of the "time for *their* purification" (2:22), intending perhaps to indicate together the prescriptions involving both the mother and the firstborn Son.

2.2 The term "purification" can surprise us, because it is referred to a Mother who had been granted, by a singular grace, to be immaculate from the first moment of her existence, and to a Child who was totally holy. However, it must be remembered that it was not a question of purifying the conscience from some stain of sin, but only of reacquiring ritual purity which, according to the ideas of the time, may be harmed by the simple fact of birth without there being any form of guilt.

2.3 The Evangelist uses the occasion to stress the special link existing between Jesus, as "first-born" (*Lk* 2:7, 23) and God's holiness, as well as to indicate the spirit of humble offering which motivated Mary and Joseph (cf. *Lk* 2:24). In fact, the "two turtledoves or two young pigeons" (*Lv* 12:8),[2] was the offering of the poor.

---

[1] "*Et postquam impleti sunt dies purgationis eorum secundum legem Moysis, tulerunt illum in Hierosolymam, ut sisterent Domino, sicut scriptum est in lege Domini: 'Omne masculinum adaperiens vulvam sanctum Domino vocabitur', et ut darent hostiam secundum quod dictum est in lege Domini: par turturum aut duos pullos columbarum*" (*Lc* 2, 22-24).
[2] "*Duos turtures vel duos pullos columbæ*" (*Lev* 12, 8).

3.1 In the temple, Joseph and Mary meet Simeon, "righteous and devout, looking for the consolation of Israel" (*Lk* 2:25).[1]

3.2 The Lucan narrative says nothing of his past or of the service he carried out in the temple; it tells of a deeply religious man who nurtures great desires in his heart and awaits the Messiah, the consolation of Israel. In fact, "the Holy Spirit was upon him" and "it had been revealed to him… that he should not see death before he had seen the Lord's Christ" (*Lk* 2:25-26).[2] Simeon invites us to look at the merciful action of God who pours out the Spirit on his faithful to bring to fulfilment his mysterious project of love.

3.3 Simeon, a man who is open to God's action, "inspired by the Spirit" (*Lk* 2:27), goes to the temple where he meets Jesus, Joseph and Mary. Taking the Child in his arms, he blesses God and says, "Lord, now let your servant depart in peace, according to your word" (*Lk* 2:29).[3]

3.4 Simeon uses an Old Testament phrase to express the joy he experiences on meeting the Messiah and feels that the purpose of his life has been fulfilled; he can therefore ask the Most High to let him depart in peace to the next world.

3.5 In the episode of the Presentation we can glimpse the meeting of Israel's hope with the Messiah. We can also see in it a prophetic sign of man's encounter with Christ. The Holy Spirit makes it possible by awakening in the human heart the desire for this salvific meeting and by bringing it about.

3.6 Nor can we neglect the role of Mary who gives the Child to the holy old man Simeon. By divine will, it is the Mother who gives Jesus to mankind.

4.1 In revealing the Saviour's future, Simeon refers to the prophecy of the "Servant" sent to the chosen people and to the nations. To him the Lord says, "I have taken you by the hand and kept you; I have given you *as a covenant to the people, a light to the nations*" (*Is* 42:6).[4] And again:

"It is too light a thing that you should be my servant to raise up the tribes of Jacob and to restore the preserved of Israel; I will give you as a light to the nations, that my salvation may reach to the end of the earth" (*Is* 49:6).[5]

---

[1] "*Iustus et timoratus, exspectans consolationem Israel*" (*Lc* 2, 25).
[2] "*Spiritus Sanctus erat super eum… responsum acceperat… non visurum se mortem nisi prius videret Christum Domini*" (*Lc* 2, 25-26).
[3] "*Nunc dimittis servum tuum, Domine, secundum verbum tuum in pace*" (*Lc* 2, 29).
[4] "*Apprehendi manum tuam; et formavi te et dedi te in fœdus populi, in lucem gentium*" (*Is* 42, 6).
[5] "*Parum est ut sis mihi servus ad suscitandas tribus Iacob et reliquias Israel reducendas: dabo te in lucem gentium, ut sit salus mea usque ad extremum terræ*" (*Is* 49, 6).

4.2 In his canticle, Simeon reverses the perspective and puts the stress on the universality of Jesus' mission:

"For my eyes have seen your salvation which you have prepared in the presence of all peoples, *a light for revelation to the Gentiles,* and *for glory for your people Israel*" (*Lk* 2:30-32).[1]

4.3 How can we fail to marvel at these words? "And his father and mother marveled at what was said about him" (*Lk* 2:33).[2] But this experience enabled Joseph and Mary to understand more clearly the importance of their act of offering: in the temple of Jerusalem they present the One who, being the glory of his people, is also the salvation of all mankind.

11 December 1996

[1] "*Quia viderunt oculi mei salutare tuum, quod parastiante faciem omnium populorum, lumen ad revelationem gentium et gloriam plebis tuæ Israel*" (*Lc* 2, 30-32).
[2] "*Et erat pater eius et mater mirantes super his, quæ dicebantur de illo*" (*Lc* 2, 33).

40
THE PROPHECY OF SIMEON ASSOCIATED MARY TO THE PAINFUL DESTINY OF THE SON

1.1 After recognising in Jesus "a light for revelation to the Gentiles" (*Lk* 2:32),[1] Simeon announces to Mary the great trial to which the Messiah is called and reveals her participation in that sorrowful destiny. His reference to the redeeming sacrifice, absent at the Annunciation, has shown in Simeon's prophecy almost a "second Annunciation" (*Redemptoris Mater*, n. 16), which will lead the Virgin to a deeper understanding of her Son's mystery.

1.2 Simeon, who up to that moment had addressed all those present, blessing Joseph and Mary in particular, now prophesies to the Virgin alone that she will share in her Son's destiny. Inspired by the Holy Spirit, he announces to her:

"Behold, this child is set for the fall and rising of many in Israel, and for a sign that is spoken against (and a sword will pierce through your own soul also), that thoughts out of many hearts may be revealed" (*Lk* 2:34-35).[2]

2.1 These words foretell a future of suffering for the Messiah. He is, in fact, "the sign of contradiction", destined to meet harsh opposition on the part of his contemporaries. But alongside Christ's suffering Simeon sets the vision of Mary's heart pierced by the sword, thus uniting the Mother with the sorrowful destiny of her Son.

2.2 In this way, while the venerable old man foresees the growing hostility the Messiah will face, he stresses its repercussion on the Mother's heart. This maternal suffering will culminate in the Passion, when she will unite with her Son in his redemptive sacrifice.

2.3 Following an allusion to the first songs of the Servant of the Lord (cf. *Is* 42:6; 49:6), cited in Luke 2:32, Simeon's words remind us of the prophecy of the Suffering Servant (*Is* 52:13; 53:12), who, "wounded for our transgressions" (*Is* 53:5),[3] "makes himself an offering for sin" (*Is* 53:10)[4] through a personal and spiritual sacrifice which far exceeds the ancient ritual sacrifices. Here we can note how Simeon's prophecy allows us to glimpse in Mary's future suffering a unique likeness to the sorrowful future of the "Servant".

---

[1] "*Lumen ad revelationem gentium*" (*Lc* 2, 32).

[2] "*Ecce positus est hic in ruinam et resurrectionem multorum in Israel et in signum, cui contradicetur— et tuam ipsius animam pertransiet gladius—ut revelentur ex multis cordibus cogitationes* " (*Lc* 2, 34-35).

[3] "*Vulneratus est propter iniquitates nostras*" (*Is* 53, 5).

[4] "*Si posuerit in piaculum animam suam*" (*Is* 53, 10).

3.1 Mary and Joseph are astounded when Simeon proclaims Jesus as a "light for revelation to the Gentiles" (*Lk* 2:32). Mary, instead, with reference to the prophecy of the sword that would pierce her heart, says nothing. Together with Joseph, she accepts in silence those mysterious words which predict a deeply sorrowful trial and situate the Presentation of Jesus in the temple in its most authentic meaning.

3.2 Indeed, according to the divine plan the sacrifice offered then "according to what is said in the law of the Lord, 'a pair of turtle-doves, or two young pigeons'" (*Lk* 2:24),[1] prefigured the sacrifice of Jesus, "for I am gentle and lowly in heart" (*Mt* 11:29);[2] in it the true "presentation" would be made (cf. *Lk* 2:22), which would see the Mother associated with her Son in the work of Redemption.

4.1 Simeon's prophecy is followed by the meeting with the prophetess Anna: "She gave thanks to God, and spoke of him to all who were looking for the redemption of Jerusalem" (*Lk* 2:38).[3] The faith and prophetic wisdom of the old woman who nurtures the expectation of the Messiah by "worshipping with fasting and prayer night and day" (*Lk* 2:37),[4] offer the Holy Family a further incentive to put their hope in the God of Israel. At this particular moment, Anna's behaviour would have appeared to Mary and Joseph as a sign from the Lord, a message of enlightened faith and persevering service.

4.2 Beginning with Simeon's prophecy, Mary intensely and mysteriously unites her life with Christ's sorrowful mission: she was to become her Son's faithful coworker for the salvation of the human race.

18 December 1996

---

[1] "*Secundum quod dictum est in lege Domini: par turturum aut duos pullos columbarum*" (*Lc* 2, 24).
[2] "*Quia mitis sum et humilis corde*" (*Mt* 11, 29).
[3] "*Confitebatur Deo et loquebatur de illo omnibus, qui exspectabant redemptionem Ierusalem*" (*Lc* 2, 38).
[4] "*Ieiuniis et obsecrationibus serviens nocte ac die*" (*Lc* 2, 37).

41
THE PRESENTATION OF JESUS IN THE TEMPLE REVEALS THE COOPERATION OF THE "WOMAN" IN THE REDEMPTION

1.1 The words of the aged Simeon, announcing to Mary her sharing in the Messiah's saving mission, shed light on woman's role in the mystery of Redemption.

1.2 Indeed, Mary is not only an individual person, but she is also the "daughter of Sion", the new woman standing at the Redeemer's side in order to share his Passion and to give birth in the Spirit to the children of God. This reality is expressed by the popular depiction of the "seven swords" that pierce Mary's heart: this image highlights the deep link between the mother, who is identified with the daughter of Sion and with the Church, and the sorrowful destiny of the Incarnate Word.

1.3 Giving back her Son, whom she had just received from God, to consecrate him for his saving mission, Mary also gives herself to this mission. It is an act of interior sharing that is not only the fruit of natural maternal affection, but above all expresses the consent of the new woman to Christ's redemptive work.

2.1 In his words Simeon indicates the purpose of Jesus' sacrifice and Mary's suffering: these will come about so "that thoughts out of many hearts may be revealed" (*Lk* 2:35).[1]

2.2 Jesus, "a sign that is spoken against" (*Lk* 2:34),[2] who involves his mother in his suffering, will lead men and women to take a stand in his regard, inviting them to make a fundamental decision. In fact, he "is set for the fall and rising of many in Israel" (*Lk* 2:34).[3]

2.3 Thus Mary is united to her divine Son in this "contradiction", in view of the work of salvation. Certainly there is a risk of ruin for those who reject Christ, but the resurrection of many is a marvellous effect of the Redemption. This proclamation alone kindles great hope in the hearts of those to whom the fruit of the sacrifice already bears witness.

2.4 Directing the Blessed Virgin's attention to these prospects of salvation before the ritual offering, Simeon seems to suggest to Mary that she perform this act

---

[1] "*Ut revelentur ex multis cordibus cogitationes*" (*Lc* 2, 35).
[2] "*In signum, cui contradicetur*" (*Lc* 2, 34).
[3] "*Positus est hic in ruinam et resurrectionem multorum in Israel*" (*Lc* 2, 34).

as a contribution to humanity's ransom. In fact, he does not speak to Joseph or about Joseph: his words are addressed to Mary, whom he associates with the destiny of her Son.

3.1 The chronological priority of Mary's action does not obscure Jesus' primacy. In describing Mary's role in the economy of salvation, the Second Vatican Council recalled that she "devoted herself totally... to the person and work of her Son, *under and with him*, serving the mystery of Redemption" (*Lumen gentium*, n. 56).[1]

3.2 At the presentation of Jesus in the temple, Mary serves the mystery of Redemption under Christ and with Christ: indeed he has the principal role in salvation and must be ransomed by a ritual offering. Mary is joined to the sacrifice of her Son by the sword that will pierce her soul.

3.3 The primacy of Christ does not rule out but supports and demands the proper, irreplaceable role of woman. By involving his mother in his own sacrifice, Christ wants to reveal its deep human roots and to show us an anticipation of the priestly offering of the cross.

3.4 The divine intention to call for the specific involvement of woman in the work of Redemption can be seen by the fact that Simeon's prophecy is addressed to Mary alone, although Joseph also took part in the offering rite.

4.1 The conclusion of the episode of Jesus' presentation in the temple seems to confirm the meaning and value of the feminine presence in the economy of salvation. The meeting with a woman, Anna, brings to a close these special moments when the Old Testament as it were is handed over to the New.

4.2 Like Simeon, this woman has no special status among the chosen people, but her life seems to have a lofty value in God's eyes. Saint Luke calls her a "prophetess", probably because many consulted her for her gift of discernment and the holy life she led under the inspiration of the Spirit of the Lord.

4.3 Anna is advanced in age, being 84 years old, and has long been a widow. Totally consecrated to God, "she never left the temple, serving God day and night with fasting and prayer" (cf. *Lk* 2:37).[2] She represents those who, having intensely lived in expectation of the Messiah, are able to accept the

---

[1] "*Semetipsam ut Domini ancillam personæ et operi Filii sui totaliter devovit, sub Ipso et cum Ipso, omnipotentis Dei gratia, mysterio redemptionis inserviens*" (Concilium Vaticanum II, Const. dogm. de Ecclesia, *Lumen gentium*, 56: *AAS* 57 (1965), p. 60).
[2] "*Quæ non discedebat de templo, ieiuniis et obsecrationibus serviens nocte ac die*" (cf. *Lc* 2, 37).

fulfilment of the promise with joyous exultation. The Evangelist mentions that "coming up at that very hour she gave thanks to God" (2:38).[1]

4.4 Staying constantly in the temple, she could, perhaps more easily than Simeon, meet Jesus at the end of a life dedicated to the Lord and enriched by listening to the Word and by prayer.

4.5 At the dawn of Redemption, we can glimpse in the prophetess Anna all women who, with holiness of life and in prayerful expectation, are ready to accept Christ's presence and to praise God every day for the marvels wrought by his everlasting mercy.

5.1 Chosen to meet the Child, Simeon and Anna have a deep experience of sharing the joy of Jesus' presence with Mary and Joseph and spreading it where they live. Anna in particular shows wonderful zeal in speaking about Jesus, thus witnessing to her simple and generous faith. This faith prepares others to accept the Messiah in their lives.

5.2 Luke's expression, "she… spoke of him to all who were looking for the redemption of Jerusalem" (2:38),[2] seems to credit her as a symbol of the women who, dedicated to spreading the Gospel, will arouse and nourish the hope of salvation.

8 January 1997

---

[1] "*Hæc ipsa hora superveniens confitebatur Deo*" (*Lc* 2, 38).
[2] "*Loquebatur de illo omnibus, qui exspectabant redemptionem Ierusalem*" (*Lc* 2, 38).

42
JESUS, LOST AND THEN FOUND IN THE TEMPLE

1.1 The Evangelist Luke describes the young Jesus' pilgrimage to the temple in Jerusalem as the last episode of the infancy narrative, before the start of John the Baptist's preaching. It is an usual occasion which sheds light on the long years of his hidden life in Nazareth.

1.2 On this occasion, with his strong personality Jesus reveals that he is aware of his mission, giving to this second "entry" into his "Father's house" the meaning of his total gift of self to God which had already marked his presentation in the temple.

1.3 This passage seems to contrast with Luke's note that Jesus was obedient to Joseph and Mary (cf. 2:51). But, if one looks closely, here he seems to put himself in a conscious and almost deliberate antithesis to his normal state as son, unexpectedly causing a definite separation from Mary and Joseph. As his rule of conduct, Jesus states that he belongs only to the Father and does not mention the ties to his earthly family. Jesus' behaviour seemed very unusual

2.1 Through this episode, Jesus prepares his Mother for the mystery of the Redemption.

During those three dramatic days when the Son withdraws from them to stay in the temple, Mary and Joseph experience an anticipation of the *triduum* of his Passion, Death and Resurrection.

2.2 Letting his Mother and Joseph depart for Galilee without telling them of his intention to stay behind in Jerusalem, Jesus brings them into the mystery of that suffering which leads to joy, anticipating what he would later accomplish with his disciples through the announcement of his Passover.

2.3 According to Luke's account, on the return journey to Nazareth Mary and Joseph, after a day's traveling, are worried and anguished over the fate of the Child Jesus. They look for him in vain among their relatives and acquaintances. Returning to Jerusalem and finding him in the temple, they are astonished to see him "sitting among the teachers, listening to them and asking them questions" (*Lk* 2:46).[1] His behaviour seems most unusual. Certainly for his parents, finding him on the third day means discovering another aspect of his person and his mission.

---

[1] "*Sedentem in medio doctorum, audientem illos et interrogantem eos*" (*Lc* 2, 46).

2.4 He takes the role of teacher, as he will later do in his public life, speaking words that arouse admiration: "And all who heard him were astounded at his understanding and his answers" (2:47).[1] Revealing a wisdom that amazes his listeners, he begins to practise the art of dialogue that will be a characteristic of his saving mission.

2.5 His Mother asked Jesus: "Son, why have you treated us so? Behold, your father and I have been looking for you anxiously" (*Lk* 2:48).[2] Here we can discern an echo of the "whys" asked by so many mothers about the suffering their children cause them, as well as the questions welling up in the heart of every man and woman in times of trial.

3.1 Jesus' reply, in the form of a question, is highly significant: "How is it that you sought me? Did you not know that I must be in my Father's house?" (*Lk* 2:49).[3]

3.2 With this response, he discloses the mystery of his person to Mary and Joseph in an unexpected, unforeseen way, inviting them to go beyond appearances and unfolding before them new horizons for his future.

3.3 In his reply to his anguished Mother, the Son immediately reveals the reason for his behaviour. Mary had said: "Your father", indicating Joseph; Jesus replies: "My Father", meaning the heavenly Father.

3.4 Referring to his divine origin, he does not so much want to state that the temple, his Father's house, is the natural "place" for his presence, as that he must be concerned about all that regards his Father and his plan. He means to stress that his Father's will is the only norm requiring his obedience.

3.5 This reference to his total dedication to God's plan is highlighted in the Gospel text by the words: "I must be", which will later appear in his prediction of the Passion (cf. *Mk* 8:31).

3.6 His parents then are asked to let him go and carry out his mission wherever the heavenly Father will lead him.

4.1 The Evangelist comments: "And they did not understand the saying which he spoke to them" (*Lk* 2:50).[4]

---

[1] "*Stupebant autem omnes, qui eum audiebant, super prudentia et responsis eius*" (*Lc* 2, 47).
[2] "*Fili, quid fecisti nobis sic? Ecce pater tuus et ego dolentes quærebamus te*" (*Lc* 2, 48).
[3] "*Quid est quod me quærebatis? Nesciebatis quia in his, quæ Patris mei sunt, oportet me esse?*" (*Lc* 2, 49).
[4] "*Et ipsi non intellexerunt verbum, quod locutus est ad illos*" (*Lc* 2, 50).

4.2 Mary and Joseph do not perceive the sense of his answer, nor the way (apparently a rejection) he reacts to their parental concern. With this attitude, Jesus intends to reveal the mysterious aspects of his intimacy with the Father, aspects which Mary intuits without knowing how to associate them with the trial she is undergoing.

4.3 Luke's words teach us how Mary lives this truly unusual episode in the depths of her being. She "kept all these things in her heart" (*Lk* 2:51).[1] The Mother of Jesus associates these events with the mystery of her Son, revealed to her at the Annunciation, and ponders them in the silence of contemplation, offering her co-operation in the spirit of a renewed *fiat*.[2]

4.4 In this way the first link is forged in a chain of events that will gradually lead Mary beyond the natural role deriving from her motherhood, to put herself at the service of her divine Son's mission.

4.5 At the temple in Jerusalem, in this prelude to his saving mission, Jesus associates his Mother with himself; no longer is she merely the One who gave him birth, but the Woman who, through her own obedience to the Father's plan, can co-operate in the mystery of Redemption.

4.6 Thus keeping in her heart an event so charged with meaning, Mary attains a new dimension of her co-operation in salvation.

15 January 1997

[1] "*Eius conservabat omnia verba in corde suo*" (*Lc* 2, 51).
[2] *Fiat* is the first word of the Gospel text "*fiat mihi secundum verbum tuum*", which is Latin for "let it be to me according to your word", the Blessed Virgin Mary's response to the Annunciation (cf. *Lk* 1:38). The word *fiat* is also found in the Lord's Prayer (*Oratio dominica*): "*fiat voluntas tua* (Thy will be done)".

43
MARY IN THE HIDDEN LIFE OF JESUS

1.1 The Gospels offer very sparse information about the years the Holy Family spent in Nazareth. Saint Matthew tells of the decision taken by Joseph, after the return from Egypt, to make Nazareth the Holy Family's permanent home (cf. *Mt* 2:22-23), but then gives no further information except that Joseph was a carpenter (*Mt* 13:55). For his part, Saint Luke twice mentions the Holy Family's return to Nazareth (cf. *Lk* 2:39, 51) and gives two brief references to the years of Jesus' childhood, before and after the episode of the pilgrimage to Jerusalem: "The child grew and became strong, filled with wisdom; and the favor of God was upon him" (*Lk* 2:40),[1] and "Jesus increased in wisdom and in stature, and in favor with God and man" (*Lk* 2:52).[2]

1.2 In relating these brief remarks about Jesus' life, Luke is probably referring to Mary's memories of a period of profound intimacy with her Son. The union between Jesus and the one who was "full of grace" goes far beyond what normally exists between mother and child, because it is rooted in a particular supernatural condition and reinforced by the special conformity of both to the divine will.

1.3 Thus we can conclude that the atmosphere of tranquillity and peace in the house of Nazareth and their constant seeking to fulfil God's plan gave an extraordinary and unique depth to the union of mother and son.

2.1 Mary's awareness that she was carrying out a task entrusted to her by God gave a higher meaning to her daily life. The simple, humble chores of everyday life took on special value in her eyes, since she performed them as a service to Christ's mission.

2.2 Mary's example enlightens and encourages the experience of so many women who carry out their daily tasks exclusively in the home. It is a question of a humble, hidden, repetitive effort, and is often not sufficiently appreciated. Nonetheless, the long years Mary spent in the house of Nazareth reveal the enormous potential of genuine love and thus of salvation. In fact, the simplicity of the lives of so many housewives, seen as a mission of service and love, is of extraordinary value in the Lord's eyes.

2.3 One can certainly say that for Mary life in Nazareth was not dominated by monotony.

---

[1] "*Puer autem crescebat et confortabatur plenus sapientia; et gratia Dei erat super illum*" (*Lc* 2, 40).
[2] "*Iesus proficiebat sapientia et ætate et gratia apud Deum et homines*" (*Lc* 2, 52).

In her contact with the growing Jesus, she strove to penetrate the mystery of her Son through contemplation and adoration. Saint Luke says: "Mary kept all these things, pondering them in her heart" (*Lk* 2:19; cf. 2:51).[1]

2.4 "All these things": they are the events in which she was both participant and spectator, starting with the Annunciation; but above all, it is the life of her Child. Every day of intimacy with him is an invitation to know him better, to discover more deeply the meaning of his presence and the mystery of his person.

3.1 Someone might think that it was easy for Mary to believe, living as she did in daily contact with Jesus. In this regard, however, we must remember that the unique aspects of her Son's personality were usually hidden; even if his way of acting was exemplary, he lived a life similar to that of his peers.

3.2 During his thirty years of life in Nazareth, Jesus did not reveal his supernatural qualities and worked no miracles. At the first extraordinary manifestations of his personality, associated with the beginning of his preaching, his relatives (called "brothers" in the Gospel), assume—according to one interpretation —responsibility for taking him home, because they feel his behaviour is not normal (cf. *Mk* 3:21).

3.3 In the dignified and hard-working atmosphere of Nazareth, Mary strove to understand the workings of Providence in her Son's mission. A subject of particular reflection for his Mother, in this regard, was certainly the statement Jesus made in the temple of Jerusalem when he was 12 years old: "Did you not know that I must be in my Father's house?" (*Lk* 2:49).[2] Meditating on this, Mary could better understand the meaning of Jesus' divine sonship and her own motherhood, as she endeavoured to discern in her Son's conduct the traits revealing his likeness to the One he called "my Father".

4.1 Communion of life with Jesus in the house of Nazareth led Mary not only to advance "in her pilgrimage of faith" (*Lumen gentium*, n. 58),[3] but also in hope. This virtue, cultivated and sustained by her memory of the Annunciation and of Simeon's words, embraced the whole span of her earthly life, but was practised especially during the thirty years of silence and hiddeness spent in Nazareth.

---

[1] "*Maria autem conservabat omnia verba haec conferens in corde suo*" (*Lc* 2, 19; cf. 2, 51).

[2] "*Nesciebatis quia in his, quæ Patris mei sunt, oportet me esse?*" (*Lc* 2, 49).

[3] "*In peregrinatione fidei*" (CONCILIUM VATICANUM II, Const. dogm. de Ecclesia, *Lumen gentium*, 58: *AAS* 57 (1965), p. 61).

4.2 At home, the Blessed Virgin experiences hope in its highest form; she knows she will not be disappointed even if she does not know the times or the ways in which God will fulfil his promise. In the darkness of faith and in the absence of extraordinary signs announcing the beginning of her Son's messianic task, she hopes, beyond all evidence, awaiting the fulfilment of God's promise.

4.3 A setting for growth in faith and hope, the house of Nazareth becomes a place of lofty witness to charity. The love that Christ wanted to pour forth in the world is kindled and burns first of all in his Mother's heart: it is precisely in the home that the proclamation of the Gospel of divine love is prepared.

4.4 Looking at Nazareth, contemplating the mystery of the hidden life of Jesus and the Blessed Virgin, we are invited to reflect on the mystery of our life which—Saint Paul recalls—"is hidden with Christ in God" (*Col* 3:3).[1]

4.5 It is often a life that seems humble and obscure in the world's eyes, but which, following Mary's example, can reveal unexpected possibilities of salvation, radiating the love and peace of Christ.

29 January 1997

[1] "*Abscondita est cum Christo in Deo*" (*Col* 3, 3).

44
MARY AT THE WEDDING OF CANA

1.1 In the episode of the wedding at Cana, Saint John presents Mary's first intervention in the public life of Jesus and highlights her co-operation in her Son's mission.

1.2 At the beginning of the account the Evangelist tells us that "the Mother of Jesus was there" (*Jn* 2:1),[1] and, as if to suggest that her presence was the reason for the couple's invitation to Jesus and his disciples (cf. *Redemptoris Mater*, n. 21), he adds "Jesus also was invited to the marriage, with his disciples" (*Jn* 2:2).[2] With these remarks, John seems to indicate that at Cana, as in the fundamental event of the Incarnation, it is Mary who introduces the Saviour.

1.3 The meaning and role of the Blessed Virgin's presence become evident when the wine runs out. As a skilled and wise housewife, she immediately notices and intervenes so that no one's joy is marred and, above all, to help the newly married couple in difficulty.

1.4 Turning to Jesus with the words: "they have no wine" (*Jn* 2:3),[3] Mary expresses her concern to him about this situation, expecting him to solve it. More precisely, according to some exegetes, his Mother is expecting an extraordinary sign, since Jesus had no wine at his disposal.

2.1 The choice made by Mary, who could perhaps have obtained the necessary wine elsewhere, shows the courage of her faith, since until that moment Jesus had worked no miracles, either in Nazareth or in his public life.

2.2 At Cana, the Blessed Virgin once again showed her total availability to God. At the Annunciation she had contributed to the miracle of the virginal conception by believing in Jesus before seeing him; here, her trust in Jesus' as yet unrevealed power causes him to perform his "first sign", the miraculous transformation of water into wine.

2.3 In that way she precedes in faith the disciples who, as John says, would believe after the miracle: Jesus "manifested his glory; and his disciples believed in him" (*Jn* 2:11).[4] Thus, Mary strengthened their faith by obtaining this miraculous sign.

---

[1] "*Erat mater Iesu ibi*" (*Io* 2, 1).
[2] "*Vocatus est autem et Iesus et discipuli eius ad nuptias*" (*Io* 2, 2).
[3] "*Vinum non habent*" (*Io* 2, 3).
[4] "*Manifestavit gloriam suam, et crediderunt in eum discipuli eius*" (*Io* 2, 11).

3.1 Jesus' answer to Mary's words, "O woman, what have you to do with me? My hour has not yet come" (*Jn* 2:4),[1] appears to express a refusal, as if putting his Mother's faith to the test.

3.2 According to one interpretation, from the moment his mission begins Jesus seems to call into question the natural relationship of son to which his mother refers. The sentence, in the local parlance, is meant to stress a distance between the persons, by excluding a communion of life. This distance does not preclude respect and esteem; the term "woman" by which he addresses his Mother is used with a nuance that will recur in the conversations with the Canaanite woman (cf. *Mt* 15:28), the Samaritan woman (cf. *Jn* 4:21), the adulteress (cf. *Jn* 8:10) and Mary Magdalene (cf. *Jn* 20:13), in contexts that show Jesus' positive relationship with his female interlocutors.

3.3 With the expression: "O woman, what have you to do with me?", Jesus intends to put Mary's co-operation on the level of salvation which, by involving her faith and hope, requires her to go beyond her natural role of mother.

4.1 Of much greater import is the reason Jesus gives: "My hour has not yet come" (*Jn* 2:4).

4.2 Some scholars who have studied this sacred text, following Saint Augustine's interpretation, identify this "hour" with the Passion event. For others, instead, it refers to the first miracle in which the prophet of Nazareth's messianic power would be revealed. Yet others hold that the sentence is interrogative and an extension of the question that precedes it: "What have you to do with me? Has my hour not yet come?". Jesus gives Mary to understand that henceforth he no longer depends on her, but must take the initiative for doing his Father's work. Then Mary docilely refrains from insisting with him and instead turns to the servants, telling them to obey him.

4.3 In any case her trust in her Son is rewarded. Jesus, whom she has left totally free to act, works the miracle, recognising his Mother's courage and docility: "Jesus said to them, 'Fill the jars with water'. And they filled them up to the brim" (*Jn* 2:7).[2] Thus their obedience also helps to procure wine in abundance.

4.4 Mary's request: "Do whatever he tells you",[3] keeps its ever timely value for Christians of every age and is destined to renew its marvellous effect in everyone's life. It is an exhortation to trust without hesitation, especially when one does not understand the meaning or benefit of what Christ asks.

---

[1] "*Quid mihi et tibi, mulier? Nondum venit hora mea*" (*Io* 2, 4).
[2] "*Dicit eis Iesus: 'Implete hydrias aqua'. Et impleverunt eas usque ad summum*" (*Io* 2, 7).
[3] "*Quodcumque dixerit vobis, facite*" (*Io* 2, 5).

4.5 As in the account of the Canaanite woman (*Mt* 15:24-26), Jesus' apparent refusal exalts the woman's faith, so that her Son's words, "My hour has not yet come", together with the working of the first miracle, demonstrate the Mother's great faith and the power of her prayer.

4.6 The episode of the wedding at Cana urges us to be courageous in faith and to experience in our lives the truth of the Gospel words: "Ask, and it will be given you" (*Mt* 7:7; *Lk* 11:9).[1]

26 February 1997

[1] "*Petite, et dabitur vobis*" (*Mt* 7, 7; *Lc* 11, 9).

45
AT CANA, MARY LEADS JESUS TO PERFORM HIS FIRST MIRACLE

1.1 Describing Mary's presence in Jesus' public life, the Second Vatican Council recalls her involvement at Cana on the occasion of the first miracle: "At the marriage feast of Cana, moved with pity, she brought about by her intercession the beginning of miracles of Jesus the Messiah (cf. *Jn* 2:1-11)" (*Lumen gentium*, n. 58).[1]

1.2 Following the Evangelist John, the Council points out the Mother's discreet and effective role, when by her words she persuades her Son to perform his "first sign". Although her influence is discreet and maternal, her presence proves decisive.

1.3 The Blessed Virgin's initiative is all the more surprising if one considers the inferior status of women in Jewish society. At Cana, in fact, Jesus does not only recognise the dignity and role of the feminine genius, but by welcoming his Mother's intervention, he gives her the opportunity to participate in his messianic work. The epithet "Woman", with which Jesus addresses Mary (cf. *Jn* 2:4), is not in contrast with his intention. Indeed it has no negative connotations, and Jesus will use it again when he addresses his Mother at the foot of the Cross (cf. *Jn* 19:26). According to some interpretations, this title "Woman" presents Mary as the New Eve, the mother in faith of all believers.

1.4 In the text cited, the Council uses the expression "moved with pity", letting it be understood that Mary was prompted by her merciful heart. Having sensed the eventual disappointment of the newly married couple and guests because of the lack of wine, the Blessed Virgin compassionately suggests to Jesus that he intervene with his messianic power.

1.5 To some, Mary's request may appear excessive, since it subordinates the beginning of the Messiah's miracles to an act of filial devotion. Jesus himself dealt with this difficulty when, by assenting to his mother's request, he shows the Lord's superabundance in responding to human expectations, manifesting also what a mother's love can do.

2.1 The expression "the beginning of his miracles", which the Council has taken from John's text, attracts our attention. The Greek term *arche*, translated as

[1] "*Ad nuptias in Cana Galilææ, misericordia permota, initium signorum Iesu Messiæ intercessione sua induxit* (cf. *Io* 2, 1-11)" (Concilium Vaticanum II, Const. dogm. de Ecclesia, *Lumen gentium*, 58: *AAS* 57 (1965), p. 61).

"beginning", is used by John in the Prologue of his Gospel: "In the *beginning* was the Word" (1:1).[1] This significant coincidence suggests a parallel between the very origins of Christ's glory in eternity and the first manifestation of this same glory in his earthly mission.

2.2 By emphasising Mary's initiative in the first miracle and then recalling her presence on Calvary at the foot of the Cross, the Evangelist helps us understand how Mary's co-operation is extended to the whole of Christ's work. The Blessed Virgin's request is placed within the divine plan of salvation.

2.3 In the first "sign" performed by Jesus, the Fathers of the Church glimpsed an important symbolic dimension, seeing the transformation of the water into wine as the announcement of the passage from the Old to the New Covenant. At Cana it is precisely the water in the jars, destined for the purification of the Jews and the fulfilment of the legal prescriptions (cf. *Mk* 7:1-15), which becomes the new wine of the wedding feast, a symbol of the definitive union between God and humanity.

3.1 The context of a wedding banquet, chosen by Jesus for his first miracle, refers to the marriage symbolism used frequently in the Old Testament to indicate the Covenant between God and his People (cf. *Hos* 2:21; *Jer* 2:1-8; *Ps* 44; etc.), and in the New Testament to signify Christ's union with the Church (cf. *Jn* 3:28-30; *Eph* 5:25-32; *Rv* 21:1-2, etc.).

3.2 Jesus' presence at Cana is also a sign of God's saving plan for marriage. In this perspective, the lack of wine can be interpreted as an allusion to the lack of love that unfortunately often threatens marital unions. Mary asks Jesus to intervene on behalf of all married couples, who can only be freed from the dangers of infidelity, misunderstanding and division by a love which is based on God. The grace of the sacrament offers the couple this superior strength of love, which can reinforce their commitment to fidelity even in difficult circumstances.

3.3 According to the interpretation of Christian authors, the miracle at Cana also has a deep Eucharistic meaning. Performing this miracle near the time of the Jewish feast Passover (cf. *Jn* 2:13), Jesus, as he did in multiplying the loaves (cf. *Jn* 6:4), shows his intention to prepare the true paschal banquet, the Eucharist. His desire at the wedding in Cana seems to be emphasised further by the presence of wine, which alludes to the blood of the New Covenant, and by the context of a banquet.

[1] "*In principio erat Verbum*" (*Io* 1, 1).

3.4 In this way, after being the reason for Jesus' presence at the celebration, Mary obtains the miracle of the new wine which prefigures the Eucharist, the supreme sign of the presence of her risen Son among the disciples.

4.1 At the end of the account of Jesus' first miracle, made possible by the firm faith of the Lord's Mother in her divine Son, the Evangelist John concludes: "and his disciples believed in him" (2:11).[1] At Cana, Mary begins the Church's journey of faith, preceding the disciples and directing the servants' attention to Christ.

4.2 Her persevering intercession likewise encourages those who at times face the experience of "God's silence". They are asked to hope beyond all hope, always trusting in the Lord's goodness.

5 March 1997

[1] "*Et crediderunt in eum discipuli eius*" (*Io* 2, 11).

46
MARY'S PARTICIPATION IN THE PUBLIC LIFE OF THE SON

And a crowd was sitting about him; and they said to him, "Your mother and your brethren are outside, asking for you." And he replied, "Who are my mother and my brethren?" And looking around on those who sat about him, he said, "Here are my mother and my brethren! Whoever does the will of God is my brother, and sister, and mother" (*Mk* 3:32-35).[1]

1.1 After recalling Mary's intervention at the wedding feast of Cana, the Second Vatican Council emphasises her participation in the public life of Jesus: "In the course of her Son's preaching she received the words whereby, in extolling a kingdom beyond the concerns and ties of flesh and blood, he declared blessed those who heard and kept the word of God (cf. *Mk* 3:35 par.; *Lk* 11: 27-28) as she was faithfully doing (cf. *Lk* 2:19, 51)" (*Lumen gentium*, n. 58).[2]

1.2 The beginning of Jesus' mission also meant separation from his Mother, who did not always follow her son in his travels on the roads of Palestine. Jesus deliberately chose separation from his Mother and from family affection, as can be inferred from the conditions he gave his disciples for following him and for dedicating themselves to proclaiming God's kingdom.

1.3 Nevertheless, Mary sometimes heard her Son's preaching. We can assume that she was present in the synagogue of Nazareth when Jesus, after reading Isaiah's prophecy, commented on the text and applied it to himself (cf. *Lk* 4:18-30). How much she must have suffered on that occasion, after sharing the general amazement at "the gracious words which proceeded out of his mouth" (*Lk* 4:22),[3] as she observed the harsh hostility of her fellow citizens who drove Jesus from the synagogue and even tried to kill him! The drama of that moment is evident in the words of the Evangelist Luke:

"They rose up and put him out of the city, and led him to the brow of the hill on which their city was built, that they might throw him down headlong. But passing through the midst of them he went away" (4:29-30).[4]

---

[1] "*Et sedebat circa eum turba, et dicunt ei: « Ecce mater tua et fratres tui et sorores tuæ foris quærunt te ». Et respondens eis ait: « Quæ est mater mea et fratres mei?* ". *Et circumspiciens eos, qui in circuitu eius sedebant, ait: « Ecce mater mea et fratres mei. Qui enim fecerit voluntatem Dei, hic frater meus et soror mea et mater est* »" (*Mc* 3, 32-35).

[2] "*In decursu prædicationis Eius suscepit verba, quibus Filius, Regnum ultra rationes et vincula carnis et sanguinis extollens, audientes et custodientes verbum Dei, sicut ipsa fideliter faciebat* (cf. Lc 2, 19 et 51), *beatos proclamavit* (cf. *Mc* 3, 35; *Lc* 11, 27-28)" (Concilium Vaticanum II, Const. dogm. de Ecclesia, *Lumen gentium*, 58: *AAS* 57 (1965), p. 61).

[3] "*In verbis gratiæ, quæ procedebant de ore ipsius*" (*Lc* 4, 22).

[4] "*Surrexerunt et eiecerunt illum extra civitatem et duxerunt illum usque ad supercilium montis, supra quem civitas illorum erat ædificata, ut præcipitarent eum. Ipse autem transiens per medium illorum ibat*" (*Lc* 4, 29-30).

1.4 Realising after this event that there would be other trials, Mary confirmed and deepened her total obedience to the Father's will, offering him her suffering as a mother and her loneliness.

2.1 According to the Gospels, Mary had the opportunity to hear her Son on other occasions as well. First at Capernaum, where Jesus went after the wedding feast of Cana, "with his mother and his brethren and his disciples" (*Jn* 2:12).[1] For the Passover, moreover, she was probably able to follow him to the temple in Jerusalem, which Jesus called his Father's house and for which he was consumed with zeal (cf. *Jn* 2:16-17). Finding herself later among the crowd and not being able to approach Jesus, she hears him replying to those who had told him that she and their relatives had arrived: "My mother and my brethren are those who hear the word of God and do it" (*Lk* 8:21).[2]

2.2 With these words, Christ, although relativising family ties, is addressing great praise to his Mother by affirming a far loftier bond with her. Indeed, in listening to her Son, Mary accepts all his words and faithfully puts them into practice.

2.3 We can imagine that, although she did not follow Jesus on his missionary journey, she was informed of her Son's apostolic activities, lovingly and anxiously receiving news of his preaching from the lips of those who had met him.

2.4 Separation did not mean distance of heart, nor did it prevent the Mother from spiritually following her Son, from keeping and meditating on his teaching as she had done during Jesus' hidden life in Nazareth. Her faith in fact enabled her to grasp the meaning of Jesus' words before and better than his disciples, who often did not understand his teaching, especially the references to his future Passion (cf. *Mt* 16:21-23; *Mk* 9:32; *Lk* 9:45).

3.1 Following the events in her Son's life, Mary shared in his drama of experiencing rejection from some of the chosen people. This rejection first appeared during his visit to Nazareth and became more and more obvious in the words and attitudes of the leaders of the people.

3.2 In this way the Blessed Virgin would often have come to know the criticism, insults and threats directed at Jesus. In Nazareth too she would have frequently been troubled by the disbelief of relatives and acquaintances who would try to use Jesus (cf. *Jn* 7:2-5) or to stop his mission (*Mk* 3:21).

---

[1] "*Mater eius et fratres eius et discipuli eius*" (*Io* 2, 12).
[2] "*Mater mea et fratres mei hi sunt, qui verbum Dei audiunt et faciunt*" (*Lc* 8, 21).

3.3 Through this suffering borne with great dignity and hiddenness, Mary shares the journey of her Son "to Jerusalem" (*Lk* 9:51) and, more and more closely united with him in faith, hope and love, she co-operates in salvation.

4 The Blessed Virgin thus becomes a model for those who accept Christ's words.

Believing in the divine message since the Annunciation and fully supporting the Person of the Son, she teaches us to listen to the Saviour with trust, to discover in him the divine Word who transforms and renews our life. Her experience also encourages us to accept the trials and suffering that come from fidelity to Christ, keeping our gaze fixed on the happiness Jesus promised those who listen to him and keep his word.

12 March 1997

47
AT THE CROSS, MARY IS A PARTICIPANT IN THE DRAMA OF REDEMPTION

So they took Jesus, and he went out, bearing his own cross, to the place called the place of a skull, which is called in Hebrew Golgotha. There they crucified him, and with him two others, one on either side, and Jesus between them. Pilate also wrote a title and put it on the cross; it read, "Jesus of Nazareth, the King of the Jews." Many of the Jews read this title, for the place where Jesus was crucified was near the city; and it was written in Hebrew, in Latin, and in Greek. The chief priests of the Jews then said to Pilate, "Do not write, 'The King of the Jews,' but, 'This man said, I am King of the Jews.'" Pilate answered, "What I have written I have written."
When the soldiers had crucified Jesus they took his garments and made four parts, one for each soldier; also his tunic. But the tunic was without seam, woven from top to bottom; so they said to one another, "Let us not tear it, but cast lots for it to see whose it shall be." This was to fulfil the Scripture, "They parted my garments among them, and for my clothing they cast lots." So the soldiers did this.
But standing by the cross of Jesus were his mother, and his mother's sister, Mary the wife of Clopas, and Mary Magdalene. When Jesus saw his mother, and the disciple whom he loved standing near, he said to his mother, "Woman, behold, your son!" Then he said to the disciple, "Behold, your mother!" And from that hour the disciple took her to his own home. After this Jesus, knowing that all was now finished, said (to fulfil the scripture), "I thirst." But standing by the cross of Jesus were his mother, and his mother's sister, Mary the wife of Clopas, and Mary Magdalene (*Jn* 19:17-28, 25).[1]

1.1 *Regína cæli, lætáre, allelúia!*

So the Church sings in this Easter season, inviting the faithful to join in the spiritual joy of Mary, Mother of the Redeemer. The Blessed Virgin's gladness at Christ's Resurrection is even greater if one considers her intimate participation in Jesus' entire life.

[1] *"Et baiulans sibi crucem exivit in eum, qui dicitur Calvariæ locum, quod Hebraice dicitur Golgotha, ubi eum crucifixerunt et cum eo alios duos hinc et hinc, medium autem Iesum. Scripsit autem et titulum Pilatus et posuit super crucem; erat autem scriptum: « Iesus Nazarenus Rex Iudaeorum". Hunc ergo titulum multi legerunt Iudæorum, quia prope civitatem erat locus, ubi crucifixus est Iesus; et erat scriptum Hebraice, Latine, Græce. Dicebant ergo Pilato pontifices Iudæorum: « Noli scribere: Rex Iudæorum, sed: Ipse dixit: "Rex sum Iudæorum" ». Respondit Pilatus: « Quod scripsi, scripsi! ».*
Milites ergo cum crucifixissent Iesum, acceperunt vestimenta eius et fecerunt quattuor partes, unicuique militi partem, et tunicam. Erat autem tunica inconsutilis, desuper contexta per totum. Dixerunt ergo ad invicem: « Non scindamus eam, sed sortiamur de illa, cuius sit », ut Scriptura impleatur dicens: « Partiti sunt vestimenta mea sibi et in vestem meam miserunt sortem ». Et milites quidem hæc fecerunt. Stabant autem iuxta crucem Iesu mater eius et soror matris eius, Maria Cleopæ, et Maria Magdalene. Cum vidisset ergo Iesus matrem et discipulum stantem, quem diligebat, dicit matri: « Mulier, ecce filius tuus ». Deinde dicit discipulo: « Ecce mater tua ». Et ex illa hora accepit eam discipulus in sua. Post hoc sciens Iesus quia iam omnia consummata sunt, ut consummaretur Scriptura, dicit: « Sitio ». Stabant autem iuxta crucem Iesu mater eius et soror matris eius, Maria Cleopæ, et Maria Magdalene" (*Io* 19, 17-28. 25).

1.2 In accepting with complete availability the words of the Angel Gabriel, who announced to her that she would become the Mother of the Messiah, Mary began her participation in the drama of Redemption. Her involvement in her Son's sacrifice, revealed by Simeon during the presentation in the Temple, continues not only in the episode of the losing and finding of the twelve-year-old Jesus, but also throughout his public life.

1.3 However, the Blessed Virgin's association with Christ's mission reaches its culmination in Jerusalem, at the time of the Redeemer's Passion and Death. As the fourth Gospel testifies, she was in the Holy City at the time, probably for the celebration of the Jewish feast of Passover.

2.1 The Council stresses the profound dimension of the Blessed Virgin's presence on Calvary, recalling that she "faithfully persevered in her union with her Son unto the Cross" (*Lumen gentium*, n. 58),[1] and points out that this union "in the work of salvation is made manifest from the time of Christ's virginal conception up to his death" (*ibid.*, n. 57).[2]

2.2 With our gaze illumined by the radiance of the Resurrection, we pause to reflect on the Mother's involvement in her Son's redeeming Passion, which was completed by her sharing in his suffering. Let us return again, but now in the perspective of the Resurrection, to the foot of the Cross where the Mother endured "with her only-begotten Son the intensity of his suffering, associated herself with his sacrifice in her mother's heart, and lovingly consented to the immolation of this victim which was born of her" (*ibid.*, n. 58).[3]

2.3 With these words, the Council reminds us of "Mary's compassion"; in her heart reverberates all that Jesus suffers in body and soul, emphasising her willingness to share in her Son's redeeming sacrifice and to join her own maternal suffering to his priestly offering.

2.4 The Council text also stresses that her consent to Jesus' immolation is not passive acceptance but a genuine act of love, by which she offers her Son as a "victim" of expiation for the sins of all humanity.

2.5 Lastly, *Lumen gentium* relates the Blessed Virgin to Christ, who has the lead role in Redemption, making it clear that in associating herself "with his sacrifice" she remains subordinate to her divine Son.

---

[1] "*Suamque unionem cum Filio fideliter sustinuit usque ad crucem*" (Concilium Vaticanum II, Const. dogm. de Ecclesia, *Lumen gentium*, 58: *AAS* 57 (1965), p. 61).

[2] "*In opere salutari coniunctio a tempore virginalis conceptionis Christi ad Eius usque mortem manifestatur*" (Ibid., 57: *AAS* 57 (1965), p. 61).

[3] "*Cum Unigenito suo condoluit et sacrificio Eius se materno animo sociavit, victimæ de se genitæ immolationi amanter consentiens*" (Ibid., 58: *AAS* 57 (1965), p. 61).

3.1 In the fourth Gospel, Saint John says that “standing by the Cross of Jesus were his mother, and his mother’s sister, Mary the wife of Clopas, and Mary Magdalene” (19:25).[1] By using the verb “to stand”, which literally means “to be on one’s feet”, “to stand erect”, perhaps the Evangelist intends to present the dignity and strength shown in their sorrow by Mary and the other women.

3.2 The Blessed Virgin’s “standing erect” at the foot of the Cross recalls her unfailing constancy and extraordinary courage in facing suffering. In the tragic events of Calvary, Mary is sustained by faith, strengthened during the events of her life and especially during Jesus’ public life. The Council recalls that “the Blessed Virgin advanced in her pilgrimage of faith and faithfully persevered in her union with her Son unto the Cross” (*Lumen gentium*, n. 58).[2]

3.3 Sharing his deepest feelings, she counters the arrogant insults addressed to the crucified Messiah with forbearance and pardon, associating herself with his prayer to the Father: “Forgive them, for they know not what they do” (*Lk* 23:34).[3] By sharing in the feeling of abandonment to the Father’s will expressed in Jesus’ last words on the Cross: “Father, into your hands I commend my spirit!” (*ibid.*, 23:46),[4] she thus offers, as the Council notes, loving consent “to the immolation of this victim which was born of her” (*Lumen gentium*, n. 58).[5]

4.1 Mary’s supreme “yes” is radiant with trusting hope in the mysterious future, begun with the death of her crucified Son. The words in which Jesus taught the disciples on his way to Jerusalem “that the Son of man must suffer many things, and be rejected by the elders and the chief priests and the scribes, and be killed, and after three days rise again” re-echo in her heart at the dramatic hour of Calvary, awakening expectation of and yearning for the Resurrection.

4.2 Mary’s hope at the foot of the Cross contains a light stronger than the darkness that reigns in many hearts: in the presence of the redeeming Sacrifice, the hope of the Church and of humanity is born in Mary.

2 April 1997

---

[1] “*Stabant autem iuxta crucem Iesu mater eius et soror matris eius, Maria Cleopæ, et Maria Magdalene*” (*Io* 19, 25).
[2] “*B. Virgo in peregrinatione fidei processit, suamque unionem cum Filio fideliter sustinuit usque ad crucem*” (Concilium Vaticanum II, Const. dogm. de Ecclesia, *Lumen gentium*, 58: *AAS* 57 (1965), p. 61).
[3] “*Dimitte illis, non enim sciunt quid faciunt*” (*Lc* 23, 34).
[4] “*Pater, in manus tuas commendo spiritum meum*” (*Lc* 23, 46).
[5] “*Victimæ de se genitæ immolationi amanter consentiens*” (Concilium Vaticanum II, Const. dogm. de Ecclesia, *Lumen gentium*, 58: *AAS* 57 (1965), p. 61).

48
MARY'S UNIQUE COOPERATION WITH REDEMPTION

But standing by the cross of Jesus were his mother, and his mother's sister, Mary the wife of Clopas, and Mary Magdalene. When Jesus saw his mother, and the disciple whom he loved standing near, he said to his mother, "Woman, behold, your son" (*Jn* 19:25-26).[1]

1.1 Down the centuries the Church has reflected on Mary's co-operation in the work of salvation, deepening the analysis of her association with Christ's redemptive sacrifice. Saint Augustine already gave the Blessed Virgin the title "co-operator" in the Redemption (cf. *De Sancta Virginitate*, 6; *PL* 40, 399), a title which emphasises Mary's joint but subordinate action with Christ the Redeemer.

1.2 Reflection has developed along these lines, particularly since the fifteenth century.

Some feared there might be a desire to put Mary on the same level as Christ. Actually the Church's teaching makes a clear distinction between the Mother and the Son in the work of salvation, explaining the Blessed Virgin's subordination, as co-operator, to the one Redeemer.

1.3 Moreover, when the Apostle Paul says: "For we are God's fellow workers" (*1 Cor* 3:9),[2] he maintains the real possibility for man to co-operate with God. The collaboration of believers, which obviously excludes any equality with him, is expressed in the proclamation of the Gospel and in their personal contribution to its taking root in human hearts.

2.1 However, applied to Mary, the term "co-operator" acquires a specific meaning.

The collaboration of Christians in salvation takes place after the Calvary event, whose fruits they endeavour to spread by prayer and sacrifice. Mary, instead, co-operated during the event itself and in the role of mother; thus her co-operation embraces the whole of Christ's saving work. She alone was associated in this way with the redemptive sacrifice that merited the salvation of all mankind. In union with Christ and in submission to him, she collaborated in obtaining the grace of salvation for all humanity.

---

[1] "*Stabant autem iuxta crucem Iesu mater eius et soror matris eius, Maria Cleopæ, et Maria Magdalene. Cum vidisset ergo Iesus matrem et discipulum stantem, quem diligebat, dicit matri: « Mulier, ecce filius tuus »*" (*Io* 19, 25-26).

[2] "*Dei enim sumus adiutores*" (*1 Cor* 3, 9).

2.2 The Blessed Virgin's role as co-operator has its source in her divine motherhood.

By giving birth to the One who was destined to achieve man's redemption, by nourishing him, presenting him in the temple and suffering with him as he died on the Cross, "in a wholly singular way she co-operated… in the work of the Saviour" (*Lumen gentium*, n. 61).[1] Although God's call to co-operate in the work of salvation concerns every human being, the participation of the Saviour's Mother in humanity's Redemption is a unique and unrepeatable fact.

2.3 Despite the uniqueness of her condition, Mary is also the recipient of salvation.

She is the first to be saved, redeemed by Christ "in the most sublime way" in her Immaculate Conception (cf. Bull *Ineffabilis Deus*, in Pius IX, *Acta*, 1, 605) and filled with the grace of the Holy Spirit.

3.1 This assertion now leads to the question: what is the meaning of Mary's unique co-operation in the plan of salvation? It should be sought in God's particular intention for the Mother of the Redemeer, whom on two solemn occasions, that is, at Cana and beneath the Cross, Jesus addresses as "Woman" (cf. *Jn* 2, 4; 19, 26). Mary is associated as a woman in the work of salvation. Having created man "male and female" (cf. *Gn* 1:27), the Lord also wants to place the New Eve beside the New Adam in the Redemption. Our first parents had chosen the way of sin as a couple; a new pair, the Son of God with his Mother's co-operation, would re-establish the human race in its original dignity.

3.2 Mary, the New Eve, thus becomes a perfect icon of the Church. In the divine plan, at the foot of the Cross, she represents redeemed humanity which, in need of salvation, is enabled to make a contribution to the unfolding of the saving work.

4.1 The Council had this doctrine in mind and made it its own, stressing the Blessed Virgin's contribution not only to the Redeemer's birth, but also to the life of his Mystical Body down the ages until the "eschaton": in the Church Mary "has co-operated" (cf. *Lumen gentium*, n. 63) and "co-operates" (cf. *ibid.*, n. 53) in the work of salvation. In describing the mystery of the

[1] "*Operi Salvatoris singulari prorsus modo cooperata est*" (Concilium Vaticanum II, Const. dogm. de Ecclesia, *Lumen gentium*, 61: *AAS* 57 (1965), p. 63).

Annunciation, the Council states that the Virgin of Nazareth, "committing herself wholeheartedly and impeded by no sin to God's saving will, devoted herself totally, as a handmaid of the Lord, to the person and work of her Son, under and with him, serving the mystery of Redemption by the grace of Almighty God" (*ibid.*, n. 56).[1]

4.2 The Second Vatican Council moreover presents Mary not only as "Mother of the divine Redeemer", but also "in a singular way [as] the generous associate", who "co-operated by her obedience, faith, hope and burning charity in the work of the Saviour". The Council also recalls that the sublime fruit of this cooperation is her universal motherhood: "For this reason she is a mother to us in the order of grace" (*ibid.*, n. 61).[2]

4.3 We can therefore turn to the Blessed Virgin, trustfully imploring her aid in the awareness of the singular role entrusted to her by God, the role of co-operator in the Redemption, which she exercised throughout her life and in a special way at the foot of the Cross.

9 April 1997

[1] "*Ac salvificam voluntatem Dei, pleno corde et nullo retardata peccato, complectens, semetipsam ut Domini ancillam personæ et operi Filii sui totaliter devovit, sub Ipso et cum Ipso, omnipotentis Dei gratia, mysterio redemptionis inserviens*" (Concilium Vaticanum II, Const. dogm. de Ecclesia, *Lumen gentium*, 56: *AAS* 57 (1965), p. 60).

[2] "*Quam ob causam mater nobis in ordine gratiæ exstitit*" (Ibid., 61: *AAS* 57 (1965), p. 63).

49
WOMAN, BEHOLD YOUR SON!

1.1 After recalling the presence of Mary and the other women at the Lord's cross, Saint John relates: "When Jesus saw his mother, and the disciple whom he loved standing near, he said to his mother, 'Woman, behold, your son!'. Then he said to the disciple, 'Behold, your mother!'" (*Jn* 19:26-27).[1]

1.2 These particularly moving words are a "revelation scene": they reveal the deep sentiments of the dying Christ and contain a great wealth of meaning for Christian faith and spirituality. At the end of his earthly life, as he addressed his Mother and the disciple he loved, the crucified Messiah establishes a new relationship of love between Mary and Christians.

1.3 Interpreted at times as no more than an expression of Jesus' filial piety towards his Mother whom he entrusts for the future to his beloved disciple, these words go far beyond the contingent need to solve a family problem. In fact, attentive consideration of the text, confirmed by the interpretation of many Fathers and by common ecclesial opinion, presents us, in Jesus' twofold entrustment, with one of the most important events for understanding the Virgin's role in the economy of salvation.

1.4 The words of the dying Jesus actually show that his first intention was not to entrust his Mother to John, but to entrust the disciple to Mary and to give her a new maternal role. Moreover, the epithet "woman", also used by Jesus at the wedding in Cana to lead Mary to a new dimension of her existence as Mother, shows how the Saviour's words are not the fruit of a simple sentiment of filial affection but are meant to be put at a higher level.

2.1 Although Jesus' death causes Mary deep sorrow, it does not in itself change her normal way of life: in fact, in departing from Nazareth to start his public life, Jesus had already left his Mother alone. Moreover, the presence at the Cross of her relative, Mary of Clopas, allows us to suppose that the Blessed Virgin was on good terms with her family and relatives, by whom she could have been welcomed after her Son's death.

2.2 Instead, Jesus' words acquire their most authentic meaning in the context of his saving mission. Spoken at the moment of the redemptive sacrifice, they draw their loftiest value precisely from this sublime circumstance. In fact, after Jesus' statements to his Mother, the Evangelist adds a significant clause: "Jesus, knowing that all was now finished..." (*Jn* 19:28),[2] as if he wished to

[1] "*Cum vidisset ergo Iesus matrem et discipulum stantem, quem diligebat, dicit matri: 'Mulier, ecce filius tuus'. Deinde dicit discipulo: 'Ecce mater tua'. Et ex illa hora accepit eam discipulus in sua*" (*Io* 19, 26-27).

[2] "*Sciens Iesus quia iam omnia consummata sunt*" (*Io* 19, 28).

stress that he had brought his sacrifice to completion by entrusting his Mother to John, and in him to all men, whose Mother she becomes in the work of salvation.

3.1 The reality brought about by Jesus' words, that is, Mary's new motherhood in relation to the disciple, is a further sign of the great love that led Jesus to offer his life for all people. On Calvary this love is shown in the gift of a mother, his mother, who thus becomes our mother too.

3.2 We must remember that, according to tradition, it is John whom the Blessed Virgin in fact recognised as her son; but this privilege has been interpreted by Christians from the beginning as the sign of a spiritual generation in relation to all humanity.

3.3 The universal motherhood of Mary, the "Woman" of the wedding at Cana and of Calvary, recalls Eve, "mother of all living" (*Gn* 3:20).[1] However, while the latter helped to bring sin into the world, the new Eve, Mary, co-operates in the saving event of Redemption. Thus in the Blessed Virgin the figure of "woman" is rehabilitated and her motherhood takes up the task of spreading the new life in Christ among men.

3.4 In view of this mission, the Mother is asked to make the acutely painful sacrifice of accepting her only Son's death. Jesus' words: "Woman, behold your son" enable Mary to sense the new maternal relationship which was to extend and broaden the preceding one. Her "yes" to this plan is therefore an assent to Christ's sacrifice, which she generously accepts by complying with the divine will. Even if in God's plan Mary's motherhood was destined from the start to extend to all humanity, only on Calvary, by virtue of Christ's sacrifice, is its universal dimension revealed.

3.5 Jesus' words, "Behold, your son", effect what they express, making Mary the mother of John and of all the disciples destined to receive the gift of divine grace.

4.1 On the Cross Jesus did not proclaim Mary's universal motherhood formally, but established a concrete maternal relationship between her and the beloved disciple. In the Lord's choice we can see his concern that this motherhood should not be interpreted in a vague way, but should point to Mary's intense, personal relationship with individual Christians.

4.2 May each one of us, precisely through the concrete reality of Mary's universal motherhood, fully acknowledge her as our own Mother, and trustingly commend ourselves to her maternal love.

23 April 1997

[1] "*Mater esset cunctorum viventium*" (*Gen* 3, 20).

50
BEHOLD, YOUR MOTHER

But standing by the cross of Jesus were his mother, and his mother's sister, Mary the wife of Clopas, and Mary Magdalene. When Jesus saw his mother, and the disciple whom he loved standing near, he said to his mother, "Woman, behold, your son!" Then he said to the disciple, "Behold, your mother!" And from that hour the disciple took her to his own home (*Jn* 19:25-27).[1]

1.1 After entrusting John to Mary with the words "Woman, behold your son!", Jesus, from the Cross, turns to his beloved disciple, saying to him, "Behold, your mother!" (*Jn* 19:26-27).[2] With these words, he reveals to Mary the height of her motherhood: as mother of the Saviour, she is also the mother of the redeemed, of all the members of the Mystical Body of her Son.

1.2 In silence the Virgin accepts the elevation to this highest degree of her motherhood of grace, having already given a response of faith with her "yes" at the Annunciation.

1.3 Jesus not only urges John to care for Mary with special love, but he entrusts her to him so that he may recognise her as his own mother.

1.4 During the Last Supper, "the disciple whom Jesus loved" listened to the Master's commandment: "Love one another as I have loved you" (*Jn* 15:12)[3] and, leaning his head against the Lord's breast, he received from him a unique sign of love. Such experiences prepared him better to perceive in Jesus' words an invitation to accept her who had been given him as mother and to love her as Jesus did with filial affection.

1.5 May all discover in Jesus' words: "Behold, your mother!", the invitation to accept Mary as mother, responding to her motherly love as true children.

2.1 In the light of this entrustment to his beloved disciple, one can understand the authentic meaning of Marian devotion in the ecclesial community. In fact, it places Christians in Jesus' filial relationship to his mother, putting them in a condition to grow in intimacy with both of them.

---

[1] "*Stabant autem iuxta crucem Iesu mater eius et soror matris eius, Maria Cleopæ, et Maria Magdalene. Cum vidisset ergo Iesus matrem et discipulum stantem, quem diligebat, dicit matri: « Mulier, ecce filius tuus ». Deinde dicit discipulo: « Ecce mater tua ». Et ex illa hora accepit eam discipulus in sua*" (*Io* 19, 25-27).

[2] "*Mulier, ecce filius tuus*"..." *Ecce mater tua*" (*Io* 19, 26-27).

[3] "*Diligatis invicem, sicut dilexi vos*" (*Io* 15, 12).

2.2 The Church's devotion to the Virgin is not only the fruit of a spontaneous response to the exceptional value of her person and the importance of her role in the work of salvation, but is based on Christ's will.

2.3 The words "Behold, your mother!", express Jesus' intention to inspire in his disciples an attitude of love for and trust in Mary, leading them to recognise her as their mother, the mother of every believer.

2.4 At the school of the Virgin, the disciples learn to know the Lord deeply, as John did, and to have an intimate and lasting relationship of love with him. They also discover the joy of entrusting themselves to the Mother's maternal love, living like affectionate and docile children.

2.5 The history of Christian piety teaches that Mary is the way which leads to Christ and that filial devotion to her takes nothing from intimacy with Jesus; indeed, it increases it and leads to the highest levels of perfection.

2.6 The countless Marian shrines throughout the world testify to the marvels wrought by grace through the intercession of Mary, Mother of the Lord and our Mother.

2.7 Turning to her, drawn by her tenderness, the men and women of our time also meet Jesus, Saviour and Lord of their lives.

2.8 Above all, the poor, tried in heart, in their affections and in their material need, find refuge and peace in the Mother of God, and discover that for all people true riches consist in the grace of conversion and of following Christ.

3.1 According to the original Greek, the Gospel text continues: "From that hour the disciple took her among his possessions" (*Jn* 19:27),[1] thus stressing John's ready and generous adherence to Jesus' words and informing us about his behaviour for the whole of his life as the faithful guardian and docile son of the Virgin.

3.2 The hour of acceptance is that of the fulfilment of the work of salvation. Mary's spiritual motherhood and the first manifestation of the new link between her and the Lord's disciples begins precisely in this context.

3.3 John took the Mother "among his possessions". These rather general words seem to highlight his initiative, full of respect and love, not only in taking Mary to his house but also in living his spiritual life in communion with her.

[1] εἶτα λέγει τῷ μαθητῇ: ἴδε ἡ μήτηρ σου. καὶ ἀπ' ἐκείνης τῆς ὥρας ἔλαβεν ὁ μαθητὴς αὐτὴν εἰς τὰ ἴδια; "*Et ex illa hora accepit eam discipulus in sua*" (*Io* 19, 27); *RSV*-2CE: "And from that hour the disciple took her to his own home" (*Jn* 19:27).

3.4 In fact, a literal translation of the Greek expression "among his possessions" does not so much refer to material possessions since John—as Saint Augustine observes (*In Ioan. Evang. tract.* 119, 3)—"possessed nothing of his own",[1] but rather to the spiritual goods or gifts received from Christ: grace (*Jn* 1:16), the Word (*Jn* 12:48; 17:8), the spirit (*Jn* 7:39; 14:17), the Eucharist (*Jn* 6:32-58)... Among these gifts which come to him from the fact that he is loved by Jesus, the disciple accepts Mary as his mother, establishing a profound communion of life with her (cf. *Redemptoris Mater*, n. 45, note 130).

3.5 May every Christian, after the beloved disciple's example, "take Mary into his house" and make room for her in his own daily life, recognising her providential role in the journey of salvation.

7 May 1997

[1] "*Suscepit ergo eam in sua, non praedia, quae nulla propria possidebat*" (Sanctus Augustinus, *In evangelium Ioannis tractatus*, tract. CXIX, 3: *PL* 35, 1951).

51
MARY AND THE RESURRECTION OF CHRIST

For I delivered to you as of first importance what I also received, that Christ died for our sins in accordance with the Scriptures, that he was buried, that he was raised on the third day in accordance with the Scriptures, and that he appeared to Cephas, then to the twelve. Then he appeared to more than five hundred brethren at one time (*1 Cor* 15:3-6a).[1]

1.1 After Jesus had been laid in the tomb, Mary "alone remains to keep alive the flame of faith, preparing to receive the joyful and astonishing announcement of the Resurrection".[2] The expectation felt on Holy Saturday is one of the loftiest moments of faith for the Mother of the Lord: in the darkness that envelops the world, she entrusts herself fully to the God of life, and thinking back to the words of her Son, she hopes in the fulfilment of the divine promises.

1.2 The Gospels mention various appearances of the risen Christ, but not a meeting between Jesus and his Mother. This silence must not lead to the conclusion that after the Resurrection Christ did not appear to Mary; rather it invites us to seek the reasons why the Evangelists made such a choice.

1.3 On the supposition of an "omission", this silence could be attributed to the fact that what is necessary for our saving knowledge was entrusted to the word of those "chosen by God as witnesses" (*Acts* 10:41),[3] that is, the Apostles, who gave their testimony of the Lord Jesus' Resurrection "with great power" (cf. *Acts* 4:33).[4] Before appearing to them, the Risen One had appeared to several faithful women because of their ecclesial function: "Go and tell my brethren to go to Galilee, and there they will see me" (*Mt* 28:10).[5]

1.4 If the authors of the New Testament do not speak of the Mother's encounter with her risen Son, this can perhaps be attributed to the fact that such a witness would have been considered too biased by those who denied the Lord's Resurrection, and therefore not worthy of belief.

---

[1] "*Tradidi enim vobis in primis, quod et accepi, quoniam Christus mortuus est pro peccatis nostris secundum Scripturas et quia sepultus est et quia suscitatus est tertia die secundum Scripturas et quia visus est Cephæ et post hæc Duodecim; deinde visus est plus quam quingentis fratribus simul* (*1 Cor* 15, 3-6a).

[2] Saint John Paul II, *Address at the General Audience*, 3 April 1996; *L'Osservatore Romano*, English edition, 10 April 1996, p. 7.

[3] "*Testibus præordinatis a Deo*" (*Act* 10, 41).

[4] "*Virtute magna*" (*Act* 4, 33).

[5] "*Ite, nuntiate fratribus meis, ut eant in Galilæam et ibi me videbunt*" (*Mt* 28, 10).

2.1 Furthermore, the Gospels report a small number of appearances by the risen Jesus and certainly not a complete summary of all that happened during the forty days after Easter. Saint Paul recalls that he appeared "to more than five hundred brethren at one time" (*1 Cor* 15:6).[1] How do we explain the fact that an exceptional event known to so many is not mentioned by the Evangelists? It is an obvious sign that other appearances of the Risen One were not recorded, although they were among the well-known events that occurred.

2.2 How could the Blessed Virgin, present in the first community of disciples (cf. *Acts* 1:14), be excluded from those who met her divine Son after he had risen from the dead?

3.1 Indeed, it is legitimate to think that the Mother was probably the first person to whom the risen Jesus appeared. Could not Mary's absence from the group of women who went to the tomb at dawn (cf. *Mk* 16:1; *Mt* 28:1) indicate that she had already met Jesus? This inference would also be confirmed by the fact that the first witnesses of the Resurrection, by Jesus' will, were the women who had remained faithful at the foot of the Cross and therefore were more steadfast in faith.

3.2 Indeed, the Risen One entrusts to one of them, Mary Magdalene, the message to be passed on to the Apostles (cf. *Jn* 20:17-18). Perhaps this fact too allows us to think that Jesus showed himself first to his Mother, who had been the most faithful and had kept her faith intact when put to the test.

3.3 Lastly, the unique and special character of the Blessed Virgin's presence at Calvary and her perfect union with the Son in his suffering on the Cross seem to postulate a very particular sharing on her part in the mystery of the Resurrection.

3.4 A fifth century author, Sedulius,[2] maintains that in the splendour of his risen life Christ first showed himself to his mother. In fact, she, who at the Annunciation was the way he entered the world, was called to spread the marvellous news of the Resurrection in order to become the herald of his glorious coming. Thus bathed in the glory of the Risen One, she anticipates the Church's splendour (cf. Sedulius, *Paschale carmen*, 5, 357-364, *CSEL* 10, 140f).

---

[1] "*Plus quam quingentis fratribus simul*" (*1 Cor* 15, 6).

[2] Sedulius was a fifth century Christian poet whose personal history is primarily known from two sources. *De viris illustribus*, the Latin phrase for "On Famous Men," is a genre of literature in which authors write biographies of noteworthy individuals from the past. Isidore of Seville places Sedulius seventh in his *De viris illustribus*, ahead of Possidius, while Avitus and Dracontius are ranked twenty-third and twenty-fourth, respectively. Some manuscripts of Sedulius also contain a biographical account, which may have been written by Gennadius. This account portrays Sedulius as a layman who initially lived in Italy and was interested in philosophy. It is likely that Sedulius wrote his works in Achaia during the reigns of Theodosius the Younger († 450) and Valentinian III († 455).

4.1 It seems reasonable to think that Mary, as the image and model of the Church which waits for the Risen One and meets him in the group of disciples during his Easter appearances, had had a personal contact with her risen Son, so that she too could delight in the fullness of paschal joy.

4.2 Present at Calvary on Good Friday (cf. *Jn* 19:25) and in the Cenacle on Pentecost (cf. *Acts* 1:14), the Blessed Virgin too was probably a privileged witness of Christ's Resurrection, completing in this way her participation in all the essential moments of the paschal mystery. Welcoming the risen Jesus, Mary is also a sign and an anticipation of humanity, which hopes to achieve its fulfilment through the resurrection of the dead.

4.3 In the Easter season, the Christian community addresses the Mother of the Lord and invites her to rejoice: *Regína cæli, lætáre, allelúia!*, "Queen of heaven, rejoice, alleluia!".[1] Thus it recalls Mary's joy at Jesus' Resurrection, prolonging in time the "rejoice" that the Angel addressed to her at the Annunciation, so that she might become a cause of "great joy" for all people.

21 May 1997

[1] For the text of the *Regína cæli*, see Appendix of Marian Prayers, p. 237.

52
MARY AND THE GIFT OF THE SPIRIT

Then they returned to Jerusalem from the mount called Olivet, which is near Jerusalem, a sabbath day's journey away; and when they had entered, they went up to the upper room. All these with one accord devoted themselves to prayer, together with the women and Mary the mother of Jesus, and with his brothers (*Acts* 1:12-13a.14).[1]

1.1 Retracing the course of the Virgin Mary's life, the Second Vatican Council recalls her presence in the community waiting for Pentecost.

"But since it had pleased God not to manifest solemnly the mystery of the salvation of the human race before he would pour forth the Spirit promised by Christ, we see the Apostles before the day of Pentecost 'persevering with one mind in prayer with the women and Mary the Mother of Jesus, and with his brethren' (*Acts* 1:14), and we also see Mary by her prayers imploring the gift of the Spirit, who had already overshadowed her in the Annunciation" (*Lumen gentium*, n. 59).[2]

1.2 The first community is the prelude to the birth of the Church; the Blessed Virgin's presence helps to sketch her definitive features, a fruit of the gift of Pentecost.

2.1 In the atmosphere of expectation that prevailed in the Cenacle after the Ascension, what was Mary's position in relation to the descent of the Holy Spirit?

2.2 The Council expressly underscores her prayerful presence while waiting for the outpouring of the Paraclete: she prays, "imploring the gift of the Spirit". This observation is particularly significant since at the Annunciation the Holy Spirit had descended upon her, "overshadowing" her and bringing about the Incarnation of the Word.

2.3 Having already had a unique experience of the effectiveness of such a gift, the Blessed Virgin was in a condition to appreciate it more than anyone; indeed, she owed her motherhood to the mysterious intervention of the Spirit, who had made her the way by which the Saviour came into the world.

---

[1] "*Tunc reversi sunt in Ierusalem a monte, qui vocatur Oliveti, qui est iuxta Ierusalem sabbati habens iter. Et cum introissent, in cenaculum ascenderunt. Hi omnes erant perseverantes unanimiter in oratione cum mulieribus et Maria matre Iesu et fratribus eius* (*Act* 1, 12-13a.14).

[2] "*Cum vero Deo placuerit humanæ salutis sacramentum non ante solemniter manifestare quam promissum a Christo Spiritum effunderet, Apostolos videmus ante diem Pentecostes 'perseverantes unanimiter in oratione cum mulieribus et Maria Matre Iesu et fratribus Eius'* (*Act* 1, 14), *Mariam quoque precibus suis implorantem donum Spiritus, qui in Annuntiatione ipsam iam obumbraverat*" (Concilium Vaticanum II, Const. dogm. de Ecclesia, *Lumen gentium*, 59: *AAS* 57 (1965), p. 62).

2.4 Unlike those in the Cenacle who were waiting in fearful expectation, she, fully aware of the importance of her Son's promise to the disciples (cf. *Jn* 14:16), helped the community to be well disposed to the coming of the "Paraclete".

2.5 Thus, while her unique experience made her ardently long for the Spirit's coming, it also involved her in preparing the minds and hearts of those around her.

3.1 During that prayer in the Cenacle, in an attitude of deep communion with the Apostles, with some women and with Jesus' "brethren", the Mother of the Lord prays for the gift of the Spirit for herself and for the community.

3.2 It was appropriate that the first outpouring of the Spirit upon her, which had happened in view of her divine motherhood, should be repeated and reinforced. Indeed, at the foot of the Cross Mary was entrusted with a new motherhood, which concerned Jesus' disciples. It was precisely this mission that demanded a renewed gift of the Spirit. The Blessed Virgin therefore wanted it for the fruitfulness of her spiritual motherhood.

3.3 While at the moment of the Incarnation the Holy Spirit had descended upon her as a person called to take part worthily in the great mystery, everything is now accomplished for the sake of the Church, whose image, model and mother Mary is called to be.

3.4 In the Church and for the Church, mindful of Jesus' promise, she waits for Pentecost and implores a multiplicity of gifts for everyone, in accordance with each one's personality and mission.

4.1 Mary's prayer has particular significance in the Christian community: it fosters the coming of the Spirit, imploring his action in the hearts of the disciples and in the world. Just as in the Incarnation the Spirit had formed the physical body of Christ in her virginal womb, now in the Cenacle the same Spirit comes down to give life to the Mystical Body.[1]

4.2 Thus Pentecost is also a fruit of the Blessed Virgin's incessant prayer, which is accepted by the Paraclete with special favour because it is an expression of her motherly love for the Lord's disciples.

4.3 In contemplating Mary's powerful intercession as she waits for the Holy Spirit, Christians of every age have frequently had recourse to her intercession on the long and tiring journey to salvation, in order to receive the gifts of the Paraclete in greater abundance.

---

[1] *Mystici Corporis* or *Mystici Corporis Christi* (Mystical Body of Christ).

5.1 Responding to the prayer of the Blessed Virgin and the community gathered in the Cenacle on the day of Pentecost, the Holy Spirit bestows the fullness of his gifts on the Blessed Virgin and those present, working a deep transformation in them for the sake of spreading the Good News. The Mother of Christ and his disciples are granted new strength and new apostolic energy for the Church's growth. In particular, the outpouring of the Spirit leads Mary to exercise her spiritual motherhood in an exceptional way, through her presence imbued with charity and her witness of faith.

5.2 In the nascent Church she passes on to the disciples her memories of the Incarnation, the infancy, the hidden life and the mission of her divine Son as a priceless treasure, thus helping to make him known and to strengthen the faith of believers.

5.3 We have no information about Mary's activity in the early Church, but we may suppose that after Pentecost her life would have continued to be hidden and discreet, watchful and effective. Since she was enlightened and guided by the Spirit, she exercised a deep influence on the community of the Lord's disciples.

28 May 1997

53
THE DORMITION OF THE MOTHER OF GOD

Christ will be honored in my body, whether by life or by death. For to me to live is Christ, and to die is gain (*Phil* 1:20b-21).[1]

1.1 Concerning the end of Mary's earthly life, the Council uses the terms of the Bull defining the dogma of the Assumption and states: "The Immaculate Virgin, preserved free from all stain of original sin, was taken up body and soul into heavenly glory, when her earthly life was over" (*Lumen gentium*, n. 59).[2] With this formula, the Dogmatic Constitution *Lumen gentium*, following my Venerable Predecessor Pius XII, made no pronouncement on the question of Mary's death. Nevertheless, Pius XII did not intend to deny the fact of her death, but merely did not judge it opportune to affirm solemnly the death of the Mother of God as a truth to be accepted by all believers.

1.2 Some theologians have in fact maintained that the Blessed Virgin did not die and was immediately raised from earthly life to heavenly glory. However, this opinion was unknown until the seventeenth century, whereas a common tradition actually exists which sees Mary's death as her entry into heavenly glory.

2.1 Could Mary of Nazareth have experienced the drama of death in her own flesh? Reflecting on Mary's destiny and her relationship with her divine Son, it seems legitimate to answer in the affirmative: since Christ died, it would be difficult to maintain the contrary for his Mother.

2.2 The Fathers of the Church, who had no doubts in this regard, reasoned along these lines. One need only quote Saint Jacob of Sarug († 521),[3] who wrote that when the time came for Mary "to walk on the way of all generations", the way, that is, of death, "the group of the Twelve Apostles" gathered to bury "the virginal body of the Blessed One" (*Discourse on the burial of the Holy Mother of God*, 87-99 in C. Vona, *Lateranum* 19 [1953], 188). Saint Modestus of Jerusalem († 634),[4] after a lengthy discussion of "the most

[1] "*Magnificabitur Christus in corpore meo, sive per vitam sive per mortem. Mihi enim vivere Christus est et mori lucrum* (*Phil* 1, 20b-21).

[2] "*Immaculata Virgo, ab omni originalis culpæ labe præservata immunis, expleto terrestris vitæ cursu, corpore et anima ad cælestem gloriam assumpta est*" (Concilium Vaticanum II, Const. dogm. de Ecclesia, *Lumen gentium*, 59: *AAS* 57 (1965), p. 62).

[3] Saint Jacob of Sarug (c. 451- 521) was a Syriac poet-theologian, best known for his more than seven-hundred verse homilies or *mêmrê*. In 519, he was elected Bishop of Batnan da-Srugh in the Eastern Roman or Byzantine Empire (modern day Turkey). His feast day is 29 November.

[4] Saint Modestus of Jerusalem lived as an ascetic on Mount Sinai until he was made abbot of the Monastery of Saint Theodosius in Palestine and later Patriarch of Jerusalem. His feast is celebrated on either 19 October or 16 December, and on 29 March, 17 May, or 17 December in the Eastern Orthodox churches.

blessed dormition of the most glorious Mother of God",[1] ends his eulogy by exalting the miraculous intervention of Christ who "raised her from the tomb",[2] to take her up with him in glory (*Enc. in dormitionem Deiparæ semperque Virginis Mariæ*, nn. 7 and 14: *PG* 86*bis*, 3293; 3311). Saint John Damascene († 704) for his part asks: "Why is it that she who in giving birth surpassed all the limits of nature should now bend to its laws, and her immaculate body be subjected to death?". And he answers:

"To be clothed in immortality, it is of course necessary that the mortal part be shed, since even the master of nature did not refuse the experience of death. Indeed, he died according to the flesh and by dying destroyed death; on corruption he bestowed incorruption and made death the source of resurrection" (*Panegyric on the Dormition of the Mother of God*, n. 10: *SC* 80, 107).[3]

3.1 It is true that in Revelation death is presented as a punishment for sin. However, the fact that the Church proclaims Mary free from original sin by a unique divine privilege does not lead to the conclusion that she also received physical immortality. The Mother is not superior to the Son who underwent death, giving it a new meaning and changing it into a means of salvation.

3.2 Involved in Christ's redemptive work and associated in his saving sacrifice, Mary was able to share in his suffering and death for the sake of humanity's Redemption. What Severus of Antioch says about Christ also applies to her: "Without a preliminary death, how could the Resurrection have taken place?" (*Antijulianistica*, Beirut 1931, 194f.). To share in Christ's Resurrection, Mary had first to share in his death.

4.1 The New Testament provides no information on the circumstances of Mary's death. This silence leads one to suppose that it happened naturally, with no detail particularly worthy of mention. If this were not the case, how could the information about it have remained hidden from her contemporaries and not have been passed down to us in some way?

4.2 As to the cause of Mary's death, the opinions that wish to exclude her from death by natural causes seem groundless. It is more important to look for the Blessed Virgin's spiritual attitude at the moment of her departure from

---

[1] "*O beatissima dormitio gloriosissimæ Deiparæ*" (Sanctus Modestus Hierosolymitanus, *Encomium in B. Virginem*, VII: *PG* 86, 3294).

[2] "*Qui illam e sepulcro excitavit*" (Ibid., 3311).

[3] "*O quomodo, quæ pariendo naturæ leges excesserat, nunc eius legibus cedit, et corpus immaculatum morti subjicitur!*

Oportet enim hoc mortali posito, induere incorruptionem, quandoquidem naturæ Dominus mortis periculum facere non recusavit. Carne etenim moritur, et morto mortem tollit; corruptione incorruptionem donat: necem denique suam resurrectionis fontem facit" (Sanctus Ioannes Damascenus, *Homilia I in Dormitionem B.V. Mariæ*, 10: *PG* 96, 714).

this world. In this regard, Saint Francis de Sales[1] maintains that Mary's death was due to a transport of love. He speaks of a dying "in love, from love and through love", going so far as to say that the Mother of God died of love for her Son Jesus (*Treatise on the Love of God*, bk. 7, ch. XIII-XIV).

4.3 Whatever from the physical point of view was the organic, biological cause of the end of her bodily life, it can be said that for Mary the passage from this life to the next was the full development of grace in glory, so that no death can ever be so fittingly described as a "dormition" as hers.

5.1 In some of the writings of the Church Fathers we find Jesus himself described as coming to take his Mother at the time of her death to bring her into heavenly glory. In this way they present the death of Mary as an event of love which conducted her to her divine Son to share his immortal life. At the end of her earthly life, she must have experienced, like Paul and more strongly, the desire to be freed from her body in order to be with Christ for ever (cf. *Phil* 1:23).

5.2 The experience of death personally enriched the Blessed Virgin: by undergoing mankind's common destiny, she can more effectively exercise her spiritual motherhood towards those approaching the last moment of their life.

25 June 1997

[1] Saint Francis de Sales (1567–1622) was Bishop of Geneva and was known for his deep faith and gentle approach to the religious divisions in his land resulting from the Protestant Pseudo-Reformation. He is also known for his writings on the topic of spiritual direction andformation, particularly the *Introduction à la vie dévote* [*Introduction to the Devout Life*] and the *Traité de l'amour de Dieu* [*Treatise on the Love of God*]. He was beatified in 1661 and canonized in 1665 by Pope Alexander VII. He was declared a Doctor of the Church in 1877 by Pope Blessed Pius IX. His feast day is 24 January in the Ordinary Form of the Roman Rite and 29 January in the Extraordinary Form.

54
THE ASSUMPTION OF MARY, THE TRUTH OF FAITH

And Mary said, "My soul magnifies the Lord, and my spirit rejoices in God my Savior, for he has regarded the low estate of his handmaiden. For behold, henceforth all generations will call me blessed; for he who is mighty has done great things for me, and holy is his name" (*Lk* 1:46-49).[1]

1.1 Following the Bull *Munificentissimus Deus* of my venerable Predecessor Pius XII, the Second Vatican Council affirms that the Immaculate Virgin "was taken up body and soul into heavenly glory, when her earthly life was over" (*Lumen gentium,* n. 59).[2]

1.2 The Council Fathers wished to stress that Mary, unlike Christians who die in God's grace, was taken up into the glory of heaven with her body. This age-old old belief is expressed in a long iconographical tradition which shows Mary "entering" heaven with her body.

1.3 The dogma of the Assumption affirms that Mary's body was glorified after her death. In fact, while for other human beings the resurrection of the body will take place at the end of the world, for Mary the glorification of her body was anticipated by a special privilege.

2.1 On 1 November 1950, in defining the dogma of the Assumption, Pius XII avoided using the term "resurrection" and did not take a position on the question of the Blessed Virgin's death as a truth of faith. The Bull *Munificentissimus Deus* limits itself to affirming the elevation of Mary's body to heavenly glory, declaring this truth a "divinely revealed dogma".

2.2 How can we not see that the Assumption of the Blessed Virgin has always been part of the faith of the Christian people who, by affirming Mary's entrance into heavenly glory, have meant to proclaim the glorification of her body?

2.3 The first trace of belief in the Virgin's Assumption can be found in the apocryphal accounts entitled *Transitus Mariæ,*[3] whose origin dates to the second and third centuries. These are popular and sometimes romanticised depictions, which in this case, however, pick up an intuition of faith on the part of the People of God.

---

[1] "*Et ait Maria: « Magnificat anima mea Dominum, et exsultavit spiritus meus in Deo salvatore meo, quia respexit humilitatem ancillæ suæ. Ecce enim ex hoc beatam me dicent omnes generationes, quia fecit mihi magna, qui potens est, et sanctum nomen eius »* (*Lc* 1, 46-49).

[2] "*Expleto terrestris vitæ cursu, corpore et anima ad cœlestem gloriam assumpta est*" (CONCILIUM VATICANUM II, Const. dogm. de Ecclesia, *Lumen gentium*, 59: *AAS* 57 (1965), p. 62).

[3] Latin for "Passage of Mary".

2.4 Later, there was a long period of growing reflection on Mary's destiny in the next world. This gradually led the faithful to believe in the glorious raising of the Mother of Jesus, in body and soul, and to the institution in the East of the liturgical feasts of the Dormition and Assumption of Mary.

2.5 Belief in the glorious destiny of the body and soul of the Lord's Mother after her death spread very rapidly from East to West, and has been widespread since the fourteenth century. In our century, on the eve of the definition of the dogma it was a truth almost universally accepted and professed by the Christian community in every corner of the world.

3.1 Therefore in May 1946, with the Encyclical *Deiparæ Virginis Mariæ*,[1] Pius XII called for a broad consultation, inquiring among the Bishops and, through them, among the clergy and the People of God as to the possibility and opportuneness of defining the bodily assumption of Mary as a dogma of faith. The result was extremely positive: only six answers out of 1,181 showed any reservations about the revealed character of this truth.

3.2 Citing this fact, the Bull *Munificentissimus Deus* states: "From the universal agreement of the Church's ordinary Magisterium we have a certain and firm proof demonstrating that the Blessed Virgin Mary's bodily Assumption into heaven… is a truth revealed by God and therefore should be firmly and faithfully believed by all the children of the Church" (Apostolic Constitution *Munificentissimus Deus*: *AAS* 42 [1950], 757).[2]

3.3 The definition of the dogma, in conformity with the universal faith of the People of God, definitively excludes every doubt and calls for the express assent of all Christians.

3.4 After stressing the Church's actual belief in the Assumption, the Bull recalls the scriptural basis for this truth.

3.5 Although the New Testament does not explicitly affirm Mary's Assumption, it offers a basis for it because it strongly emphasised the Blessed Virgin's perfect union with Jesus' destiny. This union, which is manifested, from the time of the Saviour's miraculous conception, in the Mother's participation in

---

[1] In view of worldwide request, Venerable Pope Pius XII sent this letter dated 1 May 1946 *in forma del tutto reservata* to all the bishops of the world, asking what their clergy and people thought about the Assumption and whether they themselves judged it "wise and prudent" that the dogma should be defined. The document was originally printed in *Il Monitore Ecclesiastico* (fasc. 7-12, 1946; pp. 97-98) as a letter but was published in the *Acta Apostolicæ Sedis* in 1950 as an encyclical letter (*epistula encyclica*) titled *Deiparæ Virginis Mariæ* (cf. *AAS* 42 [1950], p. 782).

[2] "*Ex ordinarii Ecclesiæ Magisterii universali consensu certum ac firmum sumitur argumentum, quo comprobatur corpoream Beatæ Mariæ Virginis in Cælum Assumptionem… veritatem esse a Deo revelatam, ideoque ab omnibus Ecclesiæ filiis firmiter fideliterque credendam*" (Pius XII, Const. ap. *Munificentissimus Deus* (1 novembris 1950), 12: *AAS* 42 (1950), p. 757; *DS* 3903).

her Son's mission and especially in her association with his redemptive sacrifice, cannot fail to require a continuation after death. Perfectly united with the life and saving work of Jesus, Mary shares his heavenly destiny in body and soul.

4.1 The Bull *Munificentissimus Deus* cited above refers to the participation of the woman of the Proto-Gospel in the struggle against the serpent, recognising Mary as the New Eve, and presents the Assumption as a consequence of Mary's union with Christ's saving work. In this regard it says: "Consequently, just as the glorious Resurrection of Christ was an essential part and the final sign of this victory, so that struggle which was common to the Blessed Virgin and her divine Son should be brought to a close by the glorification of her virginal body" (Apostolic Constitution *Munificentissimus Deus*: *AAS* 42 [1950], 768).[1]

4.2 The Assumption is therefore the culmination of the struggle which involved Mary's generous love in the redemption of humanity and is the fruit of her unique sharing in the victory of the Cross.

2 July 1997

[1] "*Quamobrem, sicut gloriosa Christi anastasis essentialis pars fuit ac postremum huius victoriæ tropæum, ita Beatæ Virginis commune cum Filio suo certamen virginei corporis « glorificatione » concludendum erat*" (Pius XII, Const. ap. *Munificentissimus Deus* (1 novembris 1950), 39: *AAS* 42 (1950), p. 768; cf. *DS* 3901).

55
THE ASSUMPTION OF MARY IN THE TRADITION OF THE CHURCH

And Elizabeth was filled with the Holy Spirit and she exclaimed with a loud cry, "Blessed are you among women, and blessed is the fruit of your womb! And blessed is she who believed that there would be a fulfilment of what was spoken to her from the Lord" (*Lk* 1:41b-42. 45).[1]

1.1 The Church's constant and unanimous Tradition shows how Mary's Assumption is part of the divine plan and is rooted in her unique sharing in the mission of her Son. In the first millennium sacred authors had already spoken in this way.

1.2 Testimonies, not yet fully developed, can be found in Saint Ambrose, Saint Epiphanius, and Timothy of Jerusalem. Saint Germanus I of Constantinople († 730) puts these words on Jesus' lips as he prepares to take his Mother to heaven: "You must be where I am, Mother inseparable from your Son..." (*Hom. 3 in Dormitionem*, *PG* 98, 360).[2]

1.3 In addition, the same ecclesial Tradition sees the fundamental reason for the Assumption in the divine motherhood.

1.4 We find an interesting trace of this conviction in a fifth century apocryphal account attributed to Pseudo-Melito. The author imagines Christ questioning Peter and the Apostles on the destiny Mary deserved, and this is the reply he received: "Lord, you chose this handmaid of yours to become an immaculate dwelling place for you... Thus it seemed right to us, your servants, that just as you reign in glory after conquering death, so you should raise your Mother's body and take her rejoicing with you to heaven" (*Transitus Mariæ*, 16, *PG* 5, 1238).[3] It can therefore be said that the divine motherhood, which made Mary's body the immaculate dwelling place of the Lord, was the basis of her glorious destiny.

2 Saint Germanus maintains in a richly poetic text that it is Jesus' affection for his Mother which requires Mary to be united with her divine Son in heaven:

---

[1] "*Et repleta est Spiritu Sancto Elisabeth et exclamavit voce magna et dixit: « Benedicta tu inter mulieres, et benedictus fructus ventris tui. Et beata, quæ credidit, quoniam perficientur ea, quæ dicta sunt ei a Domino »* (*Lc* 1, 41b-42. 45).

[2] "*Ubi igitur ego sum, debes et ipsa esse, inseparabilis mater, in Filio indivulso*" (Sanctus Germanus Constantinopolitanus, *Hom. 3 in Dormitionem*, VI: *PG* 98, 362).

[3] "*Domine, præelegisti hanc anciliam tuam fieri immaculatum tibi thalamum, et nos servulos tuos in ministerium tuum... Sic ergo visum nobis fuerat famulis tuis etiam rectum esse; ut sicut tu, devicta morte, regnas in gloria, ita resuscitans matris corpusculum, tu tecum duceres eam lætam in cælum*" (Spuria Sanctus Melitonis, *De Transitu Virginis Mariæ*, cap. XVI: *PG* 5, 1238).

"Just as a child seeks and desires its mother's presence and a mother delights in her child's company, it was fitting that you, whose motherly love for your Son and God leaves no room for doubt, should return to him. And was it not right, in any case, that this God who had a truly filial love for you, should take you into his company?" (*Hom. 1 in Dormitionem*, *PG* 98, 347).[1] In another text, the venerable author combines the private aspect of the relationship between Christ and Mary with the saving dimension of her motherhood, maintaining that "the mother of Life should share the dwelling place of Life" (*ibid.*, *PG* 98, 343).[2]

3.1 According to some of the Church Fathers, another argument for the privilege of the Assumption is taken from Mary's sharing in the work of Redemption. Saint John Damascene underscores the relationship between her participation in the Passion and her glorious destiny: "It was right that she who had seen her Son on the Cross and received the sword of sorrow in the depths of her heart... should behold this Son seated at the right hand of the Father" (*Hom. 2*, *PG* 96, 741).[3] In the light of the paschal mystery, it appears particularly clear that the Mother should also be glorified with her Son after death.

3.2 The Second Vatican Council, recalling the mystery of the Assumption in the Dogmatic Constitution on the Church, draws attention to the privilege of the Immaculate Conception: precisely because she was "preserved free from all stain of original sin" (*Lumen gentium*, n. 59),[4] Mary could not remain like other human beings in the state of death until the end of the world. The absence of original sin and her perfect holiness from the very first moment of her existence required the full glorification of the body and soul of the Mother of God.

4.1 Looking at the mystery of the Blessed Virgin's Assumption, we can understand the plan of divine Providence plan for humanity: after Christ, the Incarnate Word, Mary is the first human being to achieve the eschatological ideal, anticipating the fullness of happiness promised to the elect through the resurrection of the body.

---

[1] "*Uti enim chara proles propriam quærit ac desiderat parentem, atque parens vicissim cum prole amat versari, ita et te, quæ prolis amantibus in Filium tuum ac Deum visceribus prædita esses, confruum erat redire ad Filium; parque vicissim erat, ut pro ea, qua Deus ad Matrem haberet amoris affectione, suam sibi contubernalem, consuetudine donans, adiungeret*" (Sanctus Germanus Constantinopolitanus, *Hom. 1 in Dormitionem*, VI: *PG* 98, 347).

[2] "*Matrem Vitæ, communem secum vitam ducentem habuerunt*" (Sanctus Germanus Constantinopolitanus, *Hom. 1 in Dormitionem*, VI: *PG* 98, 343).

[3] "*Oportebat, ut quæ Filium suum in cruce conspexerat, et gladium quem pariendo effugisset, pectore tunc exceperat, ipsum Patri considentem spectaret. Oportebat denique Dei Matrem ea quae Filii essent, possidere, et ab omnibus creaturis adorari*" (Sanctus Ioannes Damascenus, *Homilia II in Dormitionem B.V. Mariæ*, 14: *PG* 96, 741).

[4] "*Ab omni originalis culpæ labe præservata immunis*" (Concilium Vaticanum II, Const. dogm. de Ecclesia, *Lumen gentium*, 59: *AAS* 57 (1965), p. 62).

4.2 In the Assumption of the Blessed Virgin we can also see the divine will to advance woman.

4.3 In a way analogous to what happened at the beginning of the human race and of salvation history, in God's plan the eschatological ideal was not to be revealed in an individual, but in a couple. Thus in heavenly glory, beside the risen Christ there is a woman who has been raised up, Mary: the new Adam and the new Eve, the first-fruits of the general resurrection of the bodies of all humanity.

4.4 The eschatological conditions of Christ and Mary should not, of course, be put on the same level. Mary, the new Eve, received from Christ, the new Adam, the fullness of grace and heavenly glory, having been raised through the Holy Spirit by the sovereign power of the Son.

5.1 Despite their brevity, these notes enable us to show clearly that Mary's Assumption reveals the nobility and dignity of the human body.

5.2 In the face of the profanation and debasement to which modern society frequently subjects the female body, the mystery of the Assumption proclaims the supernatural destiny and dignity of every human body, called by the Lord to become an instrument of holiness and to share in his glory.

5.3 Mary entered into glory because she welcomed the Son of God in her virginal womb and in her heart. By looking at her, the Christian learns to discover the value of his own body and to guard it as a temple of God, in expectation of the resurrection.

5.4 The Assumption, a privilege granted to the Mother of God, thus has immense value for the life and destiny of humanity.

9 July 1997

56
THE QUEEN OF THE UNIVERSE

And a great sign appeared in heaven, a woman clothed with the sun, with the moon under her feet, and on her head a crown of twelve stars (*Apoc* 12:1).[1]

1.1 Popular devotion invokes Mary as Queen. The Council, after recalling the Assumption of the Blessed Virgin in "body and soul into heavenly glory", explains that she was "exalted by the Lord as Queen over all things, that she might be the more fully conformed to her Son, the Lord of lords (cf. *Rv* 19:16) and conqueror of sin and death" (*Lumen gentium,* n. 59).[2]

1.2 In fact, starting from the fifth century, almost in the same period in which the Council of Ephesus proclaims her "Mother of God", the title of Queen begins to be attributed to her. With this further recognition of her sublime dignity, the Christian people want to place her above all creatures, exalting her role and importance in the life of every person and of the whole world.

1.3 But already a fragment of a homily, attributed to Origen,[3] contains this comment on the words Elizabeth spoke at the Visitation "It is I who should have come to visit you, because you are blessed above all women, you are the Mother of my Lord, you are my Lady" (*Fragment*, *PG* 13, 1902 D).[4] The text passes spontaneously from the expression "the Mother of my Lord" to the title, "my Lady", anticipating what Saint John Damascene was later to say, attributing to Mary the title of "Sovereign": "When she became Mother of the Creator, she truly became queen of all creatures" (Saint John Damascene, *De fide orthodoxa,* 4, 14, *PG* 94, 1157).[5]

2.1 My venerable Predecessor Pius XII, in his Encyclical *Ad cœli Reginam* to which the text of the Constitution *Lumen gentium* refers, indicates as the basis for Mary's queenship in addition to her motherhood, her co-operation in the work of the Redemption. The Encyclical recalls the liturgical text:

---

[1] "*Et signum magnum appa ruit in cœlo: mulier amicta sole, et luna sub pedibus eius, et super caput eius corona stellarum duodecim* (*Ap* 12, 1).

[2] "*Ac tamquam universorum Regina a Domino exaltata, ut plenius conformaretur Filio suo, Domino dominantium* (cf. *Apoc* 19, 16) *ac peccati mortisque victori*" (Concilium Vaticanum II, Const. dogm. de Ecclesia, *Lumen gentium*, 59: *AAS* 57 (1965), p. 62).

[3] Origen Adamantius of Alexandria (c. 184 – c. 253) was an early Christian theologian who wrote roughly 2,000 treatises in multiple branches of theology.

[4] "*Oportebat me ad te venire: tu enim super omnes mulieres benedicta: tu Mater domini mei: tu mea Domina*" (Origenes, *Fragmenta*, orat. II: *PG* 13, 1902d).

[5] "*Quæ vere omnis creaturæ Domina facta sit, cum Creatoris mater exstitit*" (Sanctus Ioannes Damascenus, *De fide orthodoxa*, liber IV, caput XIV: *PG* 94, 1158-1159; Greek text: 1157).

"Holy Mary, the Queen of heaven and mistress of the world, stood by the cross of our Lord Jesus Christ, full of sorrows" (*AAS* 46 [1954] 634).[1] It then establishes an analogy between Mary and Christ, which helps us understand the significance of the Blessed Virgin's royal status. Christ is King not only because he is Son of God, but also because he is the Redeemer; Mary is Queen not only because she is Mother of God, but also because, associated as the new Eve with the new Adam, she co-operated in the work of the redemption of the human race (*AAS* 46 [1954] 635).

2.2 In Mark's Gospel, we read that on the day of the Ascension the Lord Jesus "was taken up into heaven, and sat down at the right hand of God" (16:19).[2] In biblical language "to sit at the right hand of God" means sharing his sovereign power. Sitting "at the right hand of the Father", he establishes his kingdom, God's kingdom. Taken up into heaven, Mary is associated with the power of her Son and is dedicated to the extension of the Kingdom, sharing in the diffusion of divine grace in the world.

2.3 In looking at the analogy between Christ's Ascension and Mary's Assumption, we can conclude that Mary, in dependence on Christ, is the Queen who possesses and exercises over the universe a sovereignty granted to her by her Son.

3.1 The title of Queen does not of course replace that of Mother: her queenship remains a corollary of her particular maternal mission and simply expresses the power conferred on her to carry out that mission.

3.2 Citing Pius IX's Bull *Ineffabilis Deus,* the Supreme Pontiff highlights this maternal dimension of the Blessed Virgin's queenship: "Having a motherly affection for us and being concerned for our salvation, she extends her care to the whole human race. Appointed by the Lord as Queen of heaven and earth, raised above all the choirs of angels and the whole celestial hierarchy of saints, sitting at the right hand of her only Son, our Lord Jesus Christ, she obtains with great certainty what she asks with her motherly prayers; she obtains what she seeks and it cannot be denied her" (cf. *AAS* 46 [1954] 636-637).[3]

---

[1] "*Stabat sancta María, cœli Regína, et mundi Dómina, iuxta Crucem Dómini nostri Iesu Christi dolorósa*" (*Missale Romanum, editio typica 1962: Festum septem dolorum B. Mariæ Virg., Tractus*; PIUS XII, Litt. enc. *Ad cœli Reginam* (11 octobris 1954): *AAS* 46 (1954), p. 634).

[2] "*Assumptus est in cælum et sedit a dextris Dei*" (*Mc* 16, 19).

[3] "*Maternum sane in nos gerens animum nostræque salutis negotia tractans, de universo humano genere est sollicita, cœli terræque Regina a Domino constituta, ac super omnes Angelorum choros Sanctorumque Cœlitum ordines exaitata, adstans a dexteris unigeniti Filii sui Domini Nostri Iesu Christi, maternis suis precibus validissime impetrat, et quod quærit invenit, ac frustrari non potest*" (BEATUS PIUS IX, Const. ap. *Ineffabilis Deus*, 8 decembris 1854: *Acta Pii IX*, I, pp. 597-598; PIUS XII, Litt. Encycl. *Ad cœli Reginam*, 11 octobris 1954: *AAS* 46 (1954), pp. 636-637).

4.1 Therefore Christians look with trust to Mary as Queen and this not only does not diminish but indeed exalts their filial abandonment to her, who is mother in the order of grace.

4.2 Indeed, the concern Mary as Queen has for mankind can be fully effective precisely by virtue of her glorious state which derives from the Assumption. Saint Germanus I of Constantinople, highlights this very well. He holds that this state guarantees Mary's intimate relationship with her Son and enables her to intercede in our favour. Addressing Mary he says: Christ wanted "to have, so to speak, the closeness of your lips and your heart; thus he assents to all the desires you express to him, when you suffer for your children, with his divine power he does all that you ask of him" (Saint Germanus of Constantinople, *Hom. 1*, *PG* 98, 348).[1]

5.1 One can conclude that the Assumption favours Mary's full communion not only with Christ, but with each one of us: she is beside us, because her glorious state enables her to follow us in our daily earthly journey. As we read again in Saint Germanus: "You dwell spiritually with us and the greatness of your vigilance over us makes your communion of life with us stand out" (*Hom.* 1, *PG* 98, 344).[2]

5.2 Thus far from creating distance between her and us, Mary's glorious state brings about a continuous and caring closeness. She knows everything that happens in our life and supports us with maternal love in life's trials.

5.3 Taken up into heavenly glory, Mary dedicates herself totally to the work of salvation in order to communicate to every living person the happiness granted to her. She is a Queen who gives all that she possesses, participating above all in the life and love of Christ.

23 July 1997

[1] "*Suis te, ut ita dicam, et affatibus et visceribus volens proprius affixam: ideirco quidquid ab eo quæris, id ille, filiorum lugenti sortem, tribuit; ac si quid petis ab eo, divina implet virtute*" (Sanctus Germanus Constantinopolis, *In dormitionem B. Mariæ* I: *PG* 98, 343; Greek text: 344).

[2] "*Ideirco etiam magis ter beatissimos eos prædicamus, qui tui accolatus spectaculo delectati sunt, ut qui te, Matrem Vitæ, commune secum vitam ducentem habuerunt*" (Sanctus Germanus Constantinopolis, *In dormitionem B. Mariæ* I: *PG* 98, 347; Greek text: 348).

57
MARY, THE PRE-EMINENT MEMBER OF THE CHURCH

And when they had entered, they went up to the upper room, where they were staying, Peter and John and James and Andrew, Philip and Thomas, Bartholomew and Matthew, James the son of Alphaeus and Simon the Zealot and Judas the son of James. All these with one accord devoted themselves to prayer, together with the women and Mary the mother of Jesus, and with his brethren (*Acts* 1:13-14).[1]

1.1 Mary's exceptional role in the work of salvation invites us to deepen the relationship that exists between her and the Church.

1.2 According to some people Mary cannot be considered a member of the Church, since the privileges conferred on her, the Immaculate Conception, her divine motherhood and her unique cooperation in the work of salvation, place her in a condition of superiority with respect to the community of believers.

1.3 The Second Vatican Council, however, does not hesitate to present Mary as a member of the Church, nevertheless specifying that she is "pre-eminent and... wholly unique" (*Lumen gentium,* n. 53): Mary is the type of the Church, her model and mother. Differing from all the other faithful, because of the exceptional gifts she received from the Lord, the Blessed Virgin nonetheless belongs to the Church and is fully entitled to be a member.

2.1 Conciliar teaching finds a significant basis in Sacred Scripture. The Acts of the Apostles show Mary present from the beginning of the primitive community (cf. *Acts* 1:14), while she shares with the disciples and some women believers the prayerful expectation of the Holy Spirit, who will descend on them.

2.2 After Pentecost, the Blessed Virgin continues to live in fraternal communion with the community and takes part in the prayers, in listening to the Apostles' teaching, and in the "breaking of bread", that is, in the Eucharistic celebration (cf. *Acts* 2:42).

2.3 She who had lived in close union with Jesus in the house of Nazareth, now lives in the Church in intimate communion with her Son, present in the Eucharist.

---

[1] "*Et cum introissent, in cenaculum ascenderunt, ubi manebant et Petrus et Ioannes et Iacobus et Andreas, Philippus et Thomas, Bartholomæus et Matthæus, Iacobus Alphæi et Simon Zelotes et Iudas Iacobi. Hi omnes erant perseverantes unanimiter in oratione cum mulieribus et Maria matre Iesu et fratribus eius*" (*Act* 1, 13-14).

3.1 Mother of the only begotten Son of God, Mary is Mother of the community which constitutes Christ's mystical Body and guides its first steps.

3.2 In accepting this mission, she is committed to encouraging ecclesial life with her maternal and exemplary presence. This solidarity derives from her belonging to the community of the redeemed. In fact, unlike her Son, she had need of redemption since "being of the race of Adam, she is at the same time also united to all those who are to be saved" (*Lumen gentium,* n. 53).[1] The privilege of the Immaculate Conception preserved her from the stain of sin, because of the Redeemer's special saving influence.

3.3 As "pre-eminent and as a wholly unique member of the Church",[2] Mary uses the gifts God has granted her to achieve fuller solidarity with the brothers and sisters of her Son, now her children too.

4.1 As a member of the Church, Mary places her personal holiness, the fruit of God's grace and of her faithful collaboration, at the service of her brothers and sisters. The Immaculate Virgin is an unfailing support for all Christians in their fight against sin and a constant encouragement to live as those redeemed by Christ, sanctified by the Spirit, and children of the Father.

4.2 As a member of the first community, "Mary the Mother of Jesus" (*Acts* 1:14)[3] is respected and venerated by all. Each one understands the pre-eminence of her who brought forth the Son of God, the one universal Saviour. Furthermore, the virginal character of her motherhood allows her to witness to the extraordinary contribution to the Church's good offered by the one who, giving up human fruitfulness through docility to the Holy Spirit, puts herself completely at the service of God's kingdom.

4.3 Called to collaborate intimately in her Son's sacrifice and the gift of the divine life to humanity, Mary continues her motherly work after Pentecost. The mystery of love contained in the Cross inspires her apostolic zeal and commits her, as a member of the Church, to spreading the Good News.

4.4 The words of the crucified Christ on Golgotha: "Woman, behold, your Son" (*Jn* 19:26),[4] with which her role as the universal mother of believers is recognised, unfold before her motherhood with new and limitless horizons. The gift of the Holy Spirit, received at Pentecost through the exercise of this mission, induces her to offer the help of her motherly heart to all who are on their way towards the total fulfilment of God's kingdom.

---

[1] "*Cum omnibus hominibus salvandis in stirpe Adam invenitur coniuncta*" (Concilium Vaticanum II, Const. dogm. de Ecclesia, *Lumen gentium*, 53: *AAS* 57 (1965), p. 59).
[2] "*Supereminens prorsusque singulare membrum Ecclesiæ*" (Ibid., 53: *AAS* 57 (1965), p. 59).
[3] "*Maria matre Iesu*" (*Act* 1, 14).
[4] "*Mulier, ecce filius tuus*" (*Io* 19, 26).

5.1 A pre-eminent member of the Church, Mary lives a unique relationship with the divine persons of the Most Holy Trinity: with the Father, the Son and the Holy Spirit. The Council, in calling her "Mother of the Son of God", and therefore "beloved daughter of the Father and the temple of the Holy Spirit" (*Lumen gentium,* n. 53),[1] recalls the primary effect of the Father's love which is the divine motherhood.

5.2 Aware of the gift she has received, Mary shares with believers the attitudes of filial obedience and heartfelt gratitude, encouraging each one to recognise the signs of divine benevolence in his own life.

5.3 The Council uses the expression "temple" (*sacrarium*) of the Holy Spirit, intending to emphasise the link of presence, love and collaboration that exists between the Blessed Virgin and the Holy Spirit. The Blessed Virgin, who is already invoked by Francis of Assisi[2] as the "Bride of the Holy Spirit" (Antiphon *Santa Maria Vergine* in: *Fonti Francescane*, 281), by her example encourages the other members of the Church to entrust themselves generously to the mysterious action of the Paraclete, and to live with him in constant communion of love.

30 July 1997

[1] "*Genitrix Dei Filii... prædilecta filia Patris necnon sacrarium Spiritus Sancti* " (Concilium Vaticanum II, Const. dogm. de Ecclesia, *Lumen gentium*, 53: *AAS* 57 (1965), pp. 58-59).

[2] Saint Francis of Assisi (1181/1182–1226) was a deacon and the founder of the Order of Friars Minor (Franciscans). His feast day is 4 October. The feast of the Impression of the Stigmata of Saint Francis is observed on 17 September in the Extraordinary Form of the Roman Rite and throughout the Franciscan order.

58
MARY, TYPE AND MODEL OF THE CHURCH

And Mary said, "My soul magnifies the Lord, and my spirit rejoices in God my Savior, for he has regarded the low estate of his handmaiden. For behold, henceforth all generations will call me blessed" (*Lk* 1:46-48).[1]

1.1 The Dogmatic Constitution *Lumen gentium* of the Second Vatican Council, after presenting Mary as "pre-eminent and as a wholly unique member of the Church", declares her to be the Church's "type and outstanding model in faith and charity" (*Lumen gentium*, n. 53).[2]

The Council Fathers attribute to Mary the function of "type", that is, figure, "of the Church", borrowing the term from Saint Ambrose who expresses himself thus in his commentary on the Annunciation: "Yes, she [Mary] is betrothed, but she is a virgin because she is a type of the Church which is immaculate but a bride: a virgin, she conceived us by the Spirit; a virgin, she gave birth to us without pain" (*In Ev. sec. Luc.*, II, 7, *CCL*, 14, 33, 102-106).[3] Thus Mary is a type of the Church because of her immaculate holiness, her virginity, her betrothal and her motherhood.

Saint Paul uses the word "type", to give tangible form to a spiritual reality. In fact, he sees in the crossing of the Red Sea by the People of Israel a "type" or image of Christian Baptism, and in the manna and in the water which gushed from the rock, a "type" or image of the Eucharistic food and drink (cf. *1 Cor* 10:1-11).

By defining Mary as a type of the Church, the Council invites us to see in her the visible figure of the Church's spiritual reality, and in her spotless motherhood, the announcement of the Church's virginal motherhood.

2.1 It is necessary to explain that, unlike the Old Testament images or types, which are only prefigurations of future realities, in Mary the spiritual reality signified is already eminently present.

---

[1] "*Et ait Maria: « Magnificat anima mea Dominum, et exsultavit spiritus meus in Deo salvatore meo, quia respexit humilitatem ancillæ suæ. Ecce enim ex hoc beatam me dicent omnes generationes »* (*Lc* 1, 46-48).

[2] "*Supereminens prorsusque singulare membrum Ecclesiæ*"..."*in fide et caritate typus et exemplar spectatissimum*" (CONCILIUM VATICANUM II, Const. dogm. de Ecclesia, *Lumen gentium*, 53: *AAS* 57 (1965), p. 59).

[3] "*Bene desponsata, sed virgo; quia est Ecclesiæ typus, quæ est immaculate, sed nupta. Concepit nos virgo de Spiritu, parit nos virgo sine gemitu*" (S. AMBROSIUS, *Expositio Evangelii secundum Lucam*, lib. II, 7: *PL* 15, 1555; *CCL* 14, 33, 102-106).

The Red Sea crossing described in the book of Exodus is a saving event of liberation, but it was certainly not a baptism capable of remitting sins and giving new life. Likewise, the manna, a precious gift from Yahweh to his people wandering in the desert, contained nothing of the future reality of the Eucharist, the Body of the Lord, nor did the water which gushed from the rock already contain Christ's Blood, shed for the multitude.

The Exodus is the great work accomplished by Yahweh for his people, but it does not constitute the definitive spiritual redemption which Christ would achieve in the paschal mystery.

Moreover, referring to Jewish practices, Paul recalls: "These are only a shadow of what is to come; but the substance belongs to Christ" (*Col* 2:17).[1] This is echoed in the Letter to the Hebrews which, systematically developing this interpretation, presents the worship of the Old Covenant as "a copy and shadow of the heavenly sanctuary" (*Heb* 8:5).[2]

3.1 However, in affirming that Mary is a type of the Church, the Council does not intend to equate her with the figures or types of the Old Testament, but instead to affirm that in her the spiritual reality proclaimed and represented is completely fulfilled.

In fact, the Blessed Virgin is a type of the Church, not as an imperfect prefiguration, but as the spiritual fullness which will be found in various ways in the Church's life. The particular relationship that exists here between the image and the reality represented is based on the divine plan, which establishes a close bond between Mary and the Church. The plan of salvation which orders the prefigurations of the Old Testament to fulfilment in the New Covenant likewise determines that Mary would live in a perfect way what was later to be fulfilled in the Church.

The perfection God conferred upon Mary, therefore, acquires its most authentic meaning if it is interpreted as a prelude to divine life in the Church.

4.1 After saying that Mary is a "type of the Church", the Council adds that she is her "outstanding model", an example of perfection to be followed and imitated. Indeed, Mary is an "outstanding model" because her perfection surpasses that of all the other members of the Church.

---

[1] "*Quæ sunt umbra futurorum, corpus autem Christi*" (*Col* 2, 17).
[2] "*Figuræ et umbræ deserviunt cælestium*" (*Hebr* 8, 5).

Significantly, the Council adds that she carries out this role "in faith and in charity". Without forgetting that Christ is the first model, the Council suggests in this way that there are interior dispositions proper to the model realised in Mary, which help the Christian to establish an authentic relationship with Christ. In fact, by looking at Mary, the believer learns to live in deeper communion with Christ, to adhere to him with a living faith and to place his trust and his hope in him, loving him with his whole being.

The functions of "type and model of the Church" refer in particular to Mary's virginal motherhood and shed light on her particular place in the work of salvation. This basic structure of Mary's being is reflected in the motherhood and virginity of the Church.

6 August 1997

59
MARY, MODEL OF THE MOTHERHOOD OF THE CHURCH

But standing by the cross of Jesus were his mother, and his mother's sister, Mary the wife of Clopas, and Mary Magdalene. When Jesus saw his mother, and the disciple whom he loved standing near, he said to his mother, "Woman, behold, your son!" Then he said to the disciple, "Behold, your mother!" And from that hour the disciple took her to his own home (*Jn* 19:25-27).[1]

1.1 It is precisely in the divine motherhood that the Council perceives the basis of the special relationship between Mary and the Church. We read in the Dogmatic Constitution *Lumen gentium*:

"By reason of the gift and role of her divine motherhood, by which she is united with her Son, the Redeemer, and with her unique graces and functions, the Blessed Virgin is also intimately united to the Church" (n. 63).[2]

1.2 The Dogmatic Constitution on the Church constantly refers to this same presupposition to illustrate the prerogatives of "type" and "model" which the Blessed Virgin enjoys in relation to the Mystical Body of Christ: "In the mystery of the Church, which is herself rightly called mother and virgin, the Blessed Virgin stands out in eminent and singular fashion as exemplar both of virgin and mother" (*ibid.*).[3]

1.3 Mary's motherhood is defined as "eminent and singular", since it represents a unique and unrepeatable fact: Mary, before carrying out her motherly role for humanity, is the Mother of the only-begotten Son of God made man. On the other hand, the Church is a mother because she gives spiritual birth to Christ in the faithful, thus carrying out her maternal role for the members of the Mystical Body.

1.4 In this way the Blessed Virgin is a superior model for the Church, precisely because of the uniqueness of her prerogative as Mother of God.

2.1 *Lumen gentium,* in reflecting on Mary's motherhood, recalls that it is also expressed in the eminent dispositions of her soul:

---

[1] "*Stabant autem iuxta crucem Iesu mater eius et soror matris eius, Maria Cleopae, et Maria Magdalene. Cum vidisset ergo Iesus matrem et discipulum stantem, quem diligebat, dicit matri: « Mulier, ecce filius tuus ». Deinde dicit discipulo: « Ecce mater tua ». Et ex illa hora accepit eam discipulus in sua* (*Io* 19, 25-27).

[2] "*Beata autem Virgo divinæ maternitatis dono et munere, quo cum Filio Redemptore unitur, suisque singularibus gratiis et muneribus, etiam cum Ecclesia intime coniungitur*" (Concilium Vaticanum II, Const. dogm. de Ecclesia, *Lumen gentium*, 63: *AAS* 57 (1965), p. 64).

[3] "*In mysterio enim Ecclesiæ, quæ et ipsa iure mater vocatur et virgo, Beata Virgo Maria præcessit, eminenter et singulariter tum virginis tum matris exemplar præbens*" (Ibid.).

"Through her faith and obedience she gave birth on earth to the very Son of the Father, not through the knowledge of man but by the overshadowing of the Holy Spirit, in the manner of a new Eve who placed her faith not in the serpent of old, but in God's messenger without wavering in doubt" (*Lumen gentium,* n. 63).[1]

2.2 From these words it can be clearly seen that Mary's faith and obedience at the Annunciation are virtues for the Church to imitate and, in a certain sense, they begin her motherly journey in service to men called to salvation.

2.3 The divine motherhood cannot be isolated from the universal dimension given to it in God's saving plan, which the Council does not hesitate to recognise: "The Son whom she brought forth is he whom God placed as the first-born among many brethren (*Rom* 8:29), that is, the faithful, in whose generation and formation she co-operates with a mother's love" (*ibid.*).[2]

3.1 The Church becomes a mother, taking Mary as her model. In this regard the Council says:

"The Church indeed, contemplating her hidden sanctity, imitating her charity and faithfully fulfilling the Father's will, by receiving the Word of God in faith becomes herself a mother. By preaching and Baptism she brings forth sons, who are conceived of the Holy Spirit and born of God, to a new and immortal life" (*ibid.* n. 64).[3]

3.2 Analyzing this description of the Church's maternal work, we can note how the Christian's birth is linked here in a certain way to the birth of Jesus, as though a reflection of it: Christians are "conceived by the Holy Spirit", and therefore their birth, the fruit of preaching and baptism, resembles the Saviour's.

3.3 Moreover, in contemplating Mary, the Church imitates her charity, her faithful acceptance of the Word of God and her docility in fulfilling the Father's will. By following the Blessed Virgin's example, she achieves a fruitful spiritual motherhood.

---

[1] "*Credens enim et obœdiens, ipsum Filium Patris in terris genuit, et quidem viri nescia, Spiritu Sancto obumbrata, tamquam nova Heva, non serpenti antiquo, sed Dei nuntio præstans fidem, nullo dubio adulteratam*" (Concilium Vaticanum II, Const. dogm. de Ecclesia, *Lumen gentium*, 63: *AAS* 57 (1965), p. 64).

[2] "*Filium autem peperit, quem Deus posuit primogenitum in multis fratribus* (cf. *Rom* 8, 29), *fidelibus nempe, ad quos gignendos et educandos materno amore cooperatur*" (Ibid.).

[3] "*Iamvero Ecclesia, eius arcanam sanctitatem contemplans et caritatem imitans, voluntatemque Patris fideliter adimplens, per verbum Dei fideliter susceptum et ipsa fit mater: prædicatione enim ac baptismo filios, de Spiritu Sancto conceptos et ex Deo natos, ad vitam novam et immortalem generat*" (Ibid., 64: *AAS* 57 (1965), p. 64).

4.1 But the Church's motherhood does not make Mary's superfluous: continuing to exercise her influence on the life of Christians, Mary helps to give the Church a maternal face. In the light of Mary the motherhood of the ecclesial community, which might seem somewhat general, is called to be expressed in a more concrete and personal way towards every person redeemed by Christ.

4.2 By showing herself to be the Mother of all believers, Mary fosters in them relations of authentic spiritual brotherhood and constant dialogue.

4.3 The daily experience of faith, in every age and place, highlights the need many feel to entrust their daily necessities to Mary and they trustfully open their hearts to implore her motherly intercession and obtain her reassuring protection.

4.4 The prayers addressed to Mary by people in every age, the many forms and expressions of Marian devotion, the pilgrimages to shrines and places which commemorate the miracles worked by God the Father through the Mother of his Son show Mary's extraordinary influence on the Church's life. The love of the People of God for the Blessed Virgin points to the need for close personal relations with their heavenly Mother. At the same time Mary's spiritual motherhood supports and increases the Church's concrete practice of her own motherhood.

5.1 The two mothers, the Church and Mary, are both essential to Christian life. It could be said that the one is a more objective motherhood and the other more interior.

5.2 The Church becomes a mother in preaching God's Word and administering the sacraments, particularly Baptism, in celebrating the Eucharist and in forgiving sins.

5.3 Mary's motherhood is expressed in all the areas where grace is distributed, particularly within the framework of personal relations.

5.4 They are two inseparable forms of motherhood: indeed both enable us to recognise the same divine love which seeks to share itself with mankind.

13 August 1997

60
MARY, MODEL OF THE VIRGINITY OF THE CHURCH

All this took place to fulfil what the Lord had spoken by the prophet: "Behold, a virgin shall conceive and bear a son, and his name shall be called Emmanuel" (which means, God with us). When Joseph woke from sleep, he did as the angel of the Lord commanded him; he took his wife, but knew her not until she had borne a son; and he called his name Jesus (*Mt* 1:22-25).[1]

1.1 The Church is a mother and virgin. After affirming that she is a mother, modeled on Mary, the Council gives her the title of virgin, explaining its significance:

"She herself is a virgin, who keeps in its entirety and purity the faith she pledged to her spouse. Imitating the Mother of her Lord, and by the power of the Holy Spirit, she preserves with virginal purity an integral faith, firm hope and sincere charity" (*Lumen gentium*, n. 64).[2]

1.2 Thus Mary is also a model of the Church's virginity. In this regard, it is necessary to explain that virginity does not belong to the Church in the strict sense, since it does not represent the state of life of the vast majority of the faithful. Indeed, by virtue of God's providential plan, marriage is the most widespread and, we could say, common state for those called to the faith. The gift of virginity is reserved to a limited number of the faithful, who are called to a particular mission within the ecclesial community.

1.3 Nevertheless, in mentioning Saint Augustine's teaching, the Council maintains that the Church is virginal in the spiritual sense of integrity in faith, hope and charity. Therefore, the Church is not a virgin in the body of all her members, but possesses a virginity of the spirit (*virginitas mentis*), that is, "integral faith, firm hope and sincere charity" (*In Io. Tr.*, 13, 12; *PL* 35, 1499).[3]

2.1 The Constitution *Lumen gentium* therefore takes pains to recall that Mary's virginity, a model for that of the Church, also includes the physical dimension,

---

[1] "*Hoc autem totum factum est, ut adimpleretur id, quod dictum est a Domino per prophetam dicentem: « Ecce, virgo in utero habebit et pariet filium, et vocabunt nomen eius Emmanuel », quod est interpretatum Nobiscum Deus. Exsurgens autem Ioseph a somno fecit, sicut praecepit ei angelus Domini, et accepit coniugem suam; et non cognoscebat eam, donec peperit filium, et vocavit nomen eius Iesum* (*Mt* 1, 22-25).

[2] "*Et ipsa est virgo, quæ fidem Sponso datam integre et pure custodit, et imitans Domini sui Matrem, virtute Spiritus Sancti, virginaliter servat integram fidem, solidam spem, sinceram caritatem*" (Concilium Vaticanum II, Const. dogm. de Ecclesia, *Lumen gentium*, 64: *AAS* 57 (1965), p. 64).

[3] "*Integra fides, solida spes, sincera charitas*" (Sanctus Augustinus, *In evangelium Ioannis tractatus*, tract. XIII, 12: *PL* 35, 1499).

by which she virginally conceived Jesus by the power of the Holy Spirit without man's intervention.

2.2 Mary is a virgin in body and a virgin in heart, as appears from her intention to live in deep intimacy with the Lord, decisively manifested at the time of the Annunciation. Thus she who is invoked as "Virgin of virgins" is without doubt for everyone a very lofty example of purity and of total self-giving to the Lord. But she is a special source of inspiration for Christian virgins and for those who are radically and exclusively dedicated to the Lord in the various forms of consecrated life.

2.3 Thus after its important role in the work of salvation, Mary's virginity continues to have a beneficial influence on the Church's life.

3.1 Let us not forget that Christ is certainly the first and highest example for every chaste life. However Mary is a special model of chastity lived for love of the Lord Jesus.

3.2 She encourages all Christians to live chastity with particular commitment according to their own state, and to entrust themselves to the Lord in the different circumstances of life. She who is the sanctuary of the Holy Spirit *par excellence* helps believers rediscover their own body as the temple of God (cf. *1 Cor* 6:19) and to respect its nobility and holiness.

3.3 Young people seeking genuine love look to the Blessed Virgin and invoke her motherly help to persevere in purity.

3.4 Mary reminds married couples of the fundamental values of marriage by helping them overcome the temptation to discouragement and to subdue the passions that try to sway their hearts. Her total dedication to God is a strong encouragement to them to live in mutual fidelity, so that they will never give in to the difficulties that beset conjugal communion.

4.1 The Council urges the faithful to look to Mary so that they may imitate her "virginally integral" faith, hope, and charity.

4.2 To preserve the integrity of the faith is a demanding task for the Church, which is called to constant vigilance even at the cost of sacrifice and struggle. In fact, the Church's faith is not only threatened by those who reject the Gospel message, but especially by those who, in accepting only part of the revealed truth, refuse to share fully in the entire patrimony of the faith of Christ's Bride.

4.3 Unfortunately, this temptation, which we find from the Church's very beginning, continues to be present in her life, urging her to accept Revelation only in part, or to give the Word of God a limited, personal interpretation in conformity with the prevailing mentality and individual desires. Having fully adhered to the Word of the Lord, Mary represents for the Church an unsurpassable model of "virginally integral" faith, for with docility and perseverance she accepts the revealed Truth whole and entire. And by her constant intercession, she obtains for the Church the light of hope and the flame of charity, virtues of which, in her earthly life, she was an incomparable example for everyone.

20 August 1997

61
MARY, MODEL OF THE HOLINESS OF THE CHURCH

"For he who is mighty has done great things for me, and holy is his name. And his mercy is on those who fear him from generation to generation" (*Lk* 1:49-50).[1]

1.1 In the Letter to the Ephesians Saint Paul explains the spousal relationship between Christ and the Church in the following words: "Christ loved the Church and gave himself up for her, that he might sanctify her, having cleansed her by the washing of water with the word, that he might present the Church to himself in splendor, without spot or wrinkle or any such thing, that she might be holy and without blemish" (*Eph* 5:25-27).[2]

1.2 The Second Vatican Council takes up the Apostle's assertions and recalls that "in the most Blessed Virgin the Church has already reached perfection", while "the faithful still strive to conquer sin and increase in holiness" (*Lumen gentium*, n. 65).

1.3 In this way the difference between Mary and the faithful is emphasised, although both belong to the holy Church which Christ made "without spot or wrinkle". In fact, while the faithful receive holiness through Baptism, Mary was preserved from all stain of original sin and was redeemed antecedently by Christ. Futhermore, although the faithful have been freed "from the law of sin" (cf. *Rom* 8:2),[3] they can still give in to temptation, and human frailty continues to manifest itself in their lives. "We all make many mistakes", says the Letter of James (3:2).[4] For this reason the Council of Trent teaches: "No one can avoid all sins, even venial sins, throughout his life" (*DS* 1573). By divine privilege, however, the Immaculate Virgin is an exception to this rule, as the Council of Trent itself recalls (*ibid.*).

2.1 Despite the sins of her members, the Church is first and foremost the community of those who are called to holiness and strive each day to achieve it.

---

[1] *"Quia fecit mihi magna, qui potens est, et sanctum nomen eius, et misericordia eius in progenies et progenies timentibus eum"* (*Lc* 1, 49-50).
[2] *"Christus dilexit ecclesiam et seipsum tradidit pro ea, ut illam sanctificaret mundans lavacro aquæ in verbo, ut exhiberet ipse sibi gloriosam ecclesiam non habentem maculam aut rugam aut aliquid eiusmodi, sed ut sit sancta et immaculata"* (*Eph* 5, 25-27).
[3] *"A lege peccati"* (cf. *Rom* 8, 2).
[4] *"In multis enim offendimus omnes"* (*Iac* 3, 2).

2.2 In this arduous path to perfection they feel encouraged by her who is the "model of virtues". The Council notes:

"Devoutly meditating on her and contemplating her in the light of the Word made man, the Church reverently penetrates more deeply into the great mystery of the Incarnation and becomes more and more like her Spouse" (*Lumen gentium*, n. 65).[1]

2.3 So the Church looks to Mary. She not only contemplates the wondrous gift of her fullness of grace, but strives to imitate the perfection which in her is the fruit of her full compliance with Christ's command: "You, therefore, must be perfect as your heavenly Father is perfect" (*Mt* 5:48).[2] Mary is all-holy. For the community of believers she represents the paradigm of the authentic holiness that is achieved in union with Christ. The earthly life of the Mother of God is characterised by perfect harmony with the person of her Son and by her total dedication to the redeeming work he accomplished.

2.4 The Church turns her gaze to the maternal intimacy that grew in silence during life in Nazareth and reached perfection at the moment of sacrifice, and she strives to imitate it in her daily journey. In this way, she is increasingly conformed to her Spouse. United like Mary with the Redeemer's Cross, the Church, amid the difficulties, contradictions and persecutions that renew in her life the mystery of her Lord's Passion, constantly seeks to be fully configured to him.

3.1 The Church lives by faith, seeing in her "who believed that there would be a fulfilment of what was spoken to her from the Lord" (*Lk* 1:45),[3] the first and perfect expression of her faith. On this journey of trusting abandonment to the Lord, the Virgin goes before the disciples, adhering to the divine Word with an increasing intensity that embraces all the stages of her life and spreads to the very mission of the Church.

3.2 Her example encourages the People of God to practise their faith and to study and develop its content, by keeping in their heart and meditating on the events of salvation.

3.3 Mary also becomes a model of hope for the Church. In listening to the angel's message, the Virgin first directs her hope to the kingdom without end, which Jesus had been sent to establish.

---

[1] "*Ecclesia de Ea pie recogitans Eamque in lumine Verbi hominis facti contemplans, in summum incarnationis mysterium venerabunda penitius intrat, Sponsoque suo magis magisque conformatur*" (CONCILIUM VATICANUM II, Const. dogm. de Ecclesia, *Lumen gentium*, 65: *AAS* 57 (1965), p. 64).
[2] "*Estote ergo vos perfecti, sicut Pater vester cœlestis perfectus est*" (*Mt* 5, 48).
[3] "*Quæ credidit, quoniam perficientur ea, quæ dicta sunt ei a Domino*" (*Lc* 1, 45).

3.4 She stands firm near the cross of her Son, waiting for the divine promise to be fulfilled. After Pentecost, the Mother of Jesus sustains the Church's hope despite the threat of persecution. She is thus the Mother of hope for the community of believers and for individual Christians, and she encourages and guides her children as they await the kingdom, supporting them in their daily trials and throughout the events of history, however tragic.

3.5 Lastly, the Church sees in Mary the model of her charity. By looking at the situation of the first Christian community, we discover that the unanimity of their hearts, which was shown as they awaited Pentecost, is associated with the presence of the Holy Virgin (cf. *Acts* 1:14). And precisely because of Mary's radiant charity, it is possible to maintain harmony and fraternal love at all times within the Church.

4.1 The Council expressly underscores Mary's exemplary role for the Church's apostolic mission, with the following observation:

"The Church, therefore, in her apostolic work too, rightly looks to her who gave birth to Christ, who was thus conceived of the Holy Spirit and born of the Virgin, in order that through the Church he could be born and increase in the hearts of the faithful. In her life the Virgin has been a model of that motherly love with which all who join in the Church's apostolic mission for the regeneration of mankind should be animated" (*Lumen gentium*, n. 65).[1]

4.2 After having co-operated in the work of salvation by her motherhood, her association with Christ's sacrifice and her motherly aid to the newborn Church, Mary continues to support the Christian community and all believers in their generous commitment to proclaiming the Gospel.

3 September 1997

[1] "*Unde etiam in opere suo apostolico Ecclesia ad Eam merito respicit, quæ genuit Christum, ideo de Spiritu Sancto conceptum et de Virgine natum, ut per Ecclesiam in cordibus quoque fidelium nascatur et crescat. Quæ Virgo in sua vita exemplum exstitit materni illius affectus, quo cuncti in missione apostolica Ecclesiæ cooperantes ad regenerandos homines animentur oportet*" (CONCILIUM VATICANUM II, Const. dogm. de Ecclesia, *Lumen gentium*, 65: *AAS* 57 (1965), p. 65).

62
MARY, MODEL OF THE CHURCH IN DIVINE WORSHIP

And Mary said, "My soul magnifies the Lord, and my spirit rejoices in God my Savior, for he has regarded the low estate of his handmaiden. For behold, henceforth all generations will call me blessed" (*Lk* 1:46-48).[1]

1 In the Apostolic Exhortation *Marialis cultus* the Servant of God Paul VI, of venerable memory, presents the Blessed Virgin as a model of the Church at worship. This assertion is a corollary as it were to the truth that points to Mary as a paradigm for the People of God on the way to holiness:

"That the Blessed Virgin is an exemplar in this field derives from the fact that she is recognised as a most excellent exemplar of the Church in the order of faith, charity and perfect union with Christ, that is, of that interior disposition with which the Church, the beloved spouse, closely associated with her Lord, invokes Christ and through him worships the eternal Father" (n. 16).[2]

2.1 She who at the Annunciation showed total availability for the divine plan represents for all believers a sublime model of attentiveness and docility to the Word of God.

2.2 In replying to the angel: "Let it be to me according to your word" (*Lk* 1:38)[3] and in stating her readiness to fulfil perfectly the Lord's will, Mary rightly shares in the beatitude proclaimed by Jesus: "Blessed are those who hear the Word of God and keep it!" (*Lk* 11:28).[4]

2.3 With this attitude, which encompasses her entire life, the Blessed Virgin indicates the high road of listening to the Word of the Lord, an essential element of worship, which has become typical of the Christian liturgy. Her example shows us that worship does not primarily consist in expressing human thoughts and feelings, but in listening to the divine Word in order to know it, assimilate it and put it into practice in daily life.

---

[1] "*Et ait Maria: « Magnificat anima mea Dominum, et exsultavit spiritus meus in Deo salvatore meo, quia respexit humilitatem ancillæ suæ. Ecce enim ex hoc beatam me dicent omnes generationes »*" (*Lc* 1, 46-48).

[2] "*Posse autem Mariam Virginem in hac provincia exemplo esse, inde manat, quod ipsa ab Ecclesia tamquam specimen et documentum præstantissimum fidei, caritatis et absolutissimæ coniunctionis cum Christo habetur, id est interioris illius habitus, quo Ecclesia, sponsa dilectissima, cum Domino suo vehementer consociata, eum invocat et per eum æterno Patri cultum tribuit*" (Sanctus Paulus VI, Adh. ap. *Marialis cultus* (2 februarii 1974), 16: *AAS* 66 (1974), p. 128).

[3] "*Fiat mihi secundum verbum tuum*" (*Lc* 1, 38).

[4] "*Quinimmo beati, qui audiunt verbum Dei et custodiunt!*" (*Lc* 11, 28).

3.1 Every liturgical celebration is a memorial of the mystery of Christ in his salvific action for all humanity and is meant to promote the personal participation of the faithful in the paschal mystery re-expressed and made present in the gestures and words of the rite.

3.2 Mary was a witness to the historical unfolding of the saving events, which culminated in the Redeemer's Death and Resurrection, and she kept "all these things, pondering them in her heart" (*Lk* 2:19).[1] She was not merely present at the individual events, but sought to grasp their deep meaning, adhering with all her soul to what was being mysteriously accomplished in them.

3.3 Mary appears therefore as the supreme model of personal participation in the divine mysteries. She guides the Church in meditating on the mystery celebrated and in participating in the saving event, by encouraging the faithful to desire an intimate, personal relationship with Christ in order to co-operate with the gift of their own life in the salvation of all.

4.1 Mary also represents the model of the Church at prayer. In all probability Mary was absorbed in prayer when the angel Gabriel came to her house in Nazareth and greeted her. This prayerful setting certainly supported the Blessed Virgin in her reply to the angel and in her generous assent to the mystery of the Incarnation.

4.2 In the Annunciation scene, artists have almost always depicted Mary in a prayerful attitude. Of them all we recall Fra Angelico.[2] This shows to the Church and every believer the atmosphere that should prevail during worship.

4.3 We could add that for the People of God Mary represents the model of every expression of their prayer life. In particular, she teaches Christians how to turn to God to ask for his help and support in the various circumstances of life.

4.4 Her motherly intercession at the wedding in Cana and her presence in the Upper Room at the Apostles' side as they prayed in expectation of Pentecost suggest that the prayer of petition is an essential form of co-operation in furthering the work of salvation in the world. By following her model, the Church learns to be bold in her asking, to persevere in her intercessions and, above all, to implore the gift of the Holy Spirit (cf. *Lk* 11:13).

5.1 The Blessed Virgin also represents the Church's model for generously participating in sacrifice.

---

[1] "*Omnia verba hæc conferens in corde suo*" (*Lk* 2, 19).

[2] Blessed Giovanni da Fiesole (John of Fiesole) or "Fra Angelico" (c. 1395–1455), born Guido di Pietro, was a Renaissance painter.

5.2 In presenting Jesus in the temple and, especially, at the foot of the Cross, Mary completes the gift of herself which associates her as Mother with the suffering and trials of her Son. Thus in daily life as in the Eucharistic celebration, the "Virgin presenting offerings" (*Marialis cultus*, n. 20)[1] encourages Christians to "offer spiritual sacrifices acceptable to God through Jesus Christ" (*1 Pt* 2:5).[2]

10 September 1997

[1] "*Virgo offerens*" (*Marialis cultus*, n. 20).
[2] "*Offerre spiritales hostias acceptabiles Deo per Iesum Christum*" (*1 Petr* 2, 5).

63
MOTHER OF THE CHURCH

But standing by the cross of Jesus were his mother, and his mother's sister, Mary the wife of Clopas, and Mary Magdalene. When Jesus saw his mother, and the disciple whom he loved standing near, he said to his mother, "Woman, behold, your son!" Then he said to the disciple, "Behold, your mother!" And from that hour the disciple took her to his own home (*Jn* 19:25-27).[1]

1.1 After proclaiming Mary a "pre-eminent member", the "type" and "model" of the Church, the Second Vatican Council says: "The Catholic Church, taught by the Holy Spirit, honours her with filial affection and devotion as a most beloved mother" (*Lumen gentium*, n. 53).[2]

1.2 To tell the truth, the conciliar text does not explicitly attribute the title "Mother of the Church"[3] to the Blessed Virgin, but it unmistakably expresses its content by repeating a statement made in 1748, more than two centuries ago, by Pope Benedict XIV (*Bullarium Romanum*, series 2, t. 2, n. 61, p. 428).

1.3 In this document my venerable Predecessor, in describing the filial sentiments of the Church, which recognises Mary as her most beloved mother, indirectly proclaims her Mother of the Church.

2.1 This title was rather rarely used in the past, but has recently become more common in the pronouncements of the Church's Magisterium and in the devotion of the Christian people. The faithful first called upon Mary with the title "Mother of God", "Mother of the faithful" or "our Mother", to emphasise her personal relationship with each of her children.

2.2 Later, because of the greater attention paid to the mystery of the Church and to Mary's relationship to her, the Blessed Virgin began more frequently to be invoked as "Mother of the Church".

---

[1] *"Stabant autem iuxta crucem Iesu mater eius et soror matris eius, Maria Cleopae, et Maria Magdalene. Cum vidisset ergo Iesus matrem et discipulum stantem, quem diligebat, dicit matri: « Mulier, ecce filius tuus ». Deinde dicit discipulo: « Ecce mater tua ». Et ex illa hora accepit eam discipulus in sua"* (*Io* 19, 25-27).

[2] *"Catholica Ecclesia, a Spiritu Sancto edocta, filialis pietatis affectu tamquam matrem amantissimam prosequitur"* (CONCILIUM VATICANUM II, Const. dogm. de Ecclesia, *Lumen gentium*, 53: *AAS* 57 [1965]).

[3] *Mater Ecclésiæ.*

2.3 Before the Second Vatican Council, this expression was found in Pope Leo XIII's Magisterium, in which it is affirmed that Mary is "in all truth mother of the Church" (*Acta Leonis XIII*, 15, 302).[1] The title was later used many times in the teachings of John XXIII and Paul VI.

3.1 Although the title "Mother of the Church" was only recently attributed to Mary, it expresses the Blessed Virgin's maternal relationship with the Church as shown already in several New Testament texts.

3.2 Since the Annunciation, Mary was called to give her consent to the coming of the messianic kingdom, which would take place with the formation of the Church.

3.3 When at Cana Mary asked the Son to exercise his messianic power, she made a fundamental contribution to implanting the faith in the first community of disciples, and she co-operated in initiating God's kingdom, which has its "seed" and "beginning" in the Church (cf. *Lumen gentium,* n. 5).

3.4 On Calvary, Mary united herself to the sacrifice of her Son and made her own maternal contribution to the work of salvation, which took the form of labour pains, the birth of the new humanity.

3.5 In addressing the words "Woman, behold your son" to Mary, the Crucified One proclaims her motherhood not only in relation to the Apostle John but also to every disciple. The Evangelist himself, by saying that Jesus had to die "to gather into one the children of God who are scattered abroad" (*Jn* 11:52),[2] indicates the Church's birth as the fruit of the redemptive sacrifice with which Mary is maternally associated.

3.6 The Evangelist Saint Luke mentions the presence of Jesus' Mother in the first community of Jerusalem (*Acts* 1:14). In this way he stresses Mary's maternal role in the newborn Church, comparing it to her role in the Redeemer's birth. The maternal dimension thus becomes a fundamental element of Mary's relationship with the new People of the redeemed.

4.1 Following Sacred Scripture, patristic teaching recognises Mary's motherhood in the work of Christ and therefore in that of the Church, although in terms which are not always explicit.

---

[1] "*Verissime quidem mater Ecclesiæ atque magistra et regina Apostolorum...* [She was, in very truth, the Mother of the Church, the Teacher and Queen of the Apostles…]" (Leo XIII, Litt. Encycl. *Adiutricem populi*, 5 sept. 1895, n. 6: *Acta Leonis XIII*, vol. XV, p. 302; *Acta Sanctæ Sedis* 28 [1895-1896], p. 150).

[2] "*Ut filios Dei, qui erant dispersi, congregaret in unum*" (*Io* 11, 52).

4.2 According to Saint Irenaeus, Mary "became a cause of salvation for the whole human race" (*Haer.* 3, 22, 4; *PG* 7, 959),[1] and the pure womb of the Virgin "regenerates men in God" (*Haer.* 4, 33, 11; *PG* 7, 1080).[2] This is re-echoed by Saint Ambrose, who says: "A Virgin has begotten the salvation of the world, a Virgin has given life to all things" (*Ep.* 63, 33; *PL* 16, 1198),[3] and by other Fathers who call Mary "Mother of salvation" (Severian of Gabala, *Or. 6 in mundi creationem*, 10, *PG* 54, 4; Faustus of Riez, *Max. Bibl. Patrum,* VI, 620-621).[4]

4.3 In the Middle Ages, Saint Anselm addressed Mary in this way: "You are the mother of justification and of the justified, the Mother of reconciliation and of the reconciled, the mother of salvation and of the saved" (*Or.* 52, 8; *PL* 158, 957),[5] while other authors attribute to her the titles "Mother of grace" and "Mother of life".

5.1 The title "Mother of the Church" thus reflects the deep conviction of the Christian faithful, who see in Mary not only the mother of the person of Christ, but also of the faithful. She who is recognised as mother of salvation, life and grace, mother of the saved and mother of the living, is rightly proclaimed Mother of the Church.

5.2 Pope Paul VI would have liked the Second Vatican Council itself to have proclaimed "Mary Mother of the Church, that is, of the whole People of God, of the faithful and their Pastors".[6] He did so himself in his speech at the end of the Council's third session (21 November 1964), also asking that "henceforth the Blessed Virgin be honoured and invoked with this title by all the Christian people" (*AAS* 1964, 37).[7]

---

[1] "*Universo generi humano causa facta est salutis*" (Sanctus Irenæus, *Adversus hæreses (libri quinque)*, lib. III, cap. XXII, 4: *PG* 7, 959).
[2] "*Regenerat homines in Deum*" (*Ibid.*, lib. IV, cap. XXXIII, 11: *PG* 7, 1080).
[3] "*Virgo genuit mundi salute, virgo peperit vitam universorum*" (Sanctus Ambrosius, *Epistola* LXIII, 33: *PL* 16, 1198).
[4] "*Mater salutis*" (Severianus Gabalitanus, *In mundi creationem orationes sex*, 10; Dissertatio III, articulos VI, 67: *PG* 7, 317).
[5] "*Ergo, o domina, mater es iustificationis et iustificatorum, genitrix es reconciliationis et reconciliatorum, parens es salutis et salvatorum*" (Sanctus Anselmus Cantuariensis, *Orationes*, oratio LII: *PL* 158, 957 A).
[6] "*Igitur ad Beatæ Virginis gloriam ad nostrumque solacium, Mariam Sanctissimam declaramus Matrem Ecclesiæ, hoc est totius populi christiani, tam fidelium quam Pastorum...*" (Sanctus Paulus VI, *In Vaticana Basilica ad Conciliares Patres habita, die festo Præsentationis Beatæ Mariæ Virginis, post sollemnem ab ipso Summo Pontifice cum Præsulibus quibusdam peractam concelebrationem, tertia exacta Œcumenicæ Synodi Sessione promulgatisque Constitutione dogmatica de Ecclesia atque Decretis de Œcumenismo et de Ecclesiis Orientalibus catholicis*: *AAS* 56 (1964) 1015).
[7] "*Ut christianus populus maiore spe ac ferventiore studio invocet Beatissimam Virginem, eique cultum et honorem debitum exhibeat*" (Ibid., 1016).

5.3 In this way, my venerable Predecessor explicitly enunciated the doctrine contained in the eighth chapter of *Lumen gentium,* hoping that the title of Mary, Mother of the Church, would have an ever more important place in the liturgy and piety of the Christian people.[1]

17 September 1997

[1] On 3 March 2018, the Congregation for Divine Worship and the Discipline of the Sacraments issued *Decretum de celebratione Beatæ Mariæ Virginis Ecclesiæ Matris in Calendario Romano Generali* or "Decree on the celebration of the Blessed Virgin Mary Mother of the Church in the General Roman Calendar". Signed on 11 February 2018 by Robert Cardinal Sarah as prefect of the congregation, the document said: "*Summus autem Pontifex Franciscus, cum perpendisset quantum hæc fovenda devotio ad Pastorum, religiosorum, christifidelium Ecclesiæ sensum maternum ac genuinam marialem pietatem, adhuc proficere possit, decrevit ut memoriam B. Mariæ Virginis, Ecclesiæ Matris, in Calendarium Romanum inscribendam esse Feria II post Pentecosten et quotannis celebrandam.* [Having attentively considered how greatly the promotion of this devotion might encourage the growth of the maternal sense of the Church in the pastors, religious and faithful, as well as a growth of genuine Marian piety, Pope Francis has decreed that the Memorial of the Blessed Virgin Mary, Mother of the Church, should be inscribed in the Roman Calendar on the Monday after Pentecost and be now celebrated every year.]" (*AAS* 110 (2018), p. 438).

64
THE INTERCESSION OF THE HEAVENLY MOTHER OF DIVINE GRACE

Jesus answered, "Truly, truly, I say to you, unless one is born of water and the Spirit, he cannot enter the kingdom of God. That which is born of the flesh is flesh, and that which is born of the Spirit is spirit. Do not marvel that I said to you, 'You must be born anew'" (*Jn* 3:5-7).[1]

1.1 Mary is mother of humanity in the order of grace. The Second Vatican Council highlights this role of Mary, linking it to her co-operation in Christ's Redemption.

"In the designs of divine Providence, she was the gracious mother of the divine Redeemer here on earth, and above all others and in a singular way the generous associate and humble handmaid of the Lord" (*Lumen gentium*, n. 61).[2]

1.2 With these statements, the Constituion *Lumen gentium* wishes to give proper emphasis to the fact that the Blessed Virgin was intimately associated with Christ's redemptive work, becoming the Saviour's "generous associate", "in a singular way".

1.3 With the actions of any mother, from the most ordinary to the most demanding, Mary freely co-operated in the work of humanity's salvation in profound and constant harmony with her divine Son.

2.1 The Council also points out that Mary's co-operation was inspired by the Gospel virtues of obedience, faith, hope and charity, and was accomplished under the influence of the Holy Spirit. It also recalls that the gift of her universal spiritual motherhood stems precisely from this co-operation: associated with Christ in the work of Redemption, which includes the spiritual regeneration of humanity, she becomes mother of those reborn to new life.

2.2 In saying that Mary is "a mother to us in the order of grace" (cf. *ibid.*),[3] the Council stresses that her spiritual motherhood is not limited to the disciples

---

[1] "*Respondit Iesus: « Amen, amen dico tibi: Nisi quis natus fuerit ex aqua et Spiritu, non potest introire in regnum Dei. Quod natum est ex carne, caro est; et, quod natum est ex Spiritu, spiritus est. Non mireris quia dixi tibi: Oportet vos nasci denuo »* (*Io* 3, 5-7).

[2] "*Beata Virgo, ab æterno una cum divini Verbi incarnatione tamquam Mater Dei prædestinata, divinæ Providentiæ consilio, his in terris exstitit alma divini Redemptoris Mater, singulariter præ aliis generosa socia, et humilis ancilla Domini*" (CONCILIUM VATICANUM II, Const. dogm. de Ecclesia, *Lumen gentium*, 61: *AAS* 57 (1965), p. 63).

[3] "*Mater nobis in ordine gratiæ*" (IBID.).

alone, as though the words spoken by Jesus on Calvary: "Woman, behold your son" (*Jn* 19:26),[1] required a restrictive interpretation. Indeed, with these words the Crucified One established an intimate relationship between Mary and his beloved disciple, a typological figure of universal scope, intending to offer his Mother as Mother to all mankind.

2.3 On the other hand, the universal efficacy of the redeeming sacrifice and Mary's conscious co-operation with Christ's sacrificial offering does not allow any limitation of her motherly love.

2.4 Mary's universal mission is exercised in the context of her unique relationship with the Church. With her concern for every Christian, and indeed for every human creature, she guides the faith of the Church towards an ever deeper acceptance of God's Word, sustains her hope, enlivens her charity and fraternal communion and encourages her apostolic dynamism.

3.1 During her earthly life, Mary showed her spiritual motherhood to the Church for a very short time. Nonetheless, the full value of her role appeared after the Assumption and is destined to extend down the centuries to the end of the world. The Council expressly states:

"This motherhood of Mary in the order of grace continues uninterruptedly from the consent which she gave in faith at the Annunciation and which she sustained without wavering beneath the Cross, until the eternal fulfilment of all the elect" (*Lumen gentium*, n. 62).[2]

3.2 Having entered the Father's eternal kingdom, closer to her divine Son and thus closer to us all, she can more effectively exercise in the Spirit the role of maternal intercession entrusted to her by divine Providence.

4.1 The heavenly Father wanted to place Mary close to Christ and in communion with him who can "save those who draw near to God through him, since he always lives to make intercession for them" (*Heb* 7:25):[3] he wanted to unite to the Redeemer's intercession as a priest that of the Blessed Virgin as a mother. It is a role she carries out for the sake of those who are in danger and who need temporal favours and, especially, eternal salvation:

"By her maternal charity, she cares for the brethren of her Son, who still journey on earth surrounded by dangers and difficulties, until they are led into

---

[1] "*Mulier, ecce filius tuus*" (*Io* 19, 26).

[2] "*Hæc autem in gratiæ œconomia maternitas Mariæ indesinenter perdurat, inde a consensu quem in Annuntiatione fideliter præbuit, quemque sub cruce incunctanter sustinuit, usque ad perpetuam omnium electorum consummationem*" (CONCILIUM VATICANUM II, Const. dogm. de Ecclesia, *Lumen gentium*, 62: *AAS* 57 (1965), p. 63).

[3] "*Salvare in perpetuum potest accedentes per semetipsum ad Deum, semper vivens ad interpellandum pro eis*" (*Hebr* 7, 25).

their blessed home. Therefore the Blessed Virgin is invoked in the Church under the titles of Advocate, Helper, Benefactress and Mediatrix" (*Lumen gentium*, n. 62).[1]

4.2 These titles, suggested by the faith of the Christian people, help us better to understand the nature of the Mother of the Lord's intervention in the life of the Church and of the individual believer.

5.1 The title "Advocate" goes back to Saint Irenaeus. With regard to Eve's disobedience and Mary's obedience, he says that at the moment of the Annunciation "the Virgin Mary became the Advocate" of Eve (*Haer.* 5, 19, 1; *PG* 7, 1175-1176).[2] In fact, with her "yes" she defended our first mother and freed her from the consequences of her disobedience, becoming the cause of salvation for her and the whole human race.

5.2 Mary exercises her role as "Advocate" by co-operating both with the Spirit the Paraclete and with the One who interceded on the Cross for his persecutors (cf. *Lk* 23:34), whom John calls our "advocate with the Father" (*1 Jn* 2:1).[3] As a mother, she defends her children and protects them from the harm caused by their own sins.

5.3 Christians call upon Mary as "Helper", recognising her motherly love which sees her children's needs and is ready to come to their aid, especially when their eternal salvation is at stake.

5.4 The conviction that Mary is close to those who are suffering or in situations of serious danger has prompted the faithful to invoke her as "Benefactress". The same trusting certainty is expressed in the most ancient Marian prayer with the words:

"We fly to thy patronage, O holy Mother of God; despise not our petitions in our necessities but deliver us always from all dangers, O glorious and blessed Virgin" (from the *Roman Breviary*).[4]

5.5 As maternal Mediatrix, Mary presents our desires and petitions to Christ, and transmits the divine gifts to us, interceding continually on our behalf.

24 September 1997

[1] "*Materna sua caritate de fratribus Filii sui adhuc peregrinantibus necnon in periculis et angustiis versantibus curat, donec ad felicem patriam perducantur. Propterea B. Virgo in Ecclesia titulis Advocatæ, Auxiliatricis, Adiutricis, Mediatricis invocatur*" (CONCILIUM VATICANUM II, Const. dogm. de Ecclesia, *Lumen gentium*, 62: *AAS* 57 (1965), p. 63).

[2] "*Uti virginis Evae Virgo Maria fieret advocata*" (SANCTUS IRENÆUS LUGDUNENSIS, *Adversus hæreses*, lib. V, cap. 19, 1: *PG* 7, 1175).

[3] "*Advocatum habemus ad Patrem*" (*1 Io* 2, 1).

[4] For the text of the *Sub tuum præsídium* (We fly to your patronage), see Appendix of Marian Prayers, page 232.

65
MARY, MEDIATRIX

For there is one God, and there is one mediator between God and men, the man Christ Jesus, who gave himself as a ransom for all, the testimony to which was borne at the proper time (*1 Tm* 2:5-6).[1]

1.1 Among the titles attributed to Mary in the Church's devotion, the eighth chapter of *Lumen gentium* recalls that of "Mediatrix". Although some Council Fathers did not fully agree with this choice of title (cf. *Acta Synodalia* III, 8, 163-164), it was nevertheless inserted into the Dogmatic Constitution on the Church as confirmation of the value of the truth it expresses. Care was therefore taken not to associate it with any particular theology of mediation, but merely to list it among Mary's other recognised titles.

1.2 Moreover the conciliar text had already described the meaning of the title "Mediatrix" when it said that Mary "by her manifold intercession continues to bring us the gifts of eternal salvation" (*Lumen gentium*, n. 62).[2]

1.3 As I recalled in my Encyclical *Redemptoris Mater*: "Mary's mediation is intimately linked with her motherhood. It possesses a specifically maternal character, which distinguishes it from the mediation of the other creatures" (n. 38).[3]

1.4 From this point of view it is unique in its kind and singularly effective.

2.1 With regard to the objections made by some of the Council Fathers concerning the term "Mediatrix", the Council itself provided an answer by saying that Mary is "a mother to us in the order of grace" (*Lumen gentium*, n. 61).[4] We recall that Mary's mediation is essentially defined by her divine motherhood. Recognition of her role as Mediatrix is moreover implicit in the expression "our Mother", which presents the doctrine of Marian mediation by putting the accent on her motherhood. Lastly, the title "Mother in the order of grace" explains that the Blessed Virgin co-operates with Christ in humanity's spiritual rebirth.

---

[1] "*Unus enim Deus, unus et mediator Dei et hominum, homo Christus Iesus, qui dedit redemptionem semetipsum pro omnibus, testimonium temporibus suis* (*1 Tim* 2, 5-6).

[2] "*Multiplici intercessione sua pergit in æternæ salutis donis nobis conciliandis*" (Concilium Vaticanum II, Const. dogm. de Ecclesia, *Lumen gentium*, 62: *AAS* 57 (1965), p. 63).

[3] "*Mediatio enim Mariæ* intime conectitur cum eius maternitate, *indolem præ se fer ens proprie maternam, qua illa distinguitur a mediatione ceterarum creaturarum*" (Sanctus Ioannes Paulus II, Litt. enc. *Redemptoris Mater* (25 martii 1987), 38: *AAS* 79 (1987), p. 411).

[4] "*Mater nobis in ordine gratiæ*" (Concilium Vaticanum II, Const. dogm. de Ecclesia, *Lumen gentium*, 61: *AAS* 57 (1965), p. 63).

3.1 Mary's maternal mediation does not obscure the unique and perfect mediation of Christ. Indeed, after calling Mary "Mediatrix", the Council is careful to explain that this "neither takes away anything from nor adds anything to the dignity and efficacy of Christ the one Mediator" (*Lumen gentium*, n. 62).[1] And on this subject it quotes the famous text from the First Letter to Timothy: "For there is one God and there is one mediator between God and men, the man Christ Jesus, who gave himself as a ransom for all" (2:5-6).[2]

3.2 In addition, the Council states that "Mary's function as mother of men in no way obscures or diminishes this unique mediation of Christ, but rather shows its power" (*Lumen gentium*, n. 60).[3]

3.3 Therefore, far from being an obstacle to the exercise of Christ's unique mediation, Mary instead highlights its fruitfulness and efficacy.

"The Blessed Virgin's salutary influence on men originates not in any inner necessity but in the disposition of God. It flows forth from the superabundance of the merits of Christ, rests on his mediation, depends entirely on it and draws all its power from it" (*Lumen gentium*, n. 60).[4]

4.1 The value of Mary's mediation derives from Christ and thus the salutary influence of the Blessed Virgin "does not hinder in any way the immediate union of the faithful with Christ but on the contrary fosters it" (*ibid.*).[5]

4.2 The intrinsic orientation to Christ of the "Mediatrix's" work spurred the Council to recommend that the faithful turn to Mary "so that, encouraged by this maternal help they may the more closely adhere to the Mediator and Redeemer" (*Lumen gentium*, n. 62).[6]

4.3 In proclaiming Christ the one mediator (cf. *1 Tm* 2:5-6), the text of Saint Paul's Letter to Timothy excludes any other parallel mediation, but not subordinate mediation. In fact, before emphasising the one exclusive mediation of Christ,

---

[1] "*Dignitati et efficacitati Christi unius Mediatoris nihil deroget, nihil superaddat*" (Ibid., 62: *AAS* 57 (1965), p. 63).

[2] "*Unus enim Deus, unus et mediator Dei et hominum, homo Christus Iesus, qui dedit redemptionem semetipsum pro omnibus, testimonium temporibus suis*" (*1 Tim* 2, 5-6).

[3] "*Mariæ autem maternum munus erga homines hanc Christi unicam mediationem nullo modo obscurat nec minuit, sed virtutem eius ostendit*" (Concilium Vaticanum II, Const. dogm. de Ecclesia, *Lumen gentium*, 60: *AAS* 57 (1965), p. 62).

[4] "*Omnis enim salutaris Beatæ Virginis influxus in homines non ex aliqua rei necessitate, sed ex beneplacito divino exoritur et ex superabundantia meritorum Christi profluit, Eius mediationi innititur, ab illa omnino dependet, ex eademque totam virtutem haurit*" (Ibid.).

[5] "*Unionem autem immediatam credentium cum Christo nullo modo impedit sed fovet*" (Ibid., 60).

[6] "*Ut hoc materno fulti præsidio Mediatori ac Salvatori intimius adhæreant*" (Ibid., 62: *AAS* 57 (1965), p. 63).

the author urges "that supplications prayers, intercessions and thanksgivings be made for all men" (2:1).[1] Are not prayers a form of mediation? Indeed, according to Saint Paul, the unique mediation of Christ is meant to encourage other dependent, ministerial forms of mediation. By proclaiming the uniqueness of Christ's mediation, the Apostle intends only to exclude any autonomous or rival mediation, and not other forms compatible with the infinite value of the Saviour's work.

5.1 It is possible to participate in Christ's mediation in various areas of the work of salvation. After stressing that "no creature could ever be counted along with the Incarnate Word and Redeemer" (n. 62),[2] *Lumen gentium* describes how it is possible for creatures to exercise certain forms of mediation which are dependent on Christ. In fact, "just as the priesthood of Christ is shared in various ways both by his ministers and the faithful, and as the one goodness of God is radiated in different ways among his creatures, so also the unique mediation of the Redeemer does not exclude but rather gives rise to a manifold co-operation which is but a sharing in this one source" (*Lumen gentium,* n. 62).[3]

5.2 This desire to bring about various participations in the one mediation of Christ reveals the gratuitous love of God who wants to share what he possesses.

6.1 In truth, what is Mary's maternal mediation if not the Father's gift to humanity? This is why the Council concludes:

"The Church does not hesitate to profess this subordinate role of Mary, which it constantly experiences and recommends to the heartfelt attention of the faithful" (*ibid.*).[4]

6.2 Mary carries out her maternal role in constant dependence on the mediation of Christ and from him receives all that his heart wishes to give mankind.

6.3 On her earthly pilgrimage the Church "continuously" experiences the effective action of her "Mother in the order of grace".

1 October 1997

---

[1] "*Obsecrationes, orationes, postulationes, gratiarum actiones pro omnibus hominibus*" (*1 Tim* 2, 1).

[2] "*Nulla enim creatura cum Verbo incarnato ac Redemptore connumerari umquam potest*" (CONCILIUM VATICANUM II, Const. dogm. de Ecclesia, *Lumen gentium*, 62: *AAS* 57 (1965), p. 63).

[3] "*Sed sicut sacerdotium Christi variis modis tum a ministris tum a fideli populo participatur, et sicut una bonitas Dei in creaturis modis diversis realiter diffunditur, ita etiam unica mediatio Redemptoris non excludit, sed suscitat variam apud creaturas participatam ex unico fonte cooperationem*" (IBID.).

[4] "*Tale autem munus subordinatum Mariæ Ecclesia profiteri non dubitat, iugiter experitur et fidelium cordi commendat*" (IBID.).

66
THE CULT[1] OF THE BLESSED VIRGIN

But when the time had fully come, God sent forth his Son, born of woman, born under the law, to redeem those who were under the law, so that we might receive adoption as sons. And because you are sons, God has sent the Spirit of his Son into our hearts, crying, "Abba! Father!" (*Gal* 4:4-6).[2]

1.1 "When the time had fully come, God sent forth his Son, born of woman" (*Gal* 4:4).[3] Marian devotion is based on the wondrous divine decision, as the Apostle Paul recalls, to link forever the Son of God's human identity with a woman, Mary of Nazareth.

1.2 The mystery of the divine motherhood and of Mary's co-operation in the work of Redemption has filled believers in every age with an attitude of praise, both for the Saviour and for her who gave birth to him in time, thus co-operating in Redemption.

1.3 A further reason for grateful love for the Blessed Virgin is offered by her universal motherhood. By choosing her as Mother of all humanity, the heavenly Father has wished to reveal the motherly dimension, so to speak, of his divine tenderness and concern for all people in every era.

1.4 On Calvary, with the words: "Behold, your son!", "Behold, your mother!" (*Jn* 19:26-27),[4] Jesus gave Mary in advance to all who would receive the Good News of salvation, and was thus laying the foundation of their filial affection for her. Following John, the faithful would prolong Christ's love for his Mother with their own devotion, by accepting her into their own lives.

2.1 The Gospel texts attest to the presence of Marian devotion from the Church's origins.

2.2 The first two chapters of Saint Luke's Gospel seem to relate the particular attention to Jesus' Mother on the part of Jewish Christians, who expressed their appreciation of her and jealously guarded their memories of her.

---

[1] In Catholic terminology, "cult" or *cultus* in Latin refers to the outward religious practice for devotion or veneration extended to a particular saint, not to the worship of God. The Roman Catholic Church and the Eastern Orthodox Church make a major distinction between *latria*, the worship that is offered to God alone, and *dulia*, which is veneration offered to the saints, including the veneration of Mary, whose veneration is often referred to as *hyperdulia*.

[2] *"At ubi venit plenitudo temporis, misit Deus Filium suum, factum ex muliere, factum sub lege, ut eos, qui sub lege erant, redimeret, ut adoptionem filiorum reciperemus. Quoniam autem estis filii, misit Deus Spiritum Filii sui in corda nostra clamantem: « Abba, Pater! »"* (*Gal* 4, 4-6).

[3] *"At ubi venit plenitudo temporis, misit Deus Filium suum, factum ex muliere"* (*Gal* 4, 4).

[4] "*Mulier, ecce filius tuus*", " *Ecce mater tua*" (*Io* 19, 26-27),

2.3 Moreover, in the infancy narratives we can discern the initial expressions of and reasons for Marian devotion, summarised in Elizabeth's exclamations:

"Blessed are you among women… And blessed is she who believed that there would be a fulfilment of what was spoken to her from the Lord" (*Lk* 1:42, 45).[1]

2.4 Traces of a veneration already widespread among the first Christian community are present in the *Magníficat* canticle: "All generations will call me blessed" (*Lk* 1:48).[2] By putting these words on Mary's lips, Christians recognised her unique greatness, which would be proclaimed until the end of time.

2.5 In addition, the Gospel accounts (cf. *Lk* 1:24-35; *Mt* 1:23 and *Jn* 1:13), the first formulas of faith and a passage by Saint Ignatius of Antioch (cf. *Smyrn.* 1, 2: *SC* 10, 155) attest to the first communities' special admiration for Mary's virginity, closely linked to the mystery of the Incarnation.

2.6 The Gospel of John, by noting Mary's presence at the beginning and at the end of her Son's public life, suggests that the first Christians were keenly aware of Mary's role in the work of Redemption, in full loving dependence on Christ.

3.1 The Second Vatican Council, in stressing the particular character of Marian devotion, says: "Mary has by grace been exalted above all angels and men to a place second only to her Son, as the most holy Mother of God who was involved in the mysteries of Christ: she is rightly honoured by a special cult in the Church" (*Lumen gentium*, n. 66).[3]

3.2 Then, alluding to the third century Marian prayer, "*Sub tuum præsidium*"—"We fly to thy patronage"—it adds that this characteristic emerges from the very beginning: "From the earliest times the Blessed Virgin is honoured under the title of Mother of God in whose protection the faithful take refuge together in prayer in all their perils and needs" (*ibid.*).[4]

4.1 This assertion has been confirmed in iconography and in the teaching of the Fathers of the Church since the second century.

---

[1] "*Benedicta tu inter mulieres… Et beata, quæ credidit, quoniam perficientur ea, quæ dicta sunt ei a Domino* " (*Lc* 1, 42. 45).

[2] "*Beatam me dicent omnes generationes*" (*Lc* 1, 48).

[3] "*Maria, per gratiam Dei post Filium præ omnibus angelis et hominibus exaltata, utpote sanctissima Dei Mater, quæ mysteriis Christi interfuit, speciali cultu ab Ecclesia merito honoratur*" (CONCILIUM VATICANUM II, Const. dogm. de Ecclesia, *Lumen gentium*, 66: *AAS* 57 (1965), p. 65).

[4] "*Et sane ab antiquissimis temporibus Beata Virgo sub titulo 'Deiparæ' colitur, sub cuius præsidium fideles in cunctis periculis et necessitatibus suis deprecantes confugiunt*" (IBID.).

4.2 In Rome, in the catacombs of Priscilla, it is possible to admire the first depiction of the Madonna and Child, while at the same time, Saint Justin and Saint Irenaeus speak of Mary as the new Eve who by her faith and obedience makes amends for the disbelief and disobedience of the first woman. According to the Bishop of Lyons, it was not enough for Adam to be redeemed in Christ, but "it was right and necessary that Eve be restored in Mary" (*Demonstratio apostolica*, 33).[1] In this way he stresses the importance of woman in the work of salvation and lays the foundation for the inseparability of Marian devotion from that shown to Jesus, which will endure down the Christian centuries.

5.1 Marian devotion is first expressed in the invocation of Mary as *Theotókos*, a title which was authoritatively confirmed, after the Nestorian crisis, by the Council of Ephesus in 431.

5.2 The same popular reaction to the ambiguous and wavering position of Nestorius, who went so far as to deny Mary's divine motherhood, and the subsequent joyful acceptance of the Ephesian Synod's decisions, confirm how deeply rooted among Christians was devotion to the Blessed Virgin. However "following the Council of Ephesus, there was a remarkable growth in the devotion of the People of God towards Mary, in veneration and love, in invocation and imitation" (*Lumen gentium*, n. 66).[2] It was expressed especially in the liturgical feasts, among which, from the beginning of the fifth century, "the day of Mary *Theotókos* acquired particular importance. It was celebrated on 15 August in Jerusalem and later became the feast of the Dormition or the Assumption.

5.3 Under the influence of the "*Protoevangelium* of James",[3] the feasts of the Nativity, the Conception and the Presentation were also introduced, and notably contributed to highlighting some important aspects of the mystery of Mary.

---

[1] "*Et propter hoc alia creatura aliqua non factus est, sed ab eadem, quæ ab Adam genus habebat, similitudinem creaturæ servavit; nam necesse et dignum erat, rursus perficere Adam in Christo, ut submersum absorberetur mortale ab immortalitate, et Evam [perficere] in Maria ut virgo virginis advocata facta solveret et destrueret virgineam inoboedientiam per virgineum obsequium*" (SANCTUS IRENÆUS LUGDUNENSIS, *Demonstratio prædicationis apostolicæ*, pars. I, sect. III, 33: *Sources Chrétiennes*, 62; S. Weber, 1952, pp. 59-60). "For it was necessary that Adam should be summed up in Christ, that mortality might be swallowed up and overwhelmed by immortality; and Eve summed up in Mary, that a virgin should be a virgin's intercessor, and by a virgin's obedience undo and put away the disobedience of a virgin" (SAINT IRENAEUS OF LYON, *The Demonstration of the Apostolic Preaching*, 33: A. Robinson, D.D., 1920, p. 100).

[2] "*Inde praesertim ab Ephesina Synodo cultus Populi Dei erga Mariam mirabiliter crevit in veneratione et dilectione, in invocatione et imitatione*" (CONCILIUM VATICANUM II, Const. dogm. de Ecclesia, *Lumen gentium*, 66: *AAS* 57 (1965), p. 65).

[3] The *Protoevangelium* of James (*Protevangelium Iacobi*), also known as the Gospel of James, the Infancy Gospel of James, and *Liber Iacobi de nativitate Mariæ*, is an apocryphal (non-canonical) Gospel probably written between 140 and 170 AD and is considered to be the earliest surviving document attesting to the perpetual virginity of the Blessed Virgin Mary.

6.1 We can certainly say that Marian devotion has developed down to our day in wonderful continuity, alternating between flourishing periods and critical ones that, nonetheless, often had the merit of fostering its renewal even more.

6.2 Since the Second Vatican Council, Marian devotion seems destined to develop in harmony with a deeper understanding of the mystery of the Church and in dialogue with contemporary cultures, to be ever more firmly rooted in the faith and life of God's pilgrim people on earth.

15 October 1997

67
THE NATURE OF MARIAN DEVOTION

"Teacher, which is the great commandment in the law?" And he said to him, "You shall love the Lord your God with all your heart, and with all your soul, and with all your mind. This is the great and first commandment" (*Mt* 22:36-38).[1]

1.1 The Second Vatican Council states that devotion to the Blessed Virgin, "as it has always existed in the Church, for all its uniqueness, differs essentially from the cult of adoration, which is offered equally to the Incarnate Word and to the Father and the Holy Spirit, and it is most favourable to it" (*Lumen gentium*, n. 66).[2]

1.2 With these words the Constitution *Lumen gentium* stresses the characteristics of Marian devotion. Although the veneration of the faithful for Mary is superior to their devotion to the other saints, it is nevertheless inferior to the cult of adoration reserved to God, from which it essentially differs. The term "adoration" indicates the form of worship that man offers to God, acknowledging him as Creator and Lord of the universe. Enlightened by divine Revelation, the Christian adores the Father "in spirit and truth" (*Jn* 4:23).[3] With the Father, he adores Christ, the Incarnate Word, exclaiming with the Apostle Thomas: "My Lord and my God!" (*Jn* 20:28).[4] Lastly, in this same act of adoration he includes the Holy Spirit, who "with the Father and the Son is adored and glorified" (*DS* 150), as the Nicene-Constantinopolitan Creed recalls.[5]

1.3 When the faithful call upon Mary as "Mother of God" and contemplate in her the highest dignity conferred upon a creature, they are still not offering her a veneration equal to that of the divine Persons. There is an infinite distance between Marian veneration and worship of the Trinity and the Incarnate Word.

---

[1] "« *Magister, quod est mandatum magnum in Lege?* ». *Ait autem illi:* « *Diliges Dominum Deum tuum in toto corde tuo et in tota anima tua et in tota mente tua: hoc est magnum et primum mandatum* »" (*Mt* 22, 36-38).

[2] "*Prout in Ecclesia semper exstitit, singularis omnino quamquam est, essentialiter differt a cultu adorationis, qui Verbo incarnato æque ac Patri et Spiritui Sancto exhibetur, eidemque potissimum favet*" (Concilium Vaticanum II, Const. dogm. de Ecclesia, *Lumen gentium*, 66: *AAS* 57 (1965), p. 65).

[3] "*In Spiritu et veritate*" (*Io* 4, 23).

[4] "*Dominus meus et Deus meus!*" (*Io* 20, 28).

[5] "*Cum Patre et Fílio simul adorátur et conglorificátur*" (*Symbolum Nicænum-Constantinopolitanum*: *Missale Romanum*, Ordo Missæ; *DS* 150).

1.4 As a consequence, although the Christian community addresses the Blessed Virgin in language that sometimes recalls the terms used in the worship of God, it has a completely different meaning and value. Thus the love of the faithful for Mary differs from what they owe God: while the Lord must be loved above everything with all one's heart, with all one's soul and with all one's mind (cf. *Mt* 22:37), the sentiment joining Christians to the Blessed Virgin suggests, at a spiritual level, the affection of children for their mother.

2.1 Nevertheless there is a continuity between Marian devotion and the worship given to God: indeed, the honour paid to Mary is ordered and leads to adoration of the Blessed Trinity.

2.2 The Council recalls that Christian veneration of the Blessed Virgin "is most favourable to" the worship of the Incarnate Word, the Father and the Holy Spirit. It then adds from a Christological viewpoint that "the various forms of piety towards the Mother of God, which the Church has approved within the limits of sound and orthodox doctrine, according to the dispositions and understanding of the faithful, ensure that while the Mother is honoured, the Son through whom all things have their being (cf. *Col* 1:15-16) and in whom it has pleased the Father that all fullness should dwell (cf. *Col* 1:19) is rightly known, loved and glorified and his commandments are observed" (*Lumen gentium*, n. 66).[1]

2.3 Since the Church's earliest days, Marian devotion has been meant to foster faithful adherence to Christ. To venerate the Mother of God is to affirm the divinity of Christ. In fact, the Fathers of the Council of Ephesus, in proclaiming Mary *Theotókos*, "Mother of God", intended to confirm the belief in Christ, true God.

2.4 The conclusion of the account of Jesus' first miracle, obtained at Cana by Mary's intercession, shows how her action was directed to the glorification of her Son. In fact the Evangelist says: "This, the first of his signs, Jesus did at Cana in Galilee, and manifested his glory; and his disciples believed in him" (*Jn* 2:11).[2]

---

[1] "*Variæ enim formæ pietatis erga Dei Genitricem, quas Ecclesia intra limites sanae et orthodoxæ doctrinæ, pro temporum et locorum conditionibus et pro indole ingenioque fidelium approbavit, id efficiunt ut dum Mater honoratur, Filius, propter quem omnia* (cf. *Col* 1, 15-16) *et in quo æterno Patri 'complacuit omnem plenitudinem inhabitare'* (*Col* 1, 19), *rite noscatur, ametur, glorificetur, Eiusque mandata serventur*" (Concilium Vaticanum II, Const. dogm. de Ecclesia, *Lumen gentium*, 66: *AAS* 57 (1965), p. 65).

[2] "*Hoc fecit initium signorum Iesus in Cana Galilææ et manifestavit gloriam suam, et crediderunt in eum discipuli eius*" (*Io* 2, 11).

3.1 Marian devotion also encourages adoration of the Father and the Holy Spirit in those who practise it according to the Church's spirit. In fact, by recognising the value of Mary's motherhood, believers discover in it a special manifestation of God the Father's tenderness.

3.2 The mystery of the Virgin Mother highlights the action of the Holy Spirit, who brought about the conception of the child in her womb and continually guided her life.

3.3 The titles of Comforter, Advocate, Helper attributed to Mary by popular Christian piety do not overshadow but exalt the action of the Spirit, the Comforter, and dispose believers to benefit from his gifts.

4.1 Lastly, the Council recalls the "uniqueness" of Marian devotion and stresses the difference between adoration of God and veneration of the saints.

4.2 This devotion is unrepeatable because it is directed to a person whose personal perfection and mission are unique.

4.3 Indeed, the gifts conferred upon Mary by divine love, such as her immaculate holiness, her divine motherhood, her association with the work of Redemption and above all the sacrifice of the Cross, are absolutely exceptional.

4.4 Devotion to Mary expresses the Church's praise and recognition of these extraordinary gifts. To her, who is Mother of the Church and Mother of humanity, the Christian people turn, encouraged by filial trust, to request her motherly intercession and to obtain the necessary goods for earthly life in view of eternal happiness.

22 October 1997

68
MARIAN DEVOTION AND THE WORSHIP OF IMAGES

He is the image of the invisible God, the first-born of all creation; for in him all things were created, in heaven and on earth, visible and invisible, whether thrones or dominions or principalities or authorities—all things were created through him and for him. He is before all things, and in him all things hold together. He is the head of the body, the Church; he is the beginning, the first-born from the dead, that in everything he might be pre-eminent (*Col* 1:15-18).[1]

1.1 After giving doctrinal justification to veneration of the Blessed Virgin, the Second Vatican Council exhorts all the faithful to promote it:

"The Sacred Synod teaches this Catholic doctrine advisedly and at the same time admonishes all the sons of the Church that the cult, especially the liturgical cult, of the Blessed Virgin, be generously fostered, and that the practices and exercises of devotion towards her, recommended by the teaching authority of the Church in the course of centuries, be highly esteemed" (*Lumen gentium*, n. 67).[2]

1.2 With this last statement the Council Fathers, without going into particulars, intended to reaffirm the validity of certain prayers such as the Rosary and the *Angelus*, dear to the tradition of the Christian people and frequently encouraged by the Supreme Pontiffs as an effective means of nourishing the life of faith and devotion to the Blessed Virgin.

2.1 The conciliar text goes on to ask believers "that those decrees, which were given in the early days regarding the veneration of images of Christ, the Blessed Virgin and the saints, be religiously observed" (*Lumen gentium,* n. 67).[3]

---

[1] "*Qui est imago Dei invisibilis, primogenitus omnis creaturæ, quia in ipso condita sunt universa in cœlis et in terra, visibilia et invisibilia, sive throni sive dominationes sive principatus sive potestates. Omnia per ipsum et in ipsum creata sunt, et ipse est ante omnia, et omnia in ipso constant. Et ipse est caput corporis ecclesiæ; qui est principium, primogenitus ex mortuis, ut sit in omnibus ipse primatum tenens*" (*Col* 1, 15-18).

[2] "*Hanc catholicam doctrinam Sacrosancta Synodus consulto docet, simulque omnes Ecclesiæ filios admonet, ut cultum, præsertim liturgicum, erga Beatam Virginem generose foveant, praxes autem et exercitia pietatis erga Eam sæculorum cursu a Magisterio commendata magni faciant*" (CONCILIUM VATICANUM II, Const. dogm. de Ecclesia, *Lumen gentium*, 67: *AAS* 57 (1965), pp. 65-66).

[3] "*Et ea quæ anteactis temporibus de cultu imaginum Christi, Beatæ Virginis et Sanctorum decreta fuere, religiose servent*" (IBID., 67: *AAS* 57 (1965), p. 66).

2.2 Thus it re-proposes the decisions of the Second Council of Nicaea, held in 787, which confirmed the legitimacy of the veneration of sacred images in opposition to those who wished to destroy them, since they considered them inadequate for representing the divinity (cf. *Redemptoris Mater*, n. 33). "We define", said the Fathers of that Council, "with full precision and care that, like the representation of the precious life-giving Cross, so the venerated and holy images either painted or mosaic or made of any other suitable material, should be exposed in holy churches of God on sacred furnishings and vestments, on walls and panels in homes and streets, be they images of the Lord God and our Saviour Jesus Christ, or of our immaculate Lady, the Holy Mother of God, of the holy angels, or of all the saints and the just" (*DS* 600).[1]

2.2 By recalling this definition, *Lumen gentium* intended to stress the legitimacy and validity of sacred images, in contrast to certain tendencies to remove them from churches and shrines in order to focus full attention on Christ.

3.1 The Second Council of Nicaea does not only affirm the legitimacy of images, but seeks to describe their usefulness for Christian piety:

"Indeed, the more often these images are contemplated, the more those who look at them are brought to remember and desire the original models and, in kissing them, to show them respect and veneration" (*DS* 601).[2]

3.2 These directives apply in a particular way to the veneration of the Blessed Virgin.

Images, icons and statues of our Lady, present in houses, public places and countless churches and chapels, help the faithful to invoke her constant presence and her merciful patronage in the various circumstances of life. By making the Blessed Virgin's motherly tenderness concrete and almost visible, they invite us to turn to her, to pray to her trustfully and to imitate her in generously accepting the divine will.

---

[1] "*Regiæ quasi continuati semitae, sequentesque divinitus inspiratum sanctorum Patrum nostrorum magisterium, et catholicæ traditionem Ecclesiæ (nam Spiritus Sancti hanc esse novimus, qui nimirum in ipsa inhabitat), definimus in omni certitudine ac diligentia, sicut figuram pretiosæ ac vivificæ crucis, ita venerabiles ac sanctas imagines proponendas tam quæ de coloribus et tessellis, quam quæ ex alia materia congruenter in sanctis Dei ecclesiis, et sacris vasis et vestibus, et in parietibus ac tabulis, domibus et viis: tam videlicet imaginem Domini Dei et Salvatoris nostri Iesu Christi, quam intemeratae Dominæ nostræ sanctæ Dei genitricis, honrobiliumque Angelorum, et omnium Sanctorum simul et almorum virorum*" (*DS* 600).

[2] "*Quanto enim frequentius per imaginalem formationem videntur, tanto, qui has contemplantur, alacrius eriguntur ad primitivorum earum memoriam et desiderium, ad osculum et ad honorariam his adorationem tribuendam*" (*DS* 601).

3.3 None of the known images is an authentic reproduction of Mary's face, as Saint Augustine had already acknowledged (*De Trinitate*, 8, 7);[1] however they help us establish a more living relationship with her. Therefore the practice of exposing images of Mary in places of worship and in other buildings should be encouraged, in order to be aware of her help in moments of difficulty and as a reminder to lead a life that is ever more holy and faithful to God.

4.1 To encourage the proper use of sacred images, the Council of Nicaea recalls that "the honour paid to the image is really paid to the person it represents, and those who venerate the image are venerating the reality of the person it represents" (*DS* 601).[2]

4.2 Hence in adoring the Person of the Incarnate Word in the image of Christ the faithful are making a genuine act of worship, which has nothing in common with idolatry.

4.3 Similarly, when he venerates images of Mary, the believer's act is ultimately intended as a tribute to the person of the Mother of Jesus.

5.1 Therefore, the Second Vatican Council urges theologians and preachers to refrain from both exaggerating and minimising the special dignity of the Mother of God. It adds:

"Following the study of Sacred Scripture, the Fathers, the doctors and liturgy of the Church, and under the guidance of the Church's Magisterium, let them rightly illustrate the duties and privileges of the Blessed Virgin, which always refer to Christ, the source of all truth, sanctity and devotion" (*Lumen gentium*, n. 67).[3]

5.2 Authentic Marian doctrine is ensured by fidelity to Scripture and Tradition, as well as to the liturgical texts and the Magisterium. Its indispensable characteristic is the reference to Christ: everything in Mary derives from Christ and is directed to him.

---

[1] "*Neque enim novimus faciem virginis Mariae, ex qua ille a viro intacta neque in ipso partu corrupta mirabiliter natus est* [For neither do we know the countenance of the Virgin Mary; from whom, untouched by a husband, nor tainted in the birth itself, He was wonderfully born]" (Sanctus Augustinus, *De Trinitate*, lib. VIII, 7 (cap. V): *PL* 42, 952).

[2] "*Imaginis enim honor ad primitivum transit: et qui adorat imaginem, adorat in ea depicti subsistentiam*" (*DS* 601).

[3] "*Studium Sacræ Scripturæ, Sanctorum Patrum et Doctorum Ecclesiæque liturgiarum sub ductu Magisterii excolentes, recte illustrent munera et privilegia Beatæ Virginis, quæ semper Christum spectant, totius veritatis, sanctitatis et pietatis originem*" (Concilium Vaticanum II, Const. dogm. de Ecclesia, *Lumen gentium*, 67: *AAS* 57 (1965), p. 66).

6.1 Lastly, the Council offers believers several criteria for authentically living their filial relationship with Mary:

"Let the faithful remember moreover that true devotion consists neither in sterile nor transitory affection, nor in a certain vain credulity, but proceeds from true faith, by which we are led to recognise the excellence of the Mother of God, and we are moved to a filial love towards our Mother and to the imitation of her virtues" (*Lumen gentium*, n. 67).[1]

6.2 With these words, the Council Fathers put people on guard against "vain credulity" and the predominance of sentiment. They aim above all at reaffirming authentic Marian devotion, which proceeds from faith and the loving recognition of Mary's dignity, fosters filial affection for her and inspires the firm resolution to imitate her virtues.

29 October 1997

[1] "*Meminerint porro fideles veram devotionem neque in sterili et transitorio affectu, neque in vana quadam credulitate consistere, sed a vera fide procedere, qua ad Dei Genitricis excellentiam agnoscendam adducimur, et ad filialem erga Matrem nostram amorem eiusque virtutum imitationem excitamur*" (CONCILIUM VATICANUM II, Const. dogm. de Ecclesia, *Lumen gentium*, 67: *AAS* 57 (1965), p. 66).

69
PRAYER TO MARY

In the sixth month the angel Gabriel was sent from God to a city of Galilee named Nazareth, to a virgin betrothed to a man whose name was Joseph, of the house of David; and the virgin's name was Mary. And he came to her and said, "Hail, full of grace, the Lord is with you!" (*Lk* 1:26-28).[1]

1.1 Down the centuries Marian devotion has enjoyed an uninterrupted development. In addition to the traditional liturgical feasts dedicated to the Lord's Mother, there has been a flowering of countless expressions of piety, often approved and encouraged by the Church's Magisterium.

1.2 Many Marian devotions and prayers are an extension of the liturgy itself and have sometimes contributed to its overall enrichment, as is the case with the Office in honour of the Blessed Virgin and other pious compositions which have become part of the Breviary.

1.3 The first known Marian invocation goes back to the third century and begins with the words: "We fly to thy patronage (*Sub tuum præsídium*), O holy Mother of God…". However, since the fourteenth century the most common prayer among Christians has been the *Hail Mary*.

1.4 By repeating the first words the angel addressed to Mary, it leads the faithful to contemplate the mystery of the Incarnation. The Latin word *Ave* translates the Greek word *chàire*:[2] it is an invitation to joy and could be translated "Rejoice". The Eastern hymn *Akathistos*[3] repeatedly stresses this "rejoice". In the *Hail Mary* the Blessed Virgin is called "full of grace" and is thus recognised for the perfection and beauty of her soul.

1.5 The phrase "The Lord is with thee" reveals God's special personal relationship with Mary, which fits into the great plan for his covenant with all humanity. Next, the statement "Blessed art thou among women and blessed is the fruit of thy womb, Jesus" expresses the fulfilment of the divine plan in the Daughter of Sion's virginal body.

1.6 Calling upon "Holy Mary, Mother of God", Christians ask the one who was the immaculate Mother of the Lord by a unique privilege: "Pray for us sinners", and entrust themselves to her at the present moment and at the ultimate moment of death.

---

[1] "*In mense autem sexto missus est angelus Gabriel a Deo in civitatem Galilaeae, cui nomen Nazareth, ad virginem desponsatam viro, cui nomen erat Ioseph de domo David, et nomen virginis Maria. Et ingressus ad eam dixit: « Ave, gratia plena, Dominus tecum »* (*Lc* 1, 26-28).

[2] "*Khaire*" or "*Chàire*" is the transliteration of the Greek word χαῖρε.

[3] For the text of the *Akathistos* (Akathist Hymn to the *Theotókos*), see Appendix of Marian Prayers, page 242.

2.1 The traditional prayer of the *Angelus*[1] also invites Christians to meditate on the mystery of the Incarnation, urging them to take Mary as their point of reference at different times of their day in order to imitate her willingness to fulfil the divine plan of salvation. This prayer makes us relive in a way that great event in human history, the Incarnation, to which every *Hail Mary* refers. Here we find the value and attraction of the *Angelus*, expressed so many times not only by theologians and pastors but also by poets and painters.

2.2 In Marian devotion the Rosary has taken on an important role. By repeating the *Hail Mary*, it leads us to contemplate the mysteries of faith. In nourishing the Christian people's love for the Mother of God, this simple prayer also orients Marian prayer in a clearer way to its goal: the glorification of Christ.

2.3 Pope Paul VI, like his Predecessors,[2] especially Leo XIII, Pius XII and John XXIII, held the recitation of the Rosary in great esteem and wished it to be widely spread among families. Moreover, in the Apostolic Exhortation *Marialis cultus*, he explained its doctrine by recalling that it is a "Gospel prayer, centred on the mystery of the redemptive Incarnation", and stressing its "clearly Christological orientation" (n. 46).[3]

2.4 Popular piety frequently adds a litany to the Rosary. The best known is the one used at the Shrine of Loreto and is therefore called the "Litany of Loreto".[4]

2.5 With very simple invocations it helps us concentrate on Mary's person, in order to grasp the spiritual riches which the Father's love poured out in her.

3.1 As the liturgy and Christian piety demonstrate, the Church has always held devotion to Mary in high esteem, considering it inseparably linked to belief in Christ. It is in fact based on the Father's plan, the Saviour's will and the Paraclete's inspiration.

3.2 Having received salvation and grace from Christ, the Blessed Virgin is called to play an important role in humanity's redemption. Through Marian devotion Christians acknowledge the value of Mary's presence on their journey to salvation, having recourse to her for every kind of grace. They especially know that they can count on her motherly intercession to receive from the Lord everything necessary for growing in the divine life and for attaining eternal salvation.

---

[1] For the text of the *Angelus*, see Appendix of Marian Prayers, page 236.

[2] Pope Saint John Paul II would himself go on to promulgate the Apostolic Letter *Rosarium Virginis Mariæ* [The Rosary of the Virgin Mary] on 16 October 2002.

[3] "Rosarium *igitur cum in Evangelio innitatur et ad mysterium Incarnationis hominumque redemptionem tamquam ad centrum pertinent, oratio est putanda, quae ad rem christologicam prorsus convertitur*" (Sanctus Paulus VI, Adhortatio apostolica *Marialis cultus* (2 februarii 1974), 46: *AAS* 66 (1974), p. 155).

[4] For the text of the Litany of Loreto (*Litaniæ lauretanæ*), see Appendix of Marian Prayers, page 238.

3.3 As the many titles attributed to the Blessed Virgin and the continual pilgrimages to Marian shrines attest, the trust of the faithful in Jesus' Mother spurs them to call upon her for their daily needs.

3.4 They are certain that her maternal heart cannot remain indifferent to the material and spiritual distress of her children.

3.5 By encouraging the confidence and spontaneity of the faithful, devotion to the Mother of God thus helps to brighten their spiritual life and enables them to make progress on the demanding path of the Beatitudes.

4 Lastly, we would like to recall that devotion to Mary, by highlighting the human dimension of the Incarnation, helps us better to discern the face of a God who shares the joys and sufferings of humanity, the "God-with-us"[1] whom she conceived as man in her most pure womb, gave birth to, cared for and followed with unspeakable love from his days in Nazareth and Bethlehem to those of the Cross and Resurrection.

5 November 1997

[1] Emmanuel (Immanuel or Imanu'el) is Hebrew for "God-with-us", consisting of two Hebrew words: *El* (meaning "God") and *Immânû* (meaning "with us"); cf. *Isaiah* 7:14 and 8:8.

70
THE MOTHER OF UNITY AND HOPE

And when they had entered, they went up to the upper room, where they were staying, Peter and John and James and Andrew, Philip and Thomas, Bartholomew and Matthew, James the son of Alphaeus and Simon the Zealot and Judas the son of James. All these with one accord devoted themselves to prayer, together with the women and Mary the mother of Jesus, and with his brothers (*Acts* 1:13-14).[1]

1.1 After explaining the relationship between Mary and the Church, the Second Vatican Council rejoices in observing that the Blessed Virgin is also honoured by Christians who do not belong to the Catholic community:

"It gives great joy and comfort to this sacred Synod that among the separated brethren too there are those who give due honour to the Mother of our Lord and Saviour..." (*Lumen gentium*, n. 69; cf. *Redemptoris Mater*, nn. 29-34).[2]

In view of this fact, we can say that Mary's universal motherhood, even if it makes the divisions among Christians seem all the sadder, represents a great sign of hope for the ecumenical journey.

1.2 Many Protestant communities, because of a particular conception of grace and ecclesiology, are opposed to Marian doctrine and devotion, maintaining that Mary's co-operation in the work of salvation prejudices Christ's unique mediation. In this view, devotion to Mary would compete in a way with the honour owed the Son.

2.1 In recent years, however, further study of the thought of the first Reformers has shed light on positions more open to Catholic doctrine. Luther's[3] writings, for example, show love and veneration for Mary, extolled as a model of every virtue: he upholds the sublime holiness of the Mother of God and at times affirms the privilege of the Immaculate Conception, sharing with other Reformers belief in Mary's perpetual virginity.

2.2 The study of Luther and Calvin's[4] thought, as well as the analysis of some texts of Evangelical Christians, have contributed to a renewed attention by some Protestants and Anglicans to various themes of Mariological doctrine.

---

[1] "*Et cum introissent, in cenaculum ascenderunt, ubi manebant et Petrus et Ioannes et Iacobus et Andreas, Philippus et Thomas, Bartholomæus et Matthæus, Iacobus Alphæi et Simon Zelotes et Iudas Iacobi. Hi omnes erant perseverantes unanimiter in oratione cum mulieribus et Maria matre Iesu et fratribus eius* (*Act* 1, 13-14).

[2] "*Sacrosanctæ huic Synodo magnum affert gaudium et solatium, etiam inter fratres seiunctos non deesse, qui Matri Domini ac Salvatoris debitum afferunt honorem*" (Concilium Vaticanum II, Const. dogm. de Ecclesia, *Lumen gentium*, 69: *AAS* 57 (1965), p. 66).

[3] Martin Luther (1483–1546) was a German priest, theologian, and the initiator of the Protestant Pseudo-Reformation.

[4] John Calvin (1509–1564) was a French theologian and pastor during the Protestant Pseudo-Reformation.

2.3 Some have even arrived at positions very close to those of Catholics regarding the fundamental points of Marian doctrine, such as her divine motherhood, virginity, holiness, and spiritual motherhood.

2.4 The concern for stressing the presence of women in the Church encourages the effort to recognise Mary's role in salvation history.

2.5 All these facts are so many reasons to have hope for the ecumenical journey. Catholics have a deep desire to be able to share with all their brothers and sisters in Christ the joy that comes from Mary's presence in life according to the Spirit.

3.1 Among the brethren who "give due honour to the Mother of our Lord and Saviour", the Council mentions Eastern Christians, "who with devout mind and fervent impulse give honour to the Mother of God, Ever-Virgin" (*Lumen gentium*, n. 69).[1]

3.2 As we can see from their many expressions of devotion, veneration for Mary represents a significant element of communion between Catholics and Orthodox.

3.3 However, there remain some disagreements regarding the dogmas of the Immaculate Conception and the Assumption, even if these truths were first expounded by certain Eastern theologians—one need only recall great writers like Gregory Palamas († 1359), Nicholas Cabasilas († after 1369) and George Scholarios († after 1472).

3.4 These disagreements, however, are perhaps more a question of formulation than of content and must never make us forget our common belief in Mary's divine motherhood, her perpetual virginity, her perfect holiness, and her maternal intercession with her Son. As the Second Vatican Council recalled, this "fervent impulse" and "devout mind" unite Catholics and Orthodox in devotion to the Mother of God.

4.1 At the end of *Lumen gentium* the Council invites us to entrust the unity of Christians to Mary:

"The entire body of the faithful pours forth urgent supplications to the Mother of God and of men that she, who aided the beginnings of the Church by her prayers, may now, exalted as she is above all the angels and saints, intercede before her Son in the fellowship of all the saints" (*ibid.*).[2]

---

[1] "*Qui ad cultum Deiparæ semper Virginis fervido impulsu ac devoto animo concurrunt*" (CONCILIUM VATICANUM II, Const. dogm. de Ecclesia, *Lumen gentium*, 69: *AAS* 57 (1965), p. 66).

[2] "*Universi christifideles supplicationes instantes ad Matrem Dei et Matrem hominum effundant, ut Ipsa, quæ primitiis Ecclesiæ precibus suis adstitit, nunc quoque in cælo super omnes Beatos et Angelos exaltata, in omnium Sanctorum Communione apud Filium suum intercedat*" (IBID.).

4.2 Just as Mary's presence in the early community fostered oneness of heart, which prayer strengthened and made visible (cf. *Acts* 1:14), so the most intense communion with her whom Augustine called the "Mother of unity" (*Sermo* 192, 2; *PL* 38, 1013)[1] will be able to bring Christians to the point of enjoying the long-awaited gift of ecumenical unity.

4.3 We ceaselessly pray to the Blessed Virgin so that, just as at the beginning she supported the journey of the Christian community's oneness in prayer and the proclamation of the Gospel, so today she may obtain through her intercession reconciliation and full communion among all believers in Christ.

4.4 Mother of men, Mary knows well the needs and aspirations of humanity. The Council particularly asks her to intercede so that "all families of people, whether they are honoured with the title of Christian or whether they still do not know the Saviour, may be happily gathered together in peace and harmony into one People of God, for the glory of the Most Holy and Undivided Trinity" (*Lumen gentium*, n. 69).[2]

4.5 The peace, harmony and unity for which the Church and humanity hope still seem far away. Nevertheless, they are a gift of the Spirit to be constantly sought, as we learn from Mary and trust in her intercession.

5.1 With this petition Christians share the expectation of her who, filled with the virtue of hope, sustains the Church on her journey to the future with God.

5.2 Having personally achieved happiness because she "believed that there would be a fulfilment of what was spoken to her from the Lord" (*Lk* 1:45),[3] the Blessed Virgin accompanies believers—and the whole Church—so that in the world, amid the joys and sufferings of this life, they may be true prophets of the hope that never disappoints.

12 November 1997

---

[1] "*Mater est unitatis*" (SANCTUS AUGUSTINUS HIPPONENSIS, *Sermo* CXCII, cap. II, *Sermo* 192, 2: *PL* 38, 1013).

[2] "*Cunctæ familiæ populorum, sive quæ christiano nomine decorantur, sive quæ Salvatorem suum adhuc ignorant, cum pace et concordia in unum Populum Dei feliciter congregentur, ad gloriam Sanctissimæ et individuæ Trinitatis*" (IBID., 69: *AAS* 57 (1965), pp. 66-67).

[3] "*Beata, quæ credidit, quoniam perficientur ea, quæ dicta sunt ei a Domino*" (*Lc* 1, 45).

Appendix of Marian Prayers

1. The Angelic Salutation (*Salutatio angelica*)

The Angelic Salutation or Hail Mary is "the most familiar of all prayers addressed to the Blessed Virgin. It consists of three parts, of which (a) and (b) are scriptural (*Luke* 1:28, 42) and (c) added by the Church. (a) and (b) were first used as a formula of devotion during the 12th century and various petitions were added at will; the present form was fixed in 1568" (Donald Attwater, *A Catholic Dictionary*, 1958).

(a) *Ave, María, grátia plena, Dóminus tecum:*
benedícta tu in muliéribus,
(b) *et benedíctus fructus ventris tui, Iesus.*
(c) *Sancta María, Mater Dei,*
ora pro nobis peccatóribus,
nunc et in hora mortis nostræ. Amen.

(a) Hail, Mary, full of grace, the Lord is with thee:
blessed art thou among women,
(b) and blessed is the fruit of thy womb, Jesus.
(c) Holy Mary, Mother of God, pray for us sinners,
now and at the hour of our death. Amen.

2. The *Sub tuum*

The *Sub tuum* is one of the Marian antiphons that may be chosen at the conclusion of the Night Prayer of Compline in the Liturgy of the Hours. It is the oldest prayer to the Blessed Virgin Mary, dating to the third century.

Sub tuum præsídium confúgimus,
sancta Dei Génetrix;
nostras deprecatiónes ne despícias in necessitátibus,
sed a perículis cunctis líbera nos semper,
Virgo gloriósa et benedícta. Amen.

We fly to thy patronage,
O holy Mother of God;
despise not our petitions in our necessities,
but deliver us always from all dangers,
O glorious and blessed Virgin. Amen.

3. The *Salve Regina*

The *Salve Regina* is the most widely used prayer to the Blessed Virgin Mary after the Angelic Salutation (*Ave Maria*). It is one of the Marian antiphons that may be chosen at the close of the Night Prayer of Compline in the Divine Office, particularly during Ordinary Time after Pentecost (*Tempus per annum post Pentecosten*).

Salve, Regína, mater misericórdiæ;
vita, dulcédo et spes nostra, salve.
Ad te clamámus éxsules fílii Hevæ.
Ad te suspirámus geméntes et flentes
in hac lacrimárum valle.
Eia ergo, advocáta nostra,
illos tuos misericórdes óculos ad nos convérte.
Et Iesum, benedíctum fructum ventris tui,
nobis post hoc exsílium osténde.
O clemens, o pia, o dulcis Virgo María.

Hail, holy Queen, mother of mercy!
Hail, our life, our sweetness, and our hope!
To thee do we cry,
poor banished children of Eve;
to thee do we send up our sighs,
mourning and weeping in this vale of tears.
Turn, then, most gracious Advocate, thine eyes of mercy toward us.
And after this, our exile,
show unto us the blessed fruit of thy womb, Jesus.
O clement, O loving, O sweet Virgin Mary.

4. The Holy Rosary (*Sanctum Rosarium*)

Rosary (*rosárium*) is "a string of beads consisting of five sets (decades) each of ten small and one larger bead (a crucifix with two large and three small beads is ordinarily added)" or "the prayers said on these beads. Each decade is associated with a mystery of the faith and these mysteries number fifteen,[1] so that a full rosary consists of this number of decades and corresponding prayers, but these are rarely ever met with. The method of praying the rosary, in public or private, is to recite an Our Father (large bead), ten Hail Marys (small beads), and Glory be to the Father (large bead), while meditating on the appropriate mystery; the essence of the devotion consists in a loving and intelligent meditation and not a mechanical repetition of the prayers. The beads are simply a device for keeping count. The tradition that the rosary was revealed by our Lady to St Dominic is unproven; but the devotion has been particularly associated with his order for over 400 years" (Donald Attwater, *A Catholic Dictionary*, 1958).

[1] In his 2002 Apostolic Letter *Rosarium Virginis Mariæ* ("The Rosary of the Virgin Mary"), Pope Saint John Paul the Great proposed the addition of the optional Luminous Mysteries (*mystéria luminósa*) or Mysteries of Light (*mystéria lucis*), which would bring the total number of mysteries to 20.

Mystéria gaudiósa
in feria secunda et sabbato
1 *Annuntiátio.*
2 *Visitátio.*
3 *Natívitas.*
4 *Præsentátio.*
5 *Invéntio in Templo.*

The Joyful Mysteries
on Monday and Saturday
1 The Annunciation
2 The Visitation
3 The Nativity
4 The Presentation
5 The Finding in the Temple

Mystéria luminósa
in feria quinta
1 *Baptísma apud Iordánem.*
2 *Autorevelátio apud Cananénse matrimónium.*
3 *Regni Dei proclamátio coniúncta cum invitaménto ad conversiónem.*
4 *Transfigurátio.*
5 *Eucharístiæ Institútio.*

The Luminous Mysteries
on Thursday
1 The Baptism of Jesus
2 The Manifestation at the Wedding Feast of Cana
3 The Proclamation of the Kingdom, with the call to Conversion
4 The Transfiguration
5 The Institution of the Eucharist

Mystéria dolorósa
in feria tertia et feria sexta
1 *Agonía in Hortu.*
2 *Flagellátio.*
3 *Coronátio Spinis.*
4 *Baiulátio Crucis.*
5 *Crucifíxio et Mors.*

The Sorrowful Mysteries
on Tuesday and Friday
1 The Agony in the Garden
2 The Scourging at the Pillar
3 The Crowning with Thorns
4 The Carrying of the Cross
5 The Crucifixion

Mystéria gloriósa
in feria quarta et Dominica
1 *Resurréctio.*
2 *Ascénsio.*
3 *Descénsus Spíritus Sancti.*
4 *Assúmptio.*
5 *Coronátio in Cælo.*

The Glorious Mysteries
on Wednesday and Sunday
1 The Resurrection
2 The Ascension
3 The Descent of the Holy Spirit
4 The Assumption
5 The Coronation in Heaven

Oratio ad finem Rosarii dicenda

Orémus. Deus, cuius Unigénitus per vitam, mortem et resurrectiónem suam nobis salútis ætérnæ præmia comparávit, concéde, quǽsumus: ut hæc mystéria sacratíssimo beátæ Maríæ Vírginis Rosário recoléntes, et imitémur quod cóntinent, et quod promíttunt assequámur. Per Christum Dóminum nostrum. Amen.

Prayer concluding the Rosary

Let us pray. O God, whose only-begotten Son, by his life, death and resurrection, has purchased for us the rewards of eternal life, grant, we beseech thee, that meditating on these mysteries of the most holy Rosary of the Blessed Virgin Mary, we may imitate what they contain and obtain what they promise, through the same Christ our Lord. Amen.

5. The *Magníficat*

The *Magníficat* or Canticle of the Blessed Virgin Mary (*Canticum Beatæ Mariæ Virginis*) is prayed every evening at Vespers, and every morning at Lauds in the Byzantine Rite.

Canticum Beatæ Mariæ Virginis

Lc 1, 46-55

[46]*Magníficat ánima mea Dóminum,*
[47]*et exsultávit spíritus meus in Deo salvatóre meo,*
[48]*quia respéxit humilitátem ancíllæ suæ.*
Ecce enim ex hoc beátam me dicent omnes generatiónes,
[49]*quia fecit mihi magna, qui potens est, et sanctum nomen eius,*
[50]*et misericórdia eius in progénies et progenies timéntibus eum.*
[51]*Fecit poténtiam in bráchio suo,*
dispérsit supérbos mente cordis sui;
[52]*depósuit poténtes de sede et exaltávit húmiles;*
[53]*esuriéntes implévit bonis et dívites dimísit inánes.*
[54]*Suscépit Israel púerum suum, recordátus misericórdiæ,*
[55]*sicut locútus est ad patres nostros,*
Ábraham et sémini eius in sǽcula.
Glória Patri, et Fílio, et Spirítui Sancto.
Sicut erat in princípio, et nunc et semper,
et in sǽcula sæculórum. Amen.

Canticle of the Blessed Virgin Mary

Luke 1:46-55

[46]My soul magnifies the Lord,
[47]and my spirit rejoices in God my Saviour,
[48]for he has regarded the low estate of his handmaiden.
For behold, henceforth all generations will call me blessed;
[49]for he who is mighty has done great things for me, and holy is his name.
[50]And his mercy is on those who fear him from generation to generation.
[51]He has shown strength with his arm, he has scattered the proud
in the imagination of their hearts,
[52]he has put down the mighty from their thrones,
and exalted those of low degree;
[53]he has filled the hungry with good things,
and the rich he has sent empty away.
[54]He has helped his servant Israel, in remembrance of his mercy,
[55]as he spoke to our fathers,
to Abraham and to his posterity for ever.
Glory to the Father, and to the Son, and to the Holy Spirit:
as it was in the beginning, is now,
and will be for ever. Amen.

6. The *Angelus* and the *Regina Cæli* (*Angelus Domini et Regina cæli*)

The *Angelus* is a Marian prayer in honour of the Incarnation of our Lord, traditionally said in the morning, at midday, and in the evening, marked by the ringing of the angelus-bell. The ringing of the angelus-bell consists of three strokes followed by a pause three times, and then nine strokes, usually at about 6am, noon, and 6pm. The Angelus is said standing on Saturdays and Sundays (genuflecting at the third versicle) but kneeling at other times. During the Season of Easter, it is omitted altogether and the *Regina Cæli* is said instead, always standing (cf. Donald Attwater, *A Catholic Dictionary*, 1958). The *Regina Cæli* is also one of the Marian antiphons prayed at the close of the Night Prayer of Compline in the Divine Office during Easter Time.

℣. *Angelus Dómini nuntiávit Maríæ.*
℟. *Et concépit de Spíritu Sancto.*
℣. *Ave, María…* ℟. *Sancta María…*

℣. *Ecce ancílla Dómini.*
℟. *Fiat mihi secúndum verbum tuum.*
℣. *Ave, María…* ℟. *Sancta María…*

℣. *Et Verbum caro factum est.*
℟. *Et habitávit in nobis.*
℣. *Ave, María…* ℟. *Sancta María…*

℣. *Ora pro nobis, Sancta Dei Génetrix.*
℟. *Ut digni efficiámur promissionibus Christi.*

Orémus. Grátiam tuam, quǽsumus, Dómine, méntibus nostris infúnde, ut qui, ángelo nuntiánte, Christi Fílii tui incarnatiónem cognóvimus, per passiónem eius et crucem ad resurrectiónis glóriam perducámur. Per eúndem Christum Dóminum nostrum. ℟. *Amen.*

℣. The angel of the Lord declared unto Mary.
℟. And she conceived by the Holy Spirit.
℣. Hail, Mary… ℟. Holy Mary…

℣. Behold the handmaid of the Lord.
℟. Be it done unto me according to Your word.
℣. Hail, Mary… ℟. Holy Mary…

℣. And the Word was made flesh.
℟. And dwelt among us.
℣. Hail, Mary… ℟. Holy Mary…

℣. Pray for us, O holy Mother of God,
℟. That we may be made worthy of the promises of Christ.

Let us pray. Pour forth, we beseech You, O Lord, Your grace into our hearts, that we, to whom the Incarnation of Christ Your Son was made known by the message of an Angel, may by His passion and cross be brought to the glory of His resurrection. Through the same Christ our Lord. ℟. Amen.

Tempus Paschale

℣. *Regína cœli, lætáre, allelúia.*
℟. *Quia quem meruísti portáre, allelúia.*

℣. *Resurréxit, sicut dixit, allelúia.*
℟. *Ora pro nobis Deum, allelúia.*

℣. *Gaude et lætáre, Virgo María, allelúia.*
℟. *Quia surréxit Dóminus vere, allelúia.*

Orémus. Deus, qui per resurrectiónem Fílii tui, Dómini nostri Iesu Christi, mundum lætificáre dignátus es: præsta, quǽsumus; ut, per eius Genetrícem Vírginem Maríam, perpétuæ capiámus gáudia vitæ. Per eúndem Christum Dóminum nostrum. ℟. *Amen.*

Easter Season

℣. Queen of heaven, rejoice, alleluia!
℟. For He whom you did merit to bear, alleluia!

℣. Has risen, as He said, alleluia!
℟. Pray for us to God, alleluia!

℣. Rejoice and be glad, O Virgin Mary, alleluia!
℟. For the Lord is truly risen, alleluia.

Let us pray. O God, who through the resurrection of Your Son, our Lord Jesus Christ, did vouchsafe to give joy to the world; grant, we beseech You, that through His Mother, the Virgin Mary, we may obtain the joys of everlasting life. Through the same Christ our Lord. ℟. Amen.

7. The *Memorare*

The *Memoráre* is "a popular prayer to our Lady, attributed to Saint Bernard of Clairvaux, so called from its first word in Latin. Its use was greatly popularized by a French secular priest, Claude Bernard, in the early 17th century" (Donald Attwater, *A Catholic Dictionary*, 1958).

Memoráre, O piíssima Virgo María,
non esse audítum a sǽculo,
quemquam ad tua curréntem præsídia,
tua implorántem auxília, tua peténtem suffrágia, esse derelíctum.
Ego tali animátus confidéntia, ad te, Virgo Vírginum, Mater, curro;
ad te vénio; coram te gemens peccátor assísto.
Noli, Mater Verbi, verba mea despícere;
sed audi propítia et exáudi. Amen.

Remember, O most gracious Virgin Mary,
that never was it known that anyone who fled to thy protection,
implored thy help, or sought thy intercession was left unaided.
Inspired with this confidence,
I fly unto thee, O Virgin of virgins, my Mother; to thee do I come;
before thee I stand, sinful and sorrowful.
O Mother of the Word Incarnate, despise not my petitions,
but in thy mercy hear and answer me. Amen.

8. A Child's Prayer to Mary

This simple prayer is taken from the second verse of the Marian hymn *Memento, salutis Auctor*, which is the traditional hymn for the hours of Terce, Sext, None, and Compline in the Little Office of the Blessed Virgin Mary (*Officium Parvum Beatae Mariae Virginis*).

Maria, Mater gratiæ, Mater misericordiæ,
tu me ab hoste protege
et hora mortis suscipe. Amen.

Mary, mother whom we bless, full of grace and tenderness,
defend me from the devil's power
and greet me in my dying hour. Amen.

9. Mary, Help of Those in Need (*Sancta Maria, succurre miseris*)

This prayer was composed by Bishop Fulbert of Chartres (ca. 951–ca. 1029) and appears in his *Sermo IX, De Annuntiatione Dominica*.

Sancta María, succúrre míseris,
iuva pusillánimes, réfove flébiles, ora pro pópulo, intérveni pro clero,
intercéde pro devóto femíneo sexu:
séntiant omnes tuum iuvámen,
quicúmque célebrant tuam sanctam commemoratiónem. Amen.

Holy Mary, help those in need,
give strength to the weak, comfort the sorrowful,
pray for God's people, assist the clergy, intercede for religious.
May all who seek your help experience your
unfailing protection. Amen.

10. The Litany of Loreto (*Litaniæ Lauretanæ*)

The Litany of Loreto of the Blessed Virgin Mary had its origin at the sanctuary of Loreto in Italy and began to spread towards the end of the sixteenth century. It is often said during the Benediction of the Blessed Sacrament, and to conclude the recitation of the Rosary. Saint John Paul II added the invocations *Mater Ecclésiæ* (Mother of the Church) in 1980 and *Regína familiárum* (Queen of the family) in 1995. Pope Francis added the invocations *Mater misericórdiæ* (Mother of mercy), *Mater spei* (Mother of hope), and *Solácium migrantium* (Comfort of migrants) in 2020.

Kýrie eléison. ℟.	Lord, have mercy. ℟.
Christe eléison. ℟.	Christ, have mercy. ℟.
Kýrie eléison. ℟.	Lord, have mercy. ℟.
Christe, audi nos.	Christ, hear us.
℟. *Christe, exáudi nos.*	℟. Christ, graciously hear us.
Pater de cælis, Deus.	God, the Father of heaven.
℟. *Miserére nobis.*	℟. Have mercy on us.
Fili Redémptor mundi, Deus. ℟.	God the Son, Redeemer. ℟.
Spíritus Sancte, Deus. ℟.	God the Holy Spirit. ℟.
Sancta Trínitas, unus Deus. ℟.	Holy Trinity, one God. ℟.
Sancta María. ℟. *Ora pro nobis.*	Holy Mary. ℟. Pray for us.
Sancta Dei Génitrix. ℟.	Holy Mother of God. ℟.
Sancta Virgo Vírginum. ℟.	Holy Virgin of virgins. ℟.
Mater Christi. ℟.	Mother of Christ. ℟.
Mater Ecclésiæ. ℟.	Mother of the Church. ℟.
Mater misericórdiæ. ℟.	Mother of mercy.
Mater divínæ grátiæ. ℟.	Mother of divine grace. ℟.
Mater spei. ℟.	Mother of hope. ℟.
Mater puríssima. ℟.	Mother most pure. ℟.
Mater castíssima. ℟.	Mother most chaste. ℟.
Mater intemeráta. ℟.	Mother undefiled. ℟.
Mater invioláta. ℟.	Mother inviolate. ℟.
Mater amábilis. ℟.	Mother most amiable. ℟.
Mater admirábilis. ℟.	Mother most admirable. ℟.
Mater boni consílii. ℟.	Mother of good counsel. ℟.
Mater Creatóris. ℟.	Mother of our Creator. ℟.
Mater Salvatóris. ℟.	Mother of our Saviour. ℟.
Virgo prudentíssima. ℟.	Virgin most prudent. ℟.
Virgo veneránda. ℟.	Virgin most venerable. ℟.
Virgo prædicánda. ℟.	Virgin most renowned. ℟.
Virgo potens. ℟.	Virgin most powerful. ℟.
Virgo clemens. ℟.	Virgin most merciful. ℟.
Virgo fidélis. ℟.	Virgin most faithful. ℟.
Spéculum iustítiæ. ℟.	Mirror of justice. ℟.
Sedes sapiéntiæ. ℟.	Seat of wisdom. ℟.
Causa nostræ lætítiæ. ℟.	Cause of our joy. ℟.
Vas spirituále. ℟.	Spiritual vessel. ℟.
Vas honorábile. ℟.	Vessel of honour. ℟.
Vas insígne devotiónis. ℟.	Singular vessel of devotion. ℟.
Rosa mýstica. ℟.	Mystical rose. ℟.
Turris davídica. ℟.	Tower of David. ℟.
Turris ebúrnea. ℟.	Tower of ivory. ℟.

Domus áurea. ℟.	House of gold. ℟.
Fœderis arca. ℟.	Ark of the covenant. ℟.
Iánua cœli. ℟.	Gate of heaven. ℟.
Stella matutína. ℟.	Morning star. ℟.
Salus infirmórum. ℟.	Health of the sick. ℟.
Refúgium peccatórum. ℟.	Refuge of sinners. ℟.
Solácium migrantium. ℟.	Comfort of migrants. ℟.
Consolátrix afflictórum. ℟.	Comforter of the afflicted. ℟.
Auxílium Christianórum. ℟.	Help of Christians. ℟.
Regína Angelórum. ℟.	Queen of angels. ℟.
Regína Patriarchárum. ℟.	Queen of patriarchs. ℟.
Regína Prophetárum. ℟.	Queen of prophets. ℟.
Regína Apostolórum. ℟.	Queen of apostles. ℟.
Regína Mártyrum. ℟.	Queen of martyrs. ℟.
Regína Confessórum. ℟.	Queen of confessors. ℟.
Regína Vírginum. ℟.	Queen of virgins. ℟.
Regína Sanctórum ómnium. ℟.	Queen of all saints. ℟.
Regína sine labe originháli concépta. ℟.	Queen conceived without original sin. ℟.
Regína in cœlum assúmpta. ℟.	Queen assumed into heaven. ℟.
Regína sacratíssimi Rosárii. ℟.	Queen of the most holy Rosary. ℟.
Regína familiárum. ℟.	Queen of the family. ℟.
Regína pacis. ℟.	Queen of peace. ℟.
Agnus Dei, qui tollis peccáta mundi.	Lamb of God, You take away the sins of the world.
℟. *Parce nobis, Dómine.*	℟. Spare us, O Lord.
Agnus Dei, qui tollis peccáta mundi.	Lamb of God, You take away the sins of the world.
℟. *Exáudi nos, Dómine.*	℟. Graciously hear us, O Lord.
Agnus Dei, qui tollis peccáta mundi.	Lamb of God, You take away the sins of the world.
℟. *Miserére nobis.*	℟. Have mercy on us.
Ora pro nobis, Sancta Dei Génetrix.	Pray for us, O holy Mother of God.
℟. *Ut digni efficiámur promissionibus Christi.*	℟. That we may be made worthy of the promises of Christ.

Orémus. Concéde nos fámulos tuos, quǽsumus, Dómine Deus, perpétua mentis et córporis sanitáte gaudére: et gloriósa beátæ Maríæ semper Vírginis intercessióne, a præsénti liberári tristítia et ætérna pérfrui lætítia. Per Christum Dóminum nostrum. ℟. *Amen.*

Let us pray. Grant, we beg of You, O Lord God, that we Your servants may enjoy lasting health of mind and body, and by the glorious intercession of the

Blessed Mary, ever Virgin, be delivered from present sorrow and enter into the joy of eternal happiness. Through Christ our Lord. ℟. Amen.

11. Pious Invocations (*Piæ Invocationis*)

O Maria, sine labe origináli concépta, ora pro nobis.	O Mary, conceived without sin, pray for us who have recourse to thee.
Dignáre me laudáre te, Virgo sacráta; Da mihi virtútem contra hostes tuos.	Vouchsafe that I may praise thee, O sacred Virgin; Give me strength against thine enemies.
Mater mea, líbera me a peccáto mortáli.	My Mother, deliver me from mortal sin.
Sancta María, líbera nos a pœnis inférni.	Holy Mary, deliver us from the pains of hell.
O María, fac ut vivam in Deo, cum Deo et pro Deo.	O Mary, make me to live in God, with God, and for God.
Mater de Perpétuo Succúrsu, ora pro nobis.	Mother of Perpetual Succour, pray for us.

12. The Akathist Hymn to the *Theotókos*

The Akathist Hymn to the *Theotókos* (Mother of God) is a hymn in honour of the Blessed Virgin Mary attributed to Saint Roman the Melodist (fifth century). The name in Greek, *Akathistos Hymnos* (Ἀκάθιστος Ὕμνος), means "Unseated Hymn" because it is always sung standing, in honour of the Incarnation. The hymn consists of a brief hymn (*kontakion*) and 24 long and short strophes, each beginning with a succeeding letter of the Greek alphabet and concluding with "Rejoice, O Virgin Spouse" and "Alleluia." In the Byzantine Rite the hymn is sung at the Office in part on the first four Sundays of Lent and in toto on the Fifth Saturday of Lent.

Kontakion: Unto you, O *Theotókos*, invincible Champion, your City, in thanksgiving ascribes the victory for the deliverance from sufferings. And having your might unassailable, free us from all dangers, so that we may cry unto you: Rejoice, O Virgin Spouse.

1 The Archangel was sent from Heaven to cry "Rejoice!" to the *Theotókos*. And beholding You, O Lord, taking bodily form, he stood in awe, and with his bodiless voice he cried aloud to her such things as these:

Rejoice, you through whom joy shall shine forth.
Rejoice, you whom the curse will vanish.
Rejoice, the Restoration of fallen Adam.
Rejoice, the Redemption of the tears of Eve.
Rejoice, O Height beyond human logic.
Rejoice, O depth invisible even to the eyes of Angels.
Rejoice, for you are the King's throne.
Rejoice, you bear Him, Who bears the universe.
Rejoice, O Star revealing the Sun.
Rejoice, O Womb of divine Incarnation.
Rejoice, you through whom creation is renewed.
Rejoice, you through whom the Creator is born a Babe.
Rejoice, O Virgin Spouse.

2 Beholding herself in purity, the holy one courageously said to Gabriel: Your strange voice seems almost unbelievable to my soul; for how do you speak of birth-giving without seed? crying aloud: Alleluia.

3 Seeking to know the incomprehensible knowledge, the Virgin cried to him who ministered to her: How many a Son be born from a virginal womb? Tell me! To her he answered in fear, yet crying thus:

Rejoice, O seer of the ineffable Will.
Rejoice, O surety of those praying in silence.
Rejoice, you the Preface of Christ's miracles.
Rejoice, you the Pinnacle of His commandments.
Rejoice, O heavenly Ladder, by which God descended.

Rejoice, O Bridge leading those from earth to Heaven.
Rejoice, O Miracle, much marveled of Angels.
Rejoice, O trauma, much dirged of demons.
Rejoice, you who ineffably gave birth to the Light.
Rejoice, you who revealed the mystery to none.
Rejoice, O knowledge superceding the wise.
Rejoice, You who enlightens the minds of the faithful.
Rejoice, O Virgin Spouse.

4 The power of the Most High then overshadowed the Virgin, that she might conceive; and her fruitful womb He made a fertile meadow for all those desiring to reap salvation, as they chant: Alleluia.

5 Carrying God in her womb, the Virgin hastened to Elizabeth, whose unborn babe forthwith recognising Mary's salutation rejoiced, and with leaps as it were with songs, he cried out to the *Theotókos*:

Rejoice, O branch of the unwithering Vine.
Rejoice, O Land yielding the untainted Fruit.
Rejoice, O Husbandry of the merciful Husbandman.
Rejoice, O birthgiver to the Planter of our life.
Rejoice, O Field bearing abundant compassion.
Rejoice, O Table laden with an abundance of mercies.
Rejoice, for you make the meadow produce contentment.
Rejoice, for you prepare a haven for souls.
Rejoice, acceptable Incense of intercession.
Rejoice, Oblation for all the world.
Rejoice, Favour of God to mortals.
Rejoice, Access of mortals to God.
Rejoice, O Virgin Spouse.

6 Having doubtful thoughts, the righteous Joseph was troubled; for he suspected a secret union as he beheld you unwed, O blameless one; but when he learned of your conception through the Holy Spirit, he cried: Alleluia.

7 On hearing the Angels praising the incarnate presence of Christ, the shepherds hastened as to a Shepherd, and beholding Him as a spotless Lamb, pastured in Mary's womb, her they hymned, and said:

Rejoice, Mother of the Lamb and Shepherd.
Rejoice, Fold of the rational sheep.
Rejoice, O Defense against invisible foes.
Rejoice, Opener of the gates of Paradise.
Rejoice, for the things of Heaven rejoice with the earth.
Rejoice, the things of earth join chorus with the Heavens.

Rejoice, never-silent Voice of the Apostles.
Rejoice, never-conquered Courage of the Martyrs.
Rejoice, firm Support of the Faith.
Rejoice, shining Token of grace.
Rejoice, you through whom Hades was laid bare.
Rejoice, you through whom we are clothed with glory.
Rejoice, O Virgin Spouse.

8 Beholding the Godward-pointing Star, the Magi followed it radiance; and holding it as a lantern, they sought through it the mighty King. And having approached the Unreachable, they rejoiced and cried to Him: Alleluia.

9 The sons of the Chaldees saw in the hands of the Virgin Him Who by His hand fashioned man; and sensing Him as Lord, even though He had taken the form of a servant, they hastened with gifts to do homage, and they cried out to her who is blessed:

Rejoice, Mother of the never-setting Star.
Rejoice, Dawn of the mystic Day.
Rejoice, you who has quenched the fiery furnace of error.
Rejoice, you who enlightens the initiates of the Trinity.
Rejoice, you who has removed the inhuman tyrant from power.
Rejoice, you who has shown Christ, the man-befriending Lord.
Rejoice, you who has redeemed us from the pagan religion.
Rejoice, you who has rescued us from the works of mire.
Rejoice, you who ceased the worship of fire.
Rejoice, you who saves us from the flames of passions.
Rejoice, Guide of the faithful to chastity.
Rejoice, O Delight of all generations.
Rejoice, O Virgin Spouse.

10 Having become God-bearing heralds, the Magi returned to Babylon. Fulfilling Your prophecy, and having preached You as the Christ to all, they left Herod as a trifler, who knew not how to chant: Alleluia.

11 Having shed the light of truth in Egypt, You expelled the darkness of falsehood; and unable to bear Your strength, O Saviour, her idols fell; and they that were set free from them cried to the *Theotókos*:

Rejoice, Uplifting of men.
Rejoice, Downfall of demons.
Rejoice, you who trampled upon the delusion of error.
Rejoice, you who censured the deceit of the idols.
Rejoice, Sea which drowned the symbolic Pharaoh.
Rejoice, Rock which refreshed those thirsting for life.

Rejoice, Pillar of fire, guiding those in darkness.
Rejoice, Protection of the world, more spacious than a cloud.
Rejoice, Nourishment, successor to manna.
Rejoice, Minister of holy joy.
Rejoice, Land of promise.
Rejoice, you from whom flows milk and honey.
Rejoice, O Virgin Spouse.

12 When Symeon was prepared to leave from this age of deception, You were presented to him as a newborn Babe, but he recognised You as perfect God. Wherefore, he marvelled at Your ineffable wisdom, chanting: Alleluia.

13 New was the Creation which the Creator showed to us His creatures, when He sprang forth from the seedless womb; and He preserved it incorrupt, even as it was, that we, seeing this Miracle, may praise her saying:

Rejoice, Flower of incorruption.
Rejoice, Crown of self-restraint.
Rejoice, O shining Token of Resurrection.
Rejoice, you whom reflects the life of the Angels.
Rejoice, Tree of delectable Fruit that nourishes the faithful.
Rejoice, well-shaded Tree under which many find shelter.
Rejoice you who bears the Guide of those astray.
Rejoice, you who gives birth to the Redeemer of captives.
Rejoice, Intercession before the righteous Judge.
Rejoice, Forgiveness for many transgressors.
Rejoice, Robe of confidence for those bare of courage.
Rejoice, Tenderness conquering all desire.
Rejoice, O Virgin Spouse.

14 Seeing a strange childbirth, let us estrange ourselves from the world by transporting our minds to Heaven; to this end the Most High God appeared on earth a lowly man, that He might draw to the heights those who cry out to Him: Alleluia.

15 The Infinite Word was wholly present with those on earth, yet never absent from those in Heaven; for this was a divine condescension and not a mere change of place; and His birth was from a Virgin chosen of God, who heard such words as these:

Rejoice, Land of the Uncontained God.

Indices

Index of Scriptural Citations

catechesis number in brackets

OLD TESTAMENT
(*VETUS TESTAMENTUM*)

Genesis
1:27 [**7**]
1:28 [**27**]
1:31 [**7**]
3:15 [**12**]
3:15 [**21**]
3:20 [**49**]
4:1 [**14**]
15:6 [**14**]
17:15-16 [**14**]
17:17 [**14**]
17:4 [**14**]
18:1-2 [**14**]
18:14 [**14**]
30:1-2 [**14**]
30:22-23 [**14**]

Exodus
15:20-21 [**15**]

Judges
5:24 [**15**]
13:3 [**14**]

1 Samuel (1 Kings)
1:11 [**14**]
1:19-20 [**14**]
1:27-28 [**14**]
2:1 [**14**]

2 Samuel (2 Kings)
7:13-14 [**13**]

1 Kings (3 Kings)
18:13 [**16**]

Judith
13:7 [**15**]
15:9-10 [**15**]

Psalms
40 (39):7-9 [**32**]

Proverbs
18:22 [**16**]
31:10 [**16**]
31:30 [**16**]

Song of Songs (of Solomon) or Canticles of Canticles
6:3 [**17**]

Isaiah (Isaias)
7:10 [**13**]
7:13-14 [**13**]
7:14 [**13, 25**]
9:5 [**13**]
42:6 [**39**]
52:7 [**34**]
53:5 [**40**]
53:10 [**40**]
54:1 [**18**]
54:5, 7-8 [**17**]
62:4-5 [**17**]
62:11-12 [**17**]

Jeremiah (Jeremias)
3:20 [**17**]
31:1-4 [**17**]

Ezekiel (Ezechiel)
16:60 [**17**]

Daniel
7:14 [**32**]

Hosea (Osee)
1:6, 9 [**17**]
2:14 [**17**]
2:16, 19-20 [**17**]
2:2 [**17**]
2:23 [**17**]
2:7 [**17**]

Joel
2:21, 27 [**18**]

Micah (Michaes)
5:1-2 (2-3) [**13**]

Zephaniah (Sophonias)
3:14 [**18**]
3:15 [**18**]
3:16 [**18**]
3:17 [**18**]

Zechariah (Zacharias)
9:9-10 [**18**]

2 Maccabees (2 Machabees)
7:20-23 [**16**]
7:28-29 [**16**]

NEW TESTAMENT
(*NOVUM TESTAMENTUM*)

Matthew
1:20 **[26]**
1:20 **[30]**
1:21 **[30]**
1:22-23 **[13]**
1:22-25 **[60]**
1:23 **[26]**
5:48 **[61]**
7:7 **[44]**
11:29 **[40]**
13:55 **[2]**
20:28 **[32]**
22:36-38 **[67]**
28:1 **[31]**
28:10 **[51]**

Mark
3:32-35 **[46]** 3:35 **[1]**
6:3 **[2]**
10:45 **[32]**
16:19 **[56]**

Luke
1:6 **[19]**
1:18, 34 **[25]**
1:26-28 **[69]**
1:27 **[19, 30]**
1:28 **[27]**
1:32 **[34]**
1:34 **[27]**
1:35 **[25, 28]**
1:38 **[8, 32, 36, 62]**
1:39 **[34]**
1:40 **[34]**
1:41 **[34]**
1:41-42 **[34]**
1:41b-42. 45 **[55]**
1:42 **[1, 15]**
1:42, 45 **[66]**
1:43 **[34]**
1:44 **[34]**
1:45 **[25, 34, 61, 70]**
1:46-48 **[58]**
1:46-48 **[62]**
1:46-49 **[54]**
1:47-48 **[35]**
1:48 **[35, 66]**
1:49-50 **[35, 61]**
1:51-53 **[35]**
1:54 **[11]**
1:54-55 **[35]**
2:4 **[36]**
2:7 **[31, 36]**
2:10 **[36]**
2:14 **[36]**
2:15 **[36]**
2:16 **[36]**
2:17 **[36]**
2:19 **[4, 36, 43, 62]**
2:22-24 **[39]**
2:24 **[40]**
2:25 **[39]**
2:25-26 **[39]**
2:29 **[39]**
2:30-32 **[39]**
2:32 **[40]**
2:33 **[39]**
2:34 **[41]**
2:34-35 **[40]**
2:35 **[41]**
2:37 **[40, 41]**
2:38 **[40, 41]**
2:40 **[43]**
2:46 **[42]**
2:47 **[42]**
2:48 **[24, 42]**
2:49 **[24, 42, 43]**
2:50 **[42]**
2:51 **[30, 42, 43]**
2:52 **[38]**
2:52 **[43]**
4:22 **[46]**
4:29-30 **[46]**
8:20 **[24]**
8:21 **[24, 46]**
9:58 **[36]**
11:28 **[24, 33, 62]**
11:9 **[44]**
23:34 **[47]**

John
1:1 **[45]**
1:11 **[36]**
1:14 **[28]**
1:18 **[28]**
1:46 **[19]**
2:1 **[44]**
2:11 **[44]**
2:11 **[45]**
2:11 **[67]**
2:12 **[46]**
2:2 **[44]**
2:3 **[44]**
2:4 **[24]**
2:4 **[44]**
2:7 **[44]**
3:5-7 **[64]**
4:23 **[67]**
4:34 **[32]**
15:12 **[50]**
19:17-28, 25 **[47]**
19:25 **[47]**

19:25-26 **[48]**
19:25-27 **[50]**
19:25-27 **[59]**
19:25-27 **[63]**
19:26 **[31]**
19:26 **[57]**
19:26 **[64]**
19:26-27 **[49]**
19:26-27 **[50]**
19:26-27 **[66]**
19:26-27a **[49]**
19:27 **[50]**
19:28 **[49]**
20:28 **[67]**

Acts of the Apostles
1:12-13a.14 **[52]**
1:13-14 **[57]**
1:13-14 **[70]**
1:14 **[1]**
1:14 **[57]**
10:41 **[51]**

Romans
5:12, 18 **[21]**
5:20 **[21]**

1 Corinthians
15:3-6a **[50]**
15:6 **[51]**
3:9 **[48]**
6:19 **[11]**

2 Corinthians
5:21 **[21]**

Galatians
4:4 **[4, 66]**
4:4-5 **[26]**
4:4-6 **[66]**

Ephesians
2:4-5 **[11]**
5:25-27 **[61]**

Philippians
1:20b-21 **[53]**

Colossians
1:15-18 **[68]**
2:17 **[58]**
3:3 **[43]**

1 Timothy
2:5-6 **[65]**

Hebrews
7:25 **[64]**
8:5 **[58]**
10:5-7 **[32]**

James
3:2 **[61]**

1 Peter
2:5 **[62]**

1 John
2:1 **[64]**

Revelation of John (The Apocalypse)
12:1 **[21, 56]**
12:2 **[21]**
12:5 **[21]**

Index of Magisterial Documents

catechesis number in brackets

Professions of Faith

Nicene-Constantinopolitan Creed **[2, 11, 67]**

Ecumenical Councils

NICAEA II (787) [68]

VATICAN II (1962-1865)
Lumen gentium, n. 52 **[2, 11]**
Lumen gentium, n. 53 **[3, 11, 57, 58, 63]**
Lumen gentium, n. 54 **[10]**
Lumen gentium, n. 55 **[12, 18, 27]**
Lumen gentium, n. 56 **[19, 20, 33, 41, 48]**
Lumen gentium, n. 57 **[31, 36]**
Lumen gentium, n. 58 **[43, 45, 46, 47]**
Lumen gentium, n. 59 **[52, 53, 54, 55, 56]**
Lumen gentium, n. 60 **[65]**
Lumen gentium, n. 61 **[3, 48, 64, 65]**
Lumen gentium, n. 62 **[64, 65]**
Lumen gentium, n. 63 **[26, 48, 59]**
Lumen gentium, n. 64 **[60]**
Lumen gentium, n. 65 **[61]**
Lumen gentium, n. 66 **[66, 67]**
Lumen gentium, n. 67 **[10, 68]**
Lumen gentium, n. 69 **[70]**
Sacrosanctum Concilium, n. 103 **[23]**

Papal Documents

BL PIUS IX (1846-1878)
Ineffabilis Deus **[23, 48, 56]**

VEN. PIUS XII (1939-1958)
Ad cœli Reginam **[56]**
Deiparæ Virginis Mariæ **[54]**
Fulgens corona, n. 7 **[21]**
Munificentissimus Deus **[54]**

ST JOHN XXIII (1958-1963)
Allocution on the occasion of the opening of Vatican II **[9]**
Celebrandi Concilii Œcumenici **[9]**

ST PAUL VI (1963-1978)
Marialis cultus, n. 16 **[62]**
Marialis cultus, n. 37 **[29]**
Marialis cultus, n. 46 **[69]**
Message of Vatican II to Women **[7]**

St John Paul II (1978-2005)
Mulieris dignitatem, n. 1 **[7]**
Redemptoris Mater, n. 13 **[27]**
Redemptoris Mater, n. 20 **[33]**
Redemptoris Mater, n. 26 **[11]**
Redemptoris Mater, n. 38 **[65]**
Redemptoris Mater, n. 43 **[29]**
Redemptoris Mater, n. 9 **[19]**
Sollicitudo **[23]**

Ecclesiastical Documents

Catechism of the Catholic Church
404 **[21]**
500 **[31]**
501 **[28]**
502 **[28]**
504 **[28]**
511 **[33]**

Sacred Liturgy

Roman Breviary (Liturgy of the Hours) **[37, 64]**

Christian Apocrypha

Protoevangelium of James **[66]**

Index of Names

catechesis number in brackets

Alexander VII **[23]**
Ambrose of Milan, St. **[4, 55, 58]**
Andrew of Crete, St. **[20]**
Anselm d'Aosta of Canterbury, St. **[3, 63]**
Aristides **[26]**
Arnold of Chartres **[3]**
Augustine of Hippo, St. **[22, 25, 29, 37, 44, 48, 50, 60, 68]**
Benedict XIV **[63]**
Bernard, St. **[3]**
Calvin **[70]**
Eadmer **[22]**
Ephrem, St. **[20]**
Epiphanius, St. **[31, 55]**
Francis of Assisi, St. **[57]**
George Scholarios **[70]**
Germanus I of Constantinople, St. **[20, 55, 56]**
Gregory Nazianzen, St. **[20]**
Gregory of Nyssa, St. **[3]**
Gregory Palamas **[70]**
Guerric of Igny, Bl. **[3]**
Hormisdas, St. **[31]**
Ignatius of Antioch, St. **[26, 66]**
Irenaeus, St. **[3, 21, 26, 33, 64, 66]**
Jacob (James) of Sarug, St. **[20, 53]**
John (Johannes) Duns Scotus, Bl. **[22]**
John Damascene, St. **[20, 53, 55]**
John of Fiesole, Bl. **[62]**
John the Geometer **[3]**
John XXIII **[9, 63]**
Joseph, St. **[13, 23, 30, 38, 39]**
Justin, St. **[26, 66]**
Leo XIII **[30, 63, 69]**
Martin I **[26]**
Martin Luther **[70]**
Modestus of Jerusalem, St. **[53]**
Nestorius **[37, 66]**
Nicholas Cabasilas **[70]**
Origen **[56]**
Paul VI **[29, 62, 63, 69]**
Pelagius **[22]**
Pius IX **[4, 23, 56]**
Pius XII **[4, 53, 54, 56, 69, 23]**
Polycarp **[3]**
Pseudo-Melito **[55]**
Severian of Gabala **[20]**
Severus of Antioch **[53]**
Sixtus IV **[22]**
Tertullian **[26]**
Theoteknos of Livias **[20]**

Domina Nostra Publishing
555 N. Main Street, #1329
Providence, RI. 02904 USA

www.DominaNostraPublishing.com

info@DominaNostraPublishing.com

Printed in the USA
CPSIA information can be obtained
at www.ICGtesting.com
LVHW091937270124
770089LV00013B/43/J